NATION, STATE, AND ECONOMY

LUDWIG VON MISES

Nation, State, and Economy

*Contributions to the Politics and
History of Our Time*

∾ LUDWIG VON MISES

Translated by Leland B. Yeager
Edited by Bettina Bien Greaves

LIBERTY FUND   *Indianapolis*

This book is published by Liberty Fund, Inc., a foundation established to encourage
study of the ideal of a society of free and responsible individuals.

𒀮𒂼𒄄

The cuneiform inscription that serves as our logo and as the design motif for
our endpapers is the earliest-known written appearance of the word "freedom"
(*amagi*), or "liberty." It is taken from a clay document written about 2300 B.C.
in the Sumerian city-state of Lagash.

First published in 1983 by the Institute for Humane Studies in association with
New York University Press.

Front cover photograph of Ludwig von Mises used by permission of the Ludwig von
Mises Institute, Auburn, Alabama

Frontispiece courtesy of Bettina Bien Greaves

Printed in the United States of America

10 09 08 07 06 C   5   4   3   2   1
10 09 08 07 06 P   5   4   3   2   1

Library of Congress Cataloging-in-Publication Data
Von Mises, Ludwig, 1881–1973.
    [Nation, Staat, und Wirtschaft. English]
    Nation, state, and economy: contributions to the politics and history of our time / Ludwig
von Mises; translated by Leland B. Yeager; edited by Bettina Bien Greaves.
        p.   cm. — (Liberty Fund library of the works of Ludwig von Mises)
    Includes bibliographical references and index.
    ISBN-13: 978-0-86597-640-5 (hardcover: alk. paper)
    ISBN-10: 0-86597-640-6 (hardcover: alk. paper)
    ISBN-13: 978-0-86597-641-2 (pbk.: alk. paper)
    ISBN-10: 0-86597-641-4 (pbk.: alk. paper)
    1. World War, 1914–1918 — Economic aspects.   2. Germany — Economic conditions —
1888–1918.   3. Economic policy.   4. State, The.   5. Socialism.   6. Imperialism.
7. Liberalism.   I. Greaves, Bettina Bien.   II. Title.   III. Series: Von Mises, Ludwig,
1881–1973. Works. 2005.
HC56 .V6613 2006
330.9′041 — dc22   2006012311

Liberty Fund, Inc.
8335 Allison Pointe Trail, Suite 300
Indianapolis, Indiana 46250-1684

CONTENTS

Socialism and Imperialism

PREFACE

The pages that I herewith submit to the public do not presume to be more than observations about the crisis in world history that we are living through and contributions to understanding the political conditions of our time. I know that any attempt to offer more would be premature and therefore mistaken. Even if we were in a position to see interrelations clearly and to recognize where developments are heading, it would be impossible for us to confront the great events of our day objectively and not let our view be blurred by wishes and hopes. Standing in the middle of battle, one strives in vain to keep cool and calm. It exceeds human capacity to treat the vital questions of one's time *sine ira et studio* [without anger and partiality]. I should not be blamed for not being an exception to this rule.

It may perhaps seem that the topics treated in the individual parts of this book hang together only superficially. Yet I believe that they are closely connected by the purpose that this study serves. Of course, reflections of this kind, which must always remain fragmentary, cannot deal with the completeness and unity of the whole. My task can only be to direct the reader's attention to points that public discussion does not usually take sufficiently into account.

Vienna, beginning of July 1919

Professor Dr. L. Mises

Ludwig von Mises wrote *Nation, Staat, und Wirtschaft* in the same year, 1919, as John Maynard Keynes wrote *The Economic Consequences of the Peace*, a better known diagnosis of and prescription for the post-war economic situation. Mises, writing a few months earlier, presumably had less detailed knowledge of the Versailles Treaty and so was less concerned with its specific provisions. Keynes went into more detail than Mises in estimating such things as the wealth of the belligerents, the amount of destruction suffered, and the capacity of the Germans to pay reparations. His focus was narrower than that of Mises, who regarded his own analysis as one particular instance of applying lessons derived from both history and economic theory.

The two books have much in common. Both compare prewar and postwar economic conditions. Both authors recognize that each country's prosperity supports rather than undercuts that of others. Both appreciate how much the standard of living of Europe and particularly of Germany had depended on world trade and regret its interruption. Both, rightly or wrongly, perceived something of an overpopulation problem in Europe and in Germany in particular and made some not too optimistic remarks about the possibilities of emigration as a remedy. Mises even waxed wistful over loss of opportunities that Germany might have had in the nineteenth century peacefully to acquire overseas territories suitable for settlement.

Both authors more or less took it for granted that the German ruling class and segments of public opinion had been largely responsible for the war. Mises deployed history, politics, sociology, psychology, and other disciplines in exploring the intellectual and ideological background of German militarism. Keynes also engaged in psychology. His dissection of the character and personality of Woodrow Wilson is justly renowned, and he made biting comments on the immorality of Lloyd George's "Hang the Kaiser" election campaign of December 1918.

Both Mises and Keynes emphasized how currency deterioration causes social as well as economic disorder. Keynes endorsed Lenin's supposed observation about the best way to destroy the capitalist system. "Lenin was certainly right. There is no subtler, no surer means of overturning the existing basis of society than to debauch the currency. The process engages all the hidden forces of economic law on the side of destruction, and does it in a manner which not one man in a million is able to diagnose." Keynes warned against misdirecting blame onto "profiteers," and Mises, too, understood the constructive function of profit, even in wartime. Mises explained how inflation undercuts the vital functions performed by accounting. Keynes and Mises were exhibiting prescience, writing four years before the hyperinflationary collapse of the German mark would dramatize the points they were already making.

Keynes's book included no signs of anticapitalism or of support for comprehensive government economic intervention. Mises was emphatic on these issues. He exposed some of the inefficiencies of socialism, although he had not yet formulated his later demonstration of the impossibility of accurate economic calculation under socialism.

Both Keynes and Mises come across in their respective books as analytical in their diagnoses and humanitarian in their recommendations. Both were pessimistic about economic conditions on the European continent, at least in the short run. Both opposed a vindictive peace; Keynes's warnings about reparations are well known. It is too bad that Keynes's fame did not carry over more effectively into actual influence and that Mises's book was not more accessible to the English-speaking world at the time. If only the two men could have joined forces!

Mises's book illustrates the differences between the political and economic philosophies of conservatism and of liberalism (liberalism in the European and etymologically correct sense of the word). Mises was emphatically not a conservative. His book rails repeatedly against political and economic privilege. He championed political democracy as well as a free-market economy. He admired democratic revolutions against hereditary and authoritarian regimes; he sympathized with movements for national liberation and unity. As he explained, liberal nationalism — in sharp contrast with militaristic and imperialistic nationalism — can be an admirable attitude and a bulwark of peace. Different peoples should be able to respect and — to interpret a bit — even share in each one's pride in their own culture and history. (I think I can understand what Mises had in mind by recalling my feelings while traveling in Italy in 1961 at the time of celebrations and exhibitions commemorating the one hundredth anniversary of the founding of the Kingdom of Italy. As my traveling companion remarked, he almost felt like an Italian patriot.)

Mises's devotion to political democracy was tinged with a touching naiveté. Passages in his book suggest that he could hardly conceive of how the people, given the opportunity to rule through freely elected representatives, would fail to choose those politicians and policies that would serve their genuine common interest. This optimism is not to his discredit. It underlines the genuineness of his liberalism. It reminds us that he was writing more than sixty years ago, before the subsequent accumulation of sobering experience with democratic government. He was writing before the development of public-choice theory, that is, the application of economic analysis and methodological individualism to understanding government and government failure, analogous to the better publicized market failure (fragmented and inaccurate cost/benefit comparisons, externalities, and all that). But Mises certainly was not naive in relation to the experience and political analysis available in 1919. On the contrary, some of the most insightful parts of his book analyze the obstacles to the development of democracy in Germany and Austria. Mises saw the significance of the nationality and language situations in those two polyglot empires. He did not single-handedly develop an economic and psychological analysis of government, but he made an impressive beginning on that task in this and later books.

Mises could expect his German-speaking readers of over sixty years ago to recall the salient facts of German and Austrian history. Such an expectation may not hold for English-speaking readers of the 1980s. For this reason, a sketch follows of the historical background that Mises took for granted. In particular, it identifies events and persons that Mises alludes to.

German-speaking territories were ruled for centuries by dozens and even hundreds of hereditary or ecclesiastical monarchs — kings, dukes, counts, princes, archbishops, and the like. Mises speaks of "the pitiable multiplicity of several dozen patrimonial principalities, with their enclaves, their hereditary affiliations, and their family laws" and of "the farcical rule of the miniature thrones of the Reuss and Schwarzburg princes." Even after formation of the German Empire in 1871, its component states numbered four kingdoms, four grand duchies, fourteen lesser duchies and principalities, and three Hanseatic cities, as well as the conquered territory of Alsace-Lorraine.

Until beyond the middle of the nineteenth century, Germany was understood to include the German-speaking sections of Austria, which was usually the dominant German state. In the words of the *Deutschlandlied,* or national anthem (written in 1841 by the exiled liberal August Heinrich Hoffmann von Fallersleben), Germany ranged from the Maas River in the West to the Memel River in the East and from the Etsch (Adige) River in the South to the Belt (Baltic Sea passages) in the North.

The domain of German rulers was not limited, however, to German-speaking territories. Poles and other Slavic peoples lived in the eastern sections of Prussia, especially after the conquests by Frederick the Great to which Mises refers. Brandenburg, where Potsdam and Berlin are located, was the nucleus of what became the Kingdom of Prussia in 1701. The Hohenzollern family held the title of Margrave of Brandenburg from 1415 on and continued as the Prussian royal family until 1918. Frederick William, the "Great Elector" (the meaning of "elector" is explained below), ruled from 1640 to 1688. He presided over the rebuilding and expansion of his state after the Thirty Years' War and obtained full sovereignty over Prussia. His son, Frederick I, who ruled from 1688 to 1713, was crowned the first King of (technically, "in") Prussia. Frederick William I, king from 1713 to 1740, was largely the founder of the Prussian army. His son Frederick II became known to history as Frederick the Great. He wrested Silesia from Austria in 1745 and joined with Russia and Austria in the first partition of Poland in 1772. His successor, Frederick William II, joined in the second and third partitions of 1793 and 1795, which wiped Poland off the map.

The Austrian Empire included not only speakers of German but also Hungarians, Rumanians, Czechs, Slovenes, Poles, Ruthenians, Italians, and others. According to a 1910 census, the population of the Austrian part of the Austro-Hungarian Monarchy consisted of 35 percent Germans, 23 percent Czechs, 17 percent Poles, 19 percent other Slavs, 2¾ percent Italians, and scattered others.

The Holy Roman Empire of the German Nation, to use its full name, existed until 1806. It coincided roughly, but only roughly, with German-speaking territory. It sometimes included parts of northern Italy but left out the eastern parts of Prussia. It was organized (or revived) under Otto I, whom the Pope crowned Emperor in 962. (He was succeeded by Otto II and Otto III; Mises refers to the age of the Ottonians.) The

Empire was a loose confederation of princely and ecclesiastical sovereignties and free cities. Seven, eight, or nine of their rulers were Electors, who chose a new Emperor when a vacancy occurred. From 1273, except for a few intervals (notably 1308 to 1438), the Holy Roman Emperors belonged to the Habsburg family, whose domains included many lands outside the boundaries of the Empire. The dynastic expansion of the Habsburgs explains Mises's reference to the "married-together state." The male line of the family died out in 1740, when Charles VI was succeeded in his domains by his daughter Maria Theresa, an event that touched off the War of the Austrian Succession. Maria Theresa's husband was the former Duke of Lorraine and Holy Roman Emperor as Francis I from 1745 to 1765, which explains why the dynasty became known as the house of Habsburg-Lorraine.

Mises mentions several other events and personalities in the history of the Holy Roman Empire. Until his death in 1637, Ferdinand II reigned from 1617 as King of Bohemia, from 1618 as King of Hungary, and from 1619 as Emperor. His fanatical Catholicism alienated the Protestant Bohemian nobles, who rebelled in 1618 (the picturesquely named Defenestration of Prague occurred at this time), beginning the Thirty Years' War. The war, which wrought havoc on Germany, hinged not only on religious differences but also on the ambition of the Habsburgs to gain control of the entire country. The Imperial forces won the war's first major battle, fought on the White Mountain, near Prague, in 1620, ending Bohemian independence for three centuries. The Protestant side was aided at times by the Danes, the Swedes, and even the French under Louis XIII and Louis XIV. The Treaty of Westphalia, in 1648, awarded certain German provinces on the Baltic Sea to Sweden and southern Alsace to France, while the Emperor's authority over Germany became purely nominal. Acceptance of the religious split of Germany was an important step toward religious toleration. Leopold I, whom Mises mentions, was Holy Roman Emperor from 1657 to 1705. The greater part of his reign was occupied by wars with Louis XIV of France and with the Turks. Leopold II, Emperor from 1790 until his death in 1792 and the last crowned King of Bohemia, succeeded his brother Joseph II (also a son of Maria Theresa). He instigated the Declaration of Pillnitz, which helped precipitate the French Revolutionary Wars a few weeks after his death.

The Napoleonic Wars brought lasting changes to the map and the political systems of Europe. The Enactment of Delegates of the Holy

Roman Empire (*Reichsdeputationshauptschluss*) was adopted in 1803 under pressure of Napoleon. Mises mentions this Enactment as an illustration of the old idea that lands were the properties of their sovereigns and so could be bought and sold, traded, reshaped, divided, and consolidated without regard to the wishes of their inhabitants, who were mere appurtenances of the land. The Enactment greatly reduced the number of sovereignties in the Empire, in part by ending the temporal rule of dignitaries of the Catholic Church and putting their lands under the rule of neighboring princes. In 1806, again under pressure of Napoleon, who had detached the western parts of Germany—only temporarily, as things turned out—and organized them into a Confederation of the Rhine, the old Empire was liquidated. Francis II gave up his title of Holy Roman Emperor but retained the title of Emperor of Austria as Francis I.

Mises mentions two men who strove for a unified Italian state at the end of the Napoleonic Wars. Joachim Murat, a marshall of France whom Napoleon had made King of Naples in 1808, tried in 1815 to make himself king of all Italy; but he was captured and shot. Florestano Pepe, one of Murat's generals, fought against the Austrians in 1815. (Mises's allusion is presumably to Florestano Pepe rather than to his brother Guglielmo, another Neapolitan general, who organized the Carbonari and who led an unsuccessful proconstitutional revolt in 1821.)

After the Napoleonic Wars, the reigning dynasties of Europe tried to restore the old regime. The Holy Alliance, to which Mises repeatedly refers with scorn, is a phrase frequently but imprecisely used to label the reactionary policies of Russia, Prussia, and Austria in particular. Strictly speaking, the Holy Alliance was an innocuous declaration of Christian principles of statesmanship drawn up by Czar Alexander I in 1815 and signed by almost all European sovereigns. The repressive policies are more properly associated with the Congress system and the Quadruple Alliance of 1815. Mises mentions, by the way, the Polish kingdom of Alexander I. The Congress of Vienna (1814–1815) created the kingdom in personal union with Russia but with a constitution of its own (which was suspended after the Polish insurrection of 1830–1831).

With the Holy Roman Empire defunct, a decision of the Congress of Vienna loosely joined some thirty-eight (soon thirty-nine) German sovereignties together again as the German Confederation. The federal diet, which met in Frankfurt under the presidency of Austria, had little power because unanimity or a two-thirds majority was required for most decisions.

In 1834, after achieving a free-trade area within its own territories, Prussia took the lead in establishing the Zollverein among most German states, not including Austria, through the merger of two regional customs unions. The new union is considered a step toward political unification. In 1867 it was reorganized with a constitution and parliament of its own. Mises mentions one of its intellectual fathers, the economist Friedrich List. List had been forced to emigrate to the United States in 1825 for advocating administrative reforms in Württemberg but had returned to Germany in 1832 as U.S. consul at Leipzig. He favored internal free trade, together with strictly temporary tariff protection to encourage the development of infant industries.

Mises makes many admiring and wistful references to the European revolutions of 1848. The revolutions were mostly the work of the middle-class intellectuals, who were bringing mainly French ideas to bear against political repression. The February revolution in Paris, resulting in the overthrow of King Louis Philippe and establishment of the Second Republic, was emulated elsewhere. In the numerous sovereignties into which Italy was still split, a movement for liberal constitutions was followed by an unsuccessful patriotic war to eject the Austrians.

Revolutionary riots came to Austria and Germany in March 1848, which explains why Mises refers to the March revolution and compares conditions afterwards with conditions as they were "before March" (to translate the German literally). In Vienna, Prince Clemens von Metternich, minister of foreign affairs and chief minister since 1809, had to resign and flee the country. The first Pan-Slav Congress met in Prague in June 1848 under the presidency of František Palacký, the Bohemian historian and nationalist. (Mises cites Palacký's much-quoted remark to the effect that if the Austrian multinational state had not existed, it would have been necessary to invent it.) Field Marshal Prince Alfred Windischgrätz bombarded the revolutionaries in Prague into submission in June 1848 and later turned to Vienna, where a further wave of radical unrest had broken out in October. He helped restore Habsburg power, with Prince Felix Schwarzenberg as the new chief minister from November 1848. Schwarzenberg engineered the abdication of Emperor Ferdinand I in favor of his eighteen-year-old nephew Francis Joseph, who would reign until his death in 1916.

Mises alludes not only to Schwarzenberg but also to Count Eduard von Clam-Gallas, who played a decisive role in suppressing the Italian and Hungarian revolutions of 1848–1849. (Actually, Mises mentions the Clam-Martinics, who were the Bohemian wing of the same wealthy noble family.)

The Hungarian independence movement succeeded at first but was finally put down by Schwarzenberg and the Habsburgs with the aid of some of their Slavic subjects and the forces of the Russian Czar Nicholas I. After their defeat by the Russians in August 1849, the Hungarians suffered vengeance at the hands of the Austrian General Julius Freiherr von Haynau.

In Germany the revolutionaries sought both representative government in the various states and unification of the country. The King of Prussia and lesser German rulers at first granted democratic concessions but later withdrew them on observing the success of counterrevolution in Austria. The Crown Prince of Prussia, who had fled the country only shortly before, as Mises notes, was able to mount a counteroffensive. Yet some prospects seemed hopeful for a while. Aspiring for a united Germany, a self-constituted "preliminary parliament" convoked a German National Assembly, also known as the Frankfurt Parliament, which met in St. Paul's Church from 18 May 1848 to 21 April 1849. Its delegates were chosen by direct male suffrage throughout Germany and Austria. It was predominantly a middle-class body inspired by liberal and democratic ideas. This is what Mises had in mind when repeatedly referring to the ideals of St. Paul's Church. (He occasionally refers in the same sense to the "ideas of 1789," thinking of course of the aspirations for freedom and political equality expressed at the beginning of the French Revolution and not to the Terror into which the revolution later degenerated.)[1]

1. [Editor's note: Mises frequently mentioned the mid-nineteenth century drive for a unified German nation to be composed of Germany and German-Austria. He described it as really a pro-freedom movement, closely associated with the liberal revolution of 1848. However, Mises never wrote about it in any detail. He refers to it briefly in this book, as does translator Leland Yeager in this Introduction. However, it might be helpful for the reader to know something more about how the movement was started, developed, and then demolished.

As Mises describes this time in history, the drive for a "greater Germany" was closely related to the eighteenth- and nineteenth-century struggle for liberalism, individualism, freedom, and democracy. Napoleon's conquest of Europe had destroyed the independence of the German principalities and dukedoms as political entities and brought them under the control of Prussia. In the hope of bringing about political reform in Germany after the defeat of Napoleon, professors, incidentally, authorized Austria-Hungary to occupy and administer the Turkish provinces of Bosnia and Herzegovina, now in Yugoslavia. The occupation was not entirely trouble-free; Mises mentions rebellions in Herzegovina and around the Gulf of Kotor. Austria-Hungary finally annexed the occupied provinces in 1908.

Another important development in international politics was the negotiation of an alliance between Germany and Austria-Hungary in 1879. Apparently Bismarck's decision not to impose an excessively harsh peace on Austria in 1866 was paying off. This alliance, like the Russian-French alliance and others, set the stage for a chain reaction whereby the countries not directly involved in the original dispute between Austria and Serbia in 1914 got drawn into World War I.

The Wilhelministic Era, which Mises refers to, was the reign of William II as German Emperor, particularly from the dismissal of Bismarck as chancellor in 1890 until World War I.

The defeat of the Central Powers in that war split Austria-Hungary up into several states. Currency inflations gained momentum. In Germany the Spartacists, whom Mises mentions and who reorganized themselves into the German Communist Party in December 1918, seemed for a time to have prospects of gaining power in at least the major cities.

We now turn to a few explanations and identifications that did not fit into the preceding chronological survey. Cabinet ministers in both Germany and Austria were responsible to the Emperor rather than to parliament. Although a government could not be thrown out of office by a vote of no confidence, parliamentary majorities were necessary to enact specific pieces of legislation; and the government occasionally resorted to political maneuvers and tricks to achieve the necessary majorities. Mises refers scornfully to these circumstances. In Austria, in particular, the parliamentary situation and the alignment of parties was complicated by the mixture of nationalities and by such issues as what languages should be used in particular schools. Mises refers, for example, to Badeni's electoral reform of 1896. (Count Kazimierz Felix Badeni, a Polish aristocrat, became prime minister in 1895. The finance minister and foreign minister in his cabinet also came from the Polish part of the Empire. Badeni was dismissed in 1897 through the pressure of German-speaking factions, who considered his policies on use of language in the civil service too favorable to the Czechs.) Mises also notes allusions made at the time to the government's courting of the ironically nick-named "Imperial and Royal Social Democrats" (the term "Imperial and

Royal," commonly abbreviated in German as "K.k.," referred to the Austrian Empire and Kingdom of Hungary and meant something like "governmental" or "official").

The nationality situation is also in the background of Mises's reference to the Linz Program of 1882. The extreme German nationalists proposed the restoration of German dominance in Austrian affairs by detaching Galicia, Bukovina, and Dalmatia from the Monarchy, weakening the ties with Hungary to a purely personal union under the same monarch, and establishing a customs union and other close ties with the German Reich. They apparently did not realize that Bismarck had little reason to provide help, since the existing domestic situation in Austria-Hungary was consonant with his approach to international affairs. The leader of the extreme German-Austrian nationalists was Georg Ritter von Schönerer, who later made anti-Semitism a part of his program.

Employing synecdoche, Mises sometimes opposes Potsdam to Weimar. Potsdam was the home of the Prussian Monarchy, and the word symbolizes the authoritarian state and militarism. Weimar, the literary and cultural center, stands for the aspect of Germany evoked by calling it the "nation of poets and thinkers." (The "classical period" of German literature, to which Mises also refers, corresponds roughly to the time of Goethe.)

The Gracchi, referred to in a Latin saying that Mises quotes, were the brothers Tiberius and Gaius Gracchus, agrarian, social, and political reformers of the second century B.C. Both perished in separate public disturbances, one of them after having sought an unconstitutional reelection as tribune of the people.

It is quite unnecessary to identify every event, person, or school of thought that Mises refers to—Alexander the Great and so on. Still, there is no harm in adding that the Manchester School was a group of English economists of the first half of the nineteenth century, led by Richard Cobden and John Bright, who campaigned for a market economy and a free-trade policy. François Quesnay, 1694–1774, was a French physician and economist who stressed the central role of agriculture and who prepared the Tableau Economique, a kind of rudimentary input-output table.

Benedikt Franz Leo Waldeck, 1802–1870, was Mises's example of the possibility of being both a Prussian nationalist and a sincere liberal democrat. Waldeck, a member of the highest Prussian court, had been a radical deputy in the Prussian constituent assembly in 1848 and leader of a committee that drafted a constitution. Later, as an opposition member of the Prussian chamber of deputies, he continued resisting authoritarian trends in government.

This introduction might fittingly end by especially recommending the discussion with which Mises ends his book—his discussion of the respective roles of value judgments and positive analysis in the choice between socialism and liberal capitalism. Mises proceeds not only from a liberal democratic outlook but also, and especially, from a rationalist and utilitarian philosophy.

Thanks are due to the Thomas Jefferson Center Foundation and the James Madison Center of the American Enterprise Institute for contributing much of the secretarial help required in preparing the translation. Thanks for their good work also go to Mrs. Anne Hobbs, Mrs. Carolyn Southall, and Miss Linda Wilson.

NATION, STATE, AND ECONOMY

Introduction

Only from lack of historical sense could one raise the question whether and how the World War could have been avoided. The very fact that the war took place shows that the forces working to cause it were stronger than those working to prevent it. It is easy to show, after the fact, how affairs could or should have been better managed. It is clear that the German people underwent experiences during the war that would have restrained them from war if they had already undergone those experiences. But nations, like individuals, become wise only through experience, and only through experience of their own. Now, to be sure, it is easy to see that the German people would be in a quite different position today if they had shaken off the yoke of princely rule in that fateful year 1848, if Weimar had triumphed over Potsdam and not Potsdam over Weimar. But every person must take his life and every nation must take its history as it comes; nothing is more useless than complaining over errors that can no longer be rectified, nothing more vain than regret. Neither as judges allotting praise and blame nor as avengers seeking out the guilty should we face the past. We seek truth, not guilt; we want to know how things came about to understand them, not to issue condemnations. Whoever approaches history the way a prosecutor approaches the documents of a criminal case — to find material for indictments — had better stay away from it. It is not the task of history to gratify the need of the masses for heroes and scapegoats.

That is the position a nation should take toward its history. It is not the task of history to project the hatred and disagreements of the present back into the past and to draw from battles fought long ago weapons for the disputes of one's own time. History should teach us to recognize causes and to understand driving forces; and when we understand everything, we will forgive everything. That is how the English and French approach their history. The Englishman, regardless of his political affiliation, can consider the history of the religious and constitutional struggles of the seventeenth century, the history of the loss of the New England states in the eighteenth century, objectively; there is no Englishman who could see in Cromwell or Washington only the embodiment of national misfortune. And no Frenchman would want to strike Louis XIV, Robespierre, or Napoleon out of the history of his people, be he Bonapartist, royalist, or republican. And for the Catholic Czech, also, it is not hard to understand Hussites and Moravian Brethren in terms of their own time. Such a conception of history leads without difficulty to understanding and appreciation of what is foreign.

Only the German is still far from a conception of history that does not see the past with the eyes of the present. Even today Martin Luther is, for some Germans, the great liberator of minds, and, for others, the embodiment of the anti-Christ. This holds above all for recent history. For the modern period, which begins with the Peace of Westphalia, Germany has two approaches to history, the Prussian-Protestant and the Austrian-Catholic, which reach a common interpretation on scarcely a *single* point. From 1815 on, a still broader clash of views develops, the clash between the liberal and the authoritarian ideas of the state;[1] and finally, the attempt has recently been made to oppose a "proletarian" to a "capitalist" historiography. All that shows not only a striking lack of scientific sense and historical critical faculty but also a grievous immaturity of political judgment.

Where it was not possible to achieve consensus in interpreting long-past struggles, it is much less to be expected that agreement can be reached in evaluating the most recent past. Already, here also, we see two sharply contradictory myths arising. On the one hand it is asserted that the German people, misled by defeatist propaganda, had lost the will to power; and thus, through "collapse of the home front," the inevitable final victory, which would have made the earth subject to it, was transformed into disastrous defeat. It is forgotten that despair did not grip the people until the decisive victories heralded by the General Staff failed to occur, until millions of German men bled to death in purposeless struggles against an opponent far superior in numbers and better armed, and until hunger brought death and disease to those who had

---

1. On this compare Hugo Preuss, *Das deutsche Volk und die Politik* (Jena: Eugen Diederichs, 1915), pp. 97 ff.

stayed at home.[2] No less far from the truth is the other myth, which blames the war and so the defeat on capitalism, the economic system based on private ownership of the means of production. It is forgotten that liberalism was always pacifistic and antimilitaristic, that not until its overthrow, which was achieved only by the united efforts of the Prussian Junker class and the Social Democratic working class, was the way opened up for the policy of Bismarck and William II; the last trace of the liberal spirit had first to disappear from Germany and liberalism had to become regarded as a kind of dishonorable ideology before the people of poets and thinkers could become a weak-willed tool of the war party. It is forgotten that the German Social Democratic Party had unanimously supported the war policy of the government and that the defection first of individuals and then of ever-larger masses ensued only as military failures showed the inevitability of defeat ever more clearly and as famine became more strongly felt. Before the battle of the Marne and before the great defeats in the East, there was no resistance to the war policy among the German people.

Such myth-making bespeaks a lack of that political maturity that only he who must bear political responsibility achieves. The German had none to bear; he was a subject, not a citizen, of his state. To be sure, we had a state that was called the German Reich and that was praised as the fulfillment of the ideals of St. Paul's Church. Yet this Great Prussia was no more the state of the Germans than the Italian kingdom of Napoleon I had been the state of the Italians or the Polish kingdom of Alexander I the state of the Poles. This empire had not arisen from the will of the German people; against the will not only of the German people but also of the majority of the Prussian people, hanging behind its conflict-minded deputies, it had been created on the battlefield of Königgrätz. It also included Poles and Danes, but it excluded many millions of German-Austrians. It was a state of German princes but not of the German people.

Many of the best people never reconciled themselves with this state; others did so late and reluctantly. Yet it was not easy to stand aside

---

2. This is not to say that the behavior of the radical wing of the Social Democratic Party in October and November of 1918 did not entail the most frightful consequences for the German people. Without the complete collapse brought on by the revolts in the hinterland and behind the lines, the armistice conditions and the peace would have turned out quite differently. But the assertion that we would have triumphed if only we had held out a short time longer is quite groundless.

bearing a grudge. There came brilliant days for the German people, rich in outward honors and in military victories. The Prussian-German armies triumphed over imperial and over republican France, Alsace-Lorraine became German again (or rather Prussian), the venerable imperial title was restored. The German Empire assumed a respected position among the European powers; German warships plowed the oceans; the German flag floated over — rather worthless, to be sure — African, Polynesian, and East Asian possessions. All this romantic activity was bound to captivate the minds of the masses that gape at processions and court festivities. They were content because there were things to admire and because they were satiated. At the same time German prosperity was growing as never before. These were the years when the wonderful opening up of the remotest territories through development of modern means of transportation was bringing undreamed-of riches to Germany. That had nothing to do with the political and military successes of the German state, but people hastily judge *post hoc ergo propter hoc.*

The men who had filled the jails before the revolution of March 1848 and who had stood on the barricades in 1848 and then had to go into exile had in the meanwhile become old and feeble; they either made their peace with the new order or kept silent. A new generation arose that saw and noted nothing but the uninterrupted growth of prosperity, of the size of population, of trade, of shipping, in short, of everything that people are accustomed to call good times. And they began to make fun of the poverty and weakness of their fathers; they now had only contempt for the ideals of the nation of poets and thinkers. In philosophy, history, and economics, new ideas appeared; the theory of power came to the fore. Philosophy became the bodyguard of throne and altar; history proclaimed the fame of the Hohenzollerns; economics praised the socially oriented kingship and the gap-free tariff schedules and took up the struggle against the "bloodless abstractions of the English Manchester School."

To the statist school of economic policy, an economy left to its own devices appears as a wild chaos into which only state intervention can bring order. The statist puts every economic phenomenon on trial, ready to reject it if it does not conform to his ethical and political feelings. It is then the job of state authority to carry out the judgment pronounced by science and to replace the botch caused by free development with what serves the general interest. That the state, all-wise and all-just, also always wishes only the common good and that it has the power to fight against all evils effectively—this is not doubted in the slightest. Although the views of individual representatives of this school may diverge in other respects, in one point they all agree, namely, in disputing the existence of economic laws and in tracing all economic events to the operation of power factors.[3] Against economic power the state can set its superior political-military power. For all the difficulties that confronted the German people at home and abroad, the military solution was recommended; only ruthless use of power was considered rational policy.

These were the German political ideas that the world has called militarism.[4]

Nevertheless, the formula that attributes the World War simply to the machinations of this militarism is wrong. For German militarism does not spring, as it were, from the violent instincts of the "Teutonic race," as the English and French war literature says; it is not the ultimate cause

3. Böhm-Bawerk masterfully evaluates this doctrine in "Macht oder ökonomisches Gesetz," *Zeitschrift für Volkswirtschaft, Sozialpolitik und Verwaltung*, vol. 23, pp. 205–271 ["Control or Economic Law," tr. John Richard Mez, 1931, published in *Shorter Classics of Böhm-Bawerk*, vol. 1, pp. 139–199 (Libertarian Press, 1962).] The statist school of German economics has indeed reached its high point in the state theory of money of Georg Friedrich Knapp. What is notable about it is not that it has been set forth; for what it taught had already been believed for centuries by canonists, jurists, romantics, and many socialists. What was notable, rather, was the book's success. In Germany and Austria it found numerous enthusiastic adherents, and basic agreement even among those who had reservations. Abroad it was almost unanimously rejected or not noticed at all. A work recently published in the United States says regarding the *Staatliche Theorie des Geldes* [*The State Theory of Money*, tr. H. M. Lucas and J. Bonar (London, 1923; repr. Augustus M. Kelley, 1973)]: "This book has had wide influence on German thinking on money. It is typical of the tendency in German thought to make the State the centre of everything" (Anderson, *The Value of Money* [New York: 1917], p. 433 n.).

4. In Germany the opinion is very widespread that foreign countries understand by militarism the fact of strong military armaments; it is pointed out, therefore, that England and France, which have maintained powerful fleets and armies on water and land, have been at least as militaristic as Germany and Austria-Hungary. That rests on an error. By militarism one should understand not armaments and readiness for war but a particular type of society, namely, the one that was designated by pan-German, conservative, and social-imperialistic authors as that of the "German state" and of "German freedom" and that others have praised as the "ideas of 1914." Its antithesis is the industrial type of society, that is, the one that a certain line of opinion in Germany during the war scorned as the ideal of "shopkeepers," as the embodiment of the "ideas of 1789." Compare Herbert Spencer, [*Principles of Sociology* (1876–1896)] *Die Prinzipien der Soziologie*, German translation by Vetter (Stuttgart: 1889), vol. 3, pp. 668–754. In the elaboration and contrasting of the two types there exists a considerable degree of agreement between Germans and Anglo-Saxons, but not in terminology. The assessment of the two types is naturally not agreed on. Even before and during the war there were not only militarists but also antimilitarists in Germany and not only antimilitarists but also militarists in England and America.

but the result of the circumstances in which the German people has lived and lives. Not too much insight into how things are interrelated is needed to recognize that the German people would have desired the war of 1914 just as little as the English, French, or American people did if they had been in the position of England, France, or the United States. The German people trod the path from the peaceful national-ism and cosmopolitanism of the Classical period to the militant impe-rialism of the Wilhelministic era under the pressure of political and economic facts that posed quite other problems for them than for the more fortunate peoples of the West. The conditions under which it has to proceed today toward reshaping its economy and its state are, again, thoroughly different from those under which its neighbors in the West and in the East live. If one wants to grasp these conditions in all their specialness, one must not shrink from looking into things that seem only remotely related.

Nation and State

1   The Nation as a Speech Community

The concepts *nation* and *nationality* are relatively new in the sense in which we understand them. Of course, the word *nation* is very old; it derives from Latin and spread early into all modern languages. But another meaning was associated with it. Only since the second half of the eighteenth century did it gradually take on the significance that it has for us today, and not until the nineteenth century did this usage of the word become general.[1] Its political significance developed step-by-step with the concept; nationality became a central point of political thought. The word and concept *nation* belong completely to the modern sphere of ideas of political and philosophical individualism; they win importance for real life only in modern democracy.

If we wish to gain insight into the essence of nationality, we must proceed not from the nation but from the individual. We must ask ourselves what the national aspect of the individual person is and what determines his belonging to a particular nation.

We then recognize immediately that this national aspect can be neither where he lives nor his attachment to a state. Not everyone who lives in Germany or holds German citizenship is a German merely for that reason. There are Germans who neither live in Germany nor hold German citizenship. Living in the same places and having the same attachment to a state do play their role in the development of nationality,

---

1. Cf. Meinecke, *Weltbürgertum und Nationalstaat*, third edition (Munich: 1915), pp. 22 ff.; Kjellén, *Der Staat als Lebensform* (Leipzig: 1917), pp. 102 ff.

but they do not pertain to its essence. It is no different with having the same ancestry. The genealogical conception of nationality is no more useful than the geographic or the state conception. Nation and race do not coincide; there is no nation of pure blood.[2] All peoples have arisen from a mixture of races. Ancestry is not decisive for belonging to a nation. Not everyone descended from German ancestors is a German merely for that reason; how many Englishmen, Americans, Magyars, Czechs, and Russians would otherwise have to be called Germans? There are Germans whose ancestors include not one German. Among members of the higher strata of the population and among famous men and women whose family trees are commonly traced, foreign ancestors can be demonstrated more often than among members of the lower strata of the people, whose origins are lost in darkness; yet the latter, too, are more seldom of pure blood than one tends to assume.

There are writers who have worked in good faith to investigate the significance of ancestry and race for history and politics; what success they attained will not be discussed here. Again, many writers demand that political significance be attached to community of race and that race policy be pursued. People can be of different opinions about the justness of this demand; to examine it is not our concern. It may also remain an open question whether that demand has already been heeded today and whether and how race policy really is pursued. Yet we must insist that just as the concepts nation and race do not coincide, so national policy and race policy are two different things. Also, the concept of race, in the sense in which the advocates of race policy use it, is new, even considerably newer than that of nation. It was introduced into politics in deliberate opposition to the concept of nation. The individualistic idea of the national community was to be displaced by the collectivist idea of the racial community. Success has so far eluded these efforts. The slight significance accorded to the race factor in the cultural and political movements of the present day contrasts sharply with the great importance that national aspects have. Lapouge, one of the founders of the anthroposociological school, expressed the opinion a generation ago that in the twentieth century people would be slaughtered by the millions because of one or two degrees more or less in the cephalic index.[3] We

2. Cf. Kjellén, loc. cit., pp. 105 ff., and the works cited there.
3. Cf. Manouvrier, "L'indice céphalique et la pseudo-sociologie," *Revue Mensuelle de l'École d'Anthropologie de Paris*, vol. 9, 1899, p. 283.

have indeed experienced the slaughter of people by the millions, but no one can assert that dolichocephaly and brachycephaly were the rallying cries of the parties in this war. We are, of course, only at the end of the second decade of the century for which Lapouge expressed his prophecy. It may be that he will yet prove right; we cannot follow him into the field of prophecy, and we do not wish to dispute over things that still rest darkly concealed in the womb of the future. In present-day politics the race factor plays no role; that alone is important for us.

The dilettantism that pervades the writings of our race theorists should not, of course, mislead us into skipping lightly over the race problem itself. Surely there is hardly any other problem whose clarification could contribute more to deepening our historical understanding. It may be that the way to ultimate knowledge in the field of historical ebb and flow leads through anthropology and race theory. What has so far been discovered in these sciences is quite scanty, of course, and is overgrown with a thicket of error, fantasy, and mysticism. But there exists true science in this field also, and here also there are great problems. It may be that we shall never solve them, but that should not keep us from investigating further and should not make us deny the significance of the race factor in history.

If one does not see racial affinity as the essence of nationality, that does not mean that one wants to deny the influence of racial affinity on all politics and on national politics in particular. In real life many different forces work in different directions; if we want to recognize them, then we must try to distinguish them in our minds as far as possible. That does not mean, though, that in observing one force, we should quite forget that still others are working alongside it or against it.

We recognize that one of these forces is the speech community; this is indeed beyond dispute. If we now say that the essence of nationality lies in language, this is no mere terminological point about which there could be no further dispute. First, let it be stated that in saying so, we are in conformity with the general use of language. To the language we apply first, and to it alone in the original sense, the designation that then becomes the designation of the nation. We speak of the German language, and everything else that bears the label "German" gets it from the German language: when we speak of German writing, of German literature, of German men and women, the relation to the language is obvious. Moreover, it does not matter whether the designation of the language is older than that of the people or is derived from the latter; once it became the designation of the language, it is what became decisive for the further development of the use of this expression. And if we finally speak of German rivers and of German cities, of German history and of German war, we have no trouble understanding that in the last analysis this expression also traces back to the original naming of the language as German. The concept of the nation is, as already said, a political concept. If we want to know its content, we must fix our eyes on the politics in which it plays a role. Now we see that all national struggles are language struggles, that they are waged about language. What is specifically "national" lies in language.[4]

Community of language is at first the consequence of an ethnic or social community; independently of its origin, however, it itself now becomes a new bond that creates definite social relations. In learning the language, the child absorbs a way of thinking and of expressing his thoughts that is predetermined by the language, and so he receives a stamp that he can scarcely remove from his life. The language opens up the way for a person of exchanging thoughts with all those who use it; he can influence them and receive influence from them. Community of language binds and difference of language separates persons and peoples. If someone finds the explanation of the nation as a speech community perhaps too paltry, let him just consider what immense significance language has for thinking and for the expression of thought, for social relations, and for all activities of life.

If, despite recognition of these connections, people often resist seeing the essence of the nation in the speech community, this hinges on certain difficulties that the demarcation of individual nations by this criterion entails.[5] Nations and languages are not unchangeable categories but, rather, provisional results of a process in constant flux; they change from day to day, and so we see before us a wealth of intermediate forms whose classification requires some pondering.

4. Cf. Scherer, *Vorträge und Aufsätze zur Geschichte des geistigen Lebens in Deutschland und Österreich* (Berlin: 1874), pp. 45 ff. That the criterion of nation lies in language was the view of Arndt and Jacob Grimm. For Grimm, a people is "the sum total of persons who speak the same language" (*Kleinere Schriften*, vol. 7 [Berlin: 1884], p. 557). A survey of the history of doctrine about the concept of nation is given in Otto Bauer, *Die Nationalitätenfrage und die Sozialdemokratie* (Vienna: 1907), pp. 1 ff., and Spann, *Kurzgefasstes System der Gesellschaftslehre* (Berlin: 1914), pp. 195 ff.

5. Moreover, let it be expressly noted that with every other explanation of the essence of the nation, difficulties turn up in much higher degree and cannot be overcome.

A German is one who thinks and speaks German. Just as there are different degrees of mastery of the language, so there are also different degrees of being German. Educated persons have penetrated into the spirit and use of the language in a manner quite different from that of the uneducated. Ability in concept formation and mastery of words are the criterion of education: the school rightly emphasizes acquiring the ability to grasp fully what is spoken and written and to express oneself intelligibly in speech and writing. Only those are full members of the German nation who have fully mastered the German language. Uneducated persons are German only insofar as the understanding of German speech has been made accessible to them. A peasant in a village cut off from the world who knows only his home dialect and cannot make himself understood by other Germans and cannot read the written language does not count at all as a member of the German nation.[6] If all other Germans were to die out and only people who knew only their own dialect survived, then one would have to say that the German nation had been wiped out. Even those peasants are not without a tinge of nationality, only they belong not to the German nation but rather to a tiny nation consisting of those who speak the same dialect.

The individual belongs, as a rule, to only *one* nation. Yet it does now and then happen that a person belongs to two nations. That is not the case merely when he speaks two languages but rather only when he has mastered two languages in such a way that he thinks and speaks in each of the two and has fully assimilated the special way of thinking that characterizes each of them. Yet there are more such persons than people believe. In territories of mixed population and in centers of international trade and commerce, one frequently meets them among merchants, officials, etc. And they are often persons without the highest education. Among men and women with more education, bilinguists are rarer, since the highest perfection in the mastery of language, which characterizes the truly educated person, is as a rule attained in only *one* language. The educated person may have mastered more languages, and all of them far better than the bilinguist has; nevertheless, he is to be counted in only one nation if he thinks only in *one* language and processes everything he hears and sees in foreign languages through a way of thinking that has been shaped by the structure and the concept

6. That the concept of national community is a matter of degree is also recognized by Spann (loc. cit., p. 207); that it includes only educated persons is explained by Bauer (loc. cit., pp. 70 ff).

formation of his own language. Yet even among the "millionaires of education"[7] there are bilinguists, men and women who have fully assimilated the education of two cultural circles. They were and are found somewhat more frequently than elsewhere in places where an old, fully developed language with an old culture and a still slightly developed language of a people only just completing the process of acquiring culture confront each other. There it is physically and psychically easier to achieve mastery of two languages and two cultural circles. Thus, there were far more bilinguists in Bohemia among the generation which immediately preceded the one now living than at present. In a certain sense one can also count as bilinguists all those who, besides the standard language, have full mastery of a dialect also.

Everyone belongs as a rule to at least *one* nation. Only children and deaf-mutes are nationless; the former first acquire an intellectual home through entry into a speech community, the latter through development of their thinking capacity into achievement of the capability of mutual understanding with the members of a nation. The process that operates here is basically the same as that by which adults already belonging to one nation switch over to another.[8]

The language researcher finds relationships among languages; he recognizes language families and language races; he speaks of sister languages and daughter languages. Some people have wanted to extend this concept directly to nations also; others, again, have wanted to make the ethnological relationship into a national one. Both ideas are totally inadmissible. If one wants to speak of national relationship, one may do so only with reference to the possibility of mutual understanding between the members of the nations. In this sense dialects are related to each other and to one or even to several standard languages. Even between standard languages, for example, between individual Slavic languages, such a relation holds. Its significance for national development exhausts itself in the fact that it facilitates a transition from one nationality to another.

---

7. Cf. Anton Menger, *Neue Staatslehre*, second ed. (Jena: 1904), p. 213.
8. It used to happen that children of German parents who had to be brought up at the expense of the municipality (so-called boarded children) were put by the municipality of Vienna into the care of Czech foster parents in the countryside; these children then grew up as Czechs. On the other hand, children of non-German parents were Germanized by German foster parents. One aristocratic Polish lady used to relieve the city of Vienna of the care of children of Polish parents in order to have the children grow up as Poles. No one can doubt that all these children became good Czechs, Germans, or Poles without regard to what nation their parents had belonged to.

On the other hand, it is politically quite unimportant that the grammatical relationship between languages facilitates learning them. No cultural and no political affinity emerges from it; no political structures can be erected on the basis of it. The notion of the relationship of peoples originates not from the national-policy/individualistic sphere of ideas but rather from the race-policy/collectivistic sphere; it was developed in conscious opposition to the freedom-oriented notion of modern autonomy. Pan-Latinism, Pan-Slavism, and Pan-Germanism are chimeras which, in confrontation with the national strivings of individual peoples, have always come out on the short end. They sound very good in the fraternizing festivities of peoples who for the moment are following parallel political goals; they fail as soon as they are supposed to be more. They never have possessed power to form states. There is no state that has been based on them.

If people have long resisted seeing the characteristic feature of the nation in language, one of the decisive circumstances was that they could not reconcile this theory with the reality that allegedly displays cases in which *one* nation speaks several languages and other cases in which several nations use *one* language. The assertion that it is possible for the members of *one* nation to speak several languages is supported with reference to the conditions of the "Czechoslovak" and "Yugoslav" nations. Czechs and Slovaks acted in this war as a unified nation. The particularist strivings of small Slovak groups have at least not manifested themselves outwardly and have not been able to achieve any political successes. It now seems that a Czechoslovak state will be formed to which all Czechs and Slovaks will belong. However, Czechs and Slovaks do not, for that reason, yet form *one* nation. The dialects from which the Slovak language was formed are extraordinarily close to the dialects of the Czech language, and it is not difficult for a rural Slovak who knows only his own dialect to communicate with Czechs, especially Moravians, when the latter speak in their dialect. If the Slovaks, back at the time before they began developing an independent standard language, that is, around the turn from the eighteenth to the nineteenth century, had come into closer political connection with the Czechs, then the development of a Slovak standard language would doubtless no more have occurred than the development of an independent Swabian standard language in Swabia. Political motives were decisive for the effort made in Slovakia to create an independent language. This Slovak standard language, which was formed quite according to the model of Czech and was closely related to it in every respect, could not develop, however, likewise because of political circumstances. Under the rule of the Magyar state, excluded from school, office, and court, it led a miserable existence in popular almanacs and opposition leaflets. Again, it was the slight development of the Slovak language that caused efforts to adopt the Czech standard language, which had been under way in Slovakia from the very beginning, to gain more and more ground. Today two movements oppose each other in Slovakia: one that wants to root all Czechism out of the Slovak language and develop the language pure and independent and a second that wishes its assimilation to Czech. If the latter movement should prevail, then the Slovaks would become Czechs and the Czechoslovak state would evolve into a purely Czech national state. If, however, the former movement should prevail, then the Czech state would gradually be compelled, if it did not want to appear an oppressor, to grant the Slovaks autonomy and finally, perhaps, complete independence. There is no Czechoslovak nation composed of Czech speakers and Slovak speakers. What we see before us is a particular Slavic nation's struggle for life. How it will turn out will depend on political, social, and cultural circumstances. From a purely linguistic point of view, either of the two developments is possible.

The case is no different with the relation of the Slovenes to the Yugoslav nation. The Slovene language, also, has been struggling since its origin between independence and approximation to or complete blending with Croatian. The Illyrian movement wanted to include the Slovene language also in the sphere of its strivings for unity. If Slovene should be able to maintain its independence even in the future, then the Yugoslav state would have to grant the Slovenes autonomy.

The South Slavs also present one of the most frequently cited examples of two nations speaking the same language. Croats and Serbs use the same language. The national difference between them, it is asserted, lies exclusively in religion. Here is said to be a case that cannot be explained by the theory that perceives the distinctive attribute of a nation in its language.

In the Serbo-Croatian people the sharpest religious contrasts confront each other. One part of the people belongs to the Orthodox Church and another part to the Catholic Church, and even today the Mohammedans form a not inconsiderable part. In addition to these religious contrasts, there are old political enmities that still stem in part from times whose political conditions have today long ago been super-seded. The dialects of all these religiously and politically splintered peoples are, however, extraordinarily closely related. These dialects were so closely related to each other that the efforts to form a standard language proceeding from different sides always led to the same result; all efforts always resulted in the same standard language. Vuk Ste-fanović Karadžić wanted to create a Serbian language, Ljudevit Gaj a unified South Slavic; Pan-Serbism and Illyrianism bluntly confronted each other. But since they had the same dialectical material to deal with, the results of their work were identical. The languages that they created differed so little from each other that they finally blended to-gether into a unified language. If the Serbs did not use the Cyrillic al-phabet and the Croats the Latin alphabet exclusively, then there would be no external sign for attributing a written work to one nation or the other. The difference of alphabets cannot split a unified nation in the long run; the Germans also use different forms of writing without this having acquired any national significance. The political development of the last years before the war and during the war itself has shown that the religious difference between Croats and Serbs upon which the Aus-trian policy of Archduke Francis Ferdinand and his followers had built castles in the air has long since lost its earlier significance. There seems to be no doubt that in the political life of the Serbs and Croats also, the national factor of a common language will override all impeding influences and that the religious difference will play no greater role in the Serbo-Croatian nation than it does in the German people.

Two other examples commonly named to show that speech com-munity and nation do not coincide are the Anglo-Saxon and Danish-Norwegian cases. The English language, it is asserted, is used by two nations, the English and the Americans; and this alone shows that it is inadmissible to seek the criterion of nationality in language alone. In truth, the English and Americans are a single nation. The inclination to count them as two nations stems from the fact that people have be-come accustomed to interpret the nationality principle as necessarily including the demand for unifying all parts of a nation into a single state. It will be shown in the next section that this is not true at all and that, therefore, the criterion of the nation should in no way be sought in efforts to form a unified state. That Englishmen and Americans be-long to different states, that the policies of these states have not always been in consonance, and that the differences between them have occasionally even led to war—all that is still no proof that Englishmen and Americans are not *one* nation. No one could doubt that England is bound together with its dominions and with the United States by a national bond that will show its binding force in days of great political crisis. The World War brought proof that disagreements between the individual parts of the Anglo-Saxon nation can appear only when the whole does not seem threatened by other nations.

It seems even more difficult at first sight to harmonize the problem of the Irish with the linguistic theory of the nation. The Irish once formed an independent nation; they used a separate Celtic language. At the beginning of the nineteenth century, 80 percent of the population of Ireland still spoke Celtic, and more than 50 percent understood no English at all. Since then the Irish language has lost much ground. Only somewhat more than 600,000 persons still use it, and only seldom are people still to be found in Ireland who understand no English. Of course, there are also efforts in Ireland today to awaken the Irish language to new life and to make its use general. The fact is, however, that very many of those who are on the side of the political Irish movement are English by nationality. The opposition between Englishmen and Irishmen is of a social and religious and not exclusively of a national nature; and so it can happen that inhabitants of Ireland who by nationality are no Irishmen also belong to the movement in great number. If the Irish should succeed in achieving the autonomy they strive for, then it is not ruled out that a large part of today's English population of Ireland would assimilate itself to the Irish nation.

The much-cited Danish-Norwegian example also cannot undercut the assertion that nationality lies in language. During the centuries-long political union between Norway and Denmark, the old Norwegian standard language was completely driven out by the Danish standard language; it still managed a miserable existence only in the numerous dialects of the rural population. After the separation of Norway from Denmark (1814), efforts were made to create a national language of its own. But the efforts of the party striving to create a new Norwegian standard language on the basis of the old Norwegian language definitely failed. Success went to those who seek only to enrich Danish by introduction of expressions from the vocabulary of the Norwegian dialects but otherwise are in favor of retaining the Danish language. The works of the great Norwegian writers Ibsen and Björnson are written in this language.[9] Danes and Norwegians still today, then, form a single nation, even though they belong politically to two states.

2 Dialect and Standard Language

In primitive times every migration causes not only geographical but also intellectual separation of clans and tribes. Economic exchanges do not yet exist; there is no contact that could work against differentiation and the rise of new customs. The dialect of each tribe becomes more and more different from the one that its ancestors spoke when they were still living together. The splintering of dialects goes on without interruption. The descendants no longer understand one another.

A need for unification in language then arises from two sides. The beginnings of trade make understanding necessary between members of different tribes. But this need is satisfied when individual middlemen in trade achieve the necessary command of language. In early times, when the exchange of goods between distant regions had only a relatively slight significance, scarcely more than individual expressions and word families must have come into more general use in this way. Political changes had to be much more significant for the unification of dialects. Conquerers appeared and created states and political unions of all kinds. The political leaders of broad territories came into closer personal relations; members of all social strata of numerous tribes were united in military service. Partly independently of the political and military organization and partly in closest connection with it, religious institutions arise and spread from one tribe to another. Hand in hand with political and religious strivings for unity go linguistic strivings. Soon the dialect of the ruling or the priestly tribe gains predominance over the dialects of the subjects and laity; soon, out of the different dialects of fellow members of state and religion, a unified mixed dialect is formed.

Introduction of the use of writing becomes the strongest basis for the unification of language. Religious doctrines, songs, laws, and records preserved in writing give preponderance to the dialect in which they

---

9. Ibsen made fun of the efforts of the adherents of the separate "Norwegian" language in the person of Huhu in *Peer Gynt* (fourth act, madhouse scene).

have been expressed. Now the further splintering of the language is impeded; now there is an ideal speech that seems worth striving to attain and to imitate. The mystical nimbus that surrounds the letters of the alphabet in primitive times and that even today — at least in regard to their printed form — has not yet quite disappeared raises the prestige of the dialect in which the writing is done. Out of the chaos of dialects there arises the general language, the language of rulers and laws, the language of priests and singers, the literary language. It becomes the language of the higher-placed and more educated persons; it becomes the language of state and culture;[10] it appears finally as the sole correct and noble language; the dialects from which it has arisen, however, are thenceforth regarded as inferior. People consider them corruptions of the written language; people begin to despise them as the speech of the common man.

In the formation of unified languages, political and cultural influences are always working together from the very beginning. The natural element in the dialect of the people is that it draws its strength from the life of those who speak it. On the other hand, the standard and unified language is a product of studyrooms and chancelleries. Of course, it too stems in the last analysis from the spoken word of the common man and from the creations of gifted poets and writers. But it is always shot through with more or less pedantry and artificiality also. The child learns the dialect from his mother; it alone can be his mother tongue; the standard language is taught by the school.

In the struggle that now arises between standard language and dialect, the latter has the advantage that it already takes possession of the person in his most receptive years. But the former also does not stand helpless. That it is the general language, that it leads beyond regional disunity to understanding with broader circles, makes it indispensable to state and church. It is the bearer of the written heritage and the intermediary of culture. Thus it can triumph over the dialect. If, however, it is too distant from the latter, if it is or over time becomes so estranged from the latter that it is still intelligible only to persons who learn it with effort, then it must succumb; then a new standard language arises from

---

10. One must distinguish between written language and cultural or standard language. When dialects possess a written literature, it will no longer do to deny them the designation of written languages. All those languages should then be called standard languages that make the claim to express all human thoughts orally and in writing and thus also to be scientific and technical languages. The boundaries between the two naturally cannot always be sharply drawn.

the dialect. Thus Latin was displaced by Italian, Church Slavonic by Russian; thus in modern Greek the common speech will perhaps triumph over the *katharevousa* of classicism.

The luster with which the school and the grammarians are accustomed to surround the standard language, the respect they pay to its rules, and the contempt they show for anyone who sins against these rules cause the relation between the standard language and the dialect to appear in a false light. The dialect is not corrupted standard language; it is primeval language; only out of the dialects was the standard language formed, whether a single dialect or else a mixed form artificially formed out of different dialects was raised to the status of standard language. The question therefore cannot arise at all whether a particular dialect belongs to this or that standard language. The relation between standard language and dialect is not always that of unequivocal association or indeed of superiority and inferiority, and the circumstances of linguistic history and grammar are not alone decisive in that respect. Political, economic, and general cultural developments of the past and present determine to which standard language the speakers of a particular dialect incline; and it can happen that in this way a unified dialect attaches itself partly to one and partly to another standard language.

The process by which the speakers of a particular dialect make the transition to using a particular standard language thereafter, either exclusively or along with the dialect, is a special case of national assimilation. It is especially characterized by being a transition to a grammatically closely related standard language, with this way being as a rule the only conceivable one in a given case. The Bavarian peasant's son has in general no other way open to culture than through the German standard language, even though it may also happen in rare particular cases that, without this detour, he becomes French or Czech directly. Yet for the Low German there are already two possibilities: assimilation to the German or to the Dutch standard language. Which of the two courses he takes is decided neither by linguistic nor genealogical considerations but by political, economic, and social ones. Today there is no longer any purely Plattdeutsch village; at least bilingualism prevails everywhere. If a Plattdeutsch district were to be separated from Germany today and be joined to the Netherlands, with the German school and the German official and judicial language replaced by Dutch ones, then the people affected would see all that as a national rape. Yet one hundred or two hundred years ago, such a separation of a bit of German territory could have been carried out without difficulty, and the descendants of the people who were separated at that time would be just as good Hollanders today as they in fact are good Germans today.

In Eastern Europe, where school and office still do not have anywhere near as much significance as in the West, something of the kind is still possible today. The linguistic researcher will be able to determine of most of the Slavic dialects spoken in upper Hungary whether they are closer to Slovak than to Ukrainian and perhaps also to decide in many cases in Macedonia whether a particular dialect is closer to Serbian or to Bulgarian. Yet that still does not answer the question whether the people who speak this dialect are Slovaks or Ukrainians, Serbs or Bulgarians. For this depends not only on linguistic conditions but also on political, ecclesiastical, and social ones. A village with a dialect undoubtedly more closely related to Serbian can more or less adopt the Bulgarian standard language relatively quickly if it acquires a Bulgarian church and a Bulgarian school.

Only thus can one gain an understanding of the exceedingly difficult Ukrainian problem. The question whether the Ukrainians are an independent nation or only Russians who speak a particular dialect is senseless in this form. If the Ukraine had not lost its political independence in the seventeenth century to the Great Russian state of the Czars, then a separate Ukrainian standard language would probably have developed. If all Ukrainians, including those in Galicia, Bukovina, and upper Hungary, had come under the rule of the Czars as late as the first half of the nineteenth century, then this might not have hindered the development of a separate Ukrainian literature; but this literature would probably have assumed a position in relation to Great Russian no different from that of Plattdeutsch writings in relation to German. It would have remained dialect poetry without particular cultural and political pretensions. However, the circumstance that several million Ukrainians were under Austrian rule and were also religiously independent of Russia created the preconditions for the formation of a separate Ruthenian standard language. No doubt the Austrian government and the Catholic Church preferred that the Austrian Reussens develop a separate language instead of adopting Russian. In this sense there is a spark of truth in the assertion of the Poles that the Ruthenians are an Austrian invention. The Poles are wrong only in saying that without this official support of the early beginnings of the Ruthenian aspirations there would have been no Reussen movement at all in East

Galicia. The national rising of the East Galicians could no more have been suppressed than could the awakening of other new nations. If state and church had not sought to guide it into other channels, then it would probably have developed from the beginning with a stronger Great Russian orientation.

The Ukrainian movement in Galicia, then, significantly furthered, at least, the separatist strivings of the Ukrainians in South Russia and perhaps even breathed life into them. The most recent political and social upheavals have furthered South Russian Ukrainianism so much that it is not entirely impossible that it can no longer be overcome by Great Russianism. But that is no ethnographic or linguistic problem. Not the degree of relationship of languages and races will decide whether the Ukrainian or the Russian language will win out but rather political, economic, religious, and general cultural circumstances. It is easily possible for that reason that the final outcome will be different in the former Austrian and Hungarian parts of the Ukraine than in the part that has long been Russian.

Conditions are similar in Slovakia. The independence of the Slovakian language from Czech is also a product of an, in a certain sense, accidental development. If there had been no religious differences between the Moravians and Slovaks and if Slovakia had been politically linked with Bohemia and Moravia no later than the eighteenth century, then a separate Slovak written and standard language would hardly have evolved. On the other hand, if the Hungarian government had given less emphasis to Magyarization of the Slovaks and had allowed their language more scope in school and administration, then it would probably have developed more strongly and would today possess more power of resistance against Czech.[11]

To the language researcher it may in general seem not impossible to draw language boundaries by classifying individual dialects with

---

11. Still more examples could be cited, including, for example, the Slovene language also. Particular interest attaches to those cases in which something similar was attempted on a smaller scale. Thus—according to information for which I am indebted to the Vienna Slavicist Dr. Norbert Jokl—the Hungarian government tried in the county of Ung to make the Slovak and Ruthenian local dialects used there independent; it had newspapers appear in these dialects in which, for the Ruthenian dialect, Latin letters and a Magyarizing orthography were used. Again, in the county of Zala the effort was made to make a Slovene dialect independent, which was facilitated by the fact that the population, in contrast to the Austrian Slovenes, was Protestant. Schoolbooks were published in this language. In Papa there was a special faculty for training teachers of this language.

particular standard languages. Yet his decision does not prejudice the historical course of events. Political and cultural events are decisive. Linguistics cannot explain why Czechs and Slovaks became two separate nations, and it would have no explanation if the two in the future should perhaps blend into *one* nation.

3   National Changes

For a long time nations have been regarded as unchanging categories, and it has not been noticed that peoples and languages are subject to very great changes in the course of history. The German nation of the tenth century is a different one from the German nation of the twentieth century. That is even outwardly evident in the fact that the Germans of today speak a different language from that of the contemporaries of the Ottonians.

For an individual, belonging to a nation is no unchangeable characteristic. One can come closer to one's nation or become alienated from it; one can even leave it entirely and exchange it for another.

National assimilation, which must of course be distinguished from the blending and turnover of races, with which it undergoes certain interactions, is a phenomenon whose historical significance cannot be assessed too highly. It is one manifestation of those forces whose operation shapes the history of peoples and states. We see it at work everywhere. If we could fully understand it in its conditions and in its essence, then we would have taken a good step further on the path that leads to understanding of historical development. In striking contrast to this importance of the problem is the disregard with which historical science and sociology have so far passed it by.

Language serves for intercourse with one's fellow men. Whoever wants to speak with his fellow men and to understand what they say must use their language. Everyone must therefore strive to understand and speak the language of his environment. For that reason individuals and minorities adopt the language of the majority. It is always a precondition for that, however, that contacts occur between the majority and the minority; if this is not the case, then no national assimilation ensues either. Assimilation proceeds the faster the closer are the contacts of the minority with the majority and the weaker the contacts within the minority itself and the weaker its contacts with fellow nationals living at a distance. From that it immediately follows that the social positions of the different nationalities must be of special significance in this regard, for personal contacts are more or less bound up with class membership. Thus, particular social strata in an environment of a foreign nation can not only maintain their own customs and own languages for centuries but also assimilate others to them. A German nobleman who immigrated to Eastern Galicia around 1850 did not become a Ruthenian but a Pole; a Frenchman who settled in Prague around 1800 became not a Czech but a German. However, the Ruthenian peasant in Eastern Galicia who by upward social mobility joined the ruling class also became a Pole, and the Czech peasant's son who rose into the bourgeoisie became a German.[12]

In a society organized by classes or castes, different nations can live side by side in the same territory for centuries without losing their national distinctness. History provides enough examples of that. In the Baltic lands of Livonia, Estonia, and Courland, in Carniola and in South Styria, the German nobility maintained itself for many generations amidst the environment of a different people; so did the German bourgeoisie in the Bohemian, Hungarian, and Polish cities. Another example is the Gypsies. If social contacts between the nations are lacking, if between them no *connubium* and only to a restricted extent *commercium* exists, if changing one's class or caste is possible only in rare exceptional cases, then the conditions for national assimilation are rarely present. Thus, self-contained peasant settlements inside a country inhabited by a population with another language could maintain themselves as long as the agricultural strata were bound to the soil. As, however, the liberal economic order set aside all bonds, removed the special privileges of classes, and gave the workers freedom of movement, the rigid national stratification was loosened. Upward social mobility and migrations made national minorities disappear rapidly, or at least pushed them into defensive positions tenable only with difficulty.

The tearing down of barriers that guarded against shifting from one social class to another, freedom of movement of the person, everything that has made modern man free, has very much facilitated the advance of standard languages against dialects. "Where the so greatly improved means of transport and communication have shaken people up today

---

12. Cf. Otto Bauer, "Die Bedingungen der Nationalen Assimilation," *Der Kampf*, vol. V, pp. 246 ff.

and mingled them together in an undreamed-of manner, this signals the end of local dialects, of local manners, traditions and usages; the railroad whistle has sung their funeral dirge. In a few years they will disappear; in a few years it will be too late to collect them and perhaps still protect them," an English philologist already remarked decades ago.[13] Today one can no longer live even as a peasant or worker in Germany without at least understanding the standard High German language and being able, if necessary, to use it. The school is making its contribution to hastening this process.

Quite distinct from natural assimilation through personal contact with people speaking other languages is artificial assimilation — denationalization by state or other compulsion. As a social process, assimilation hinges on certain preconditions; it can only occur when its preconditions exist. Compulsory methods then remain powerless; they can never succeed when the preconditions are not at hand or are not created. Administrative compulsion can sometimes bring about these conditions and so indirectly bring about assimilation; it cannot bring about national transformation directly. If individuals are put into an environment where they are cut off from contact with their fellow nationals and made exclusively dependent on contacts with foreigners, then the way is prepared for their assimilation. But if one can use only compulsory means that do not influence the colloquial language, then attempts at national oppression have scarcely any prospect of success.

Before the opening of the age of modern democracy, when national questions did not yet have the political significance that they have today, for this reason alone there could be no question of national oppression. If the Catholic Church and the Habsburg state suppressed Czech literature in the seventeenth century in Bohemia, they were motivated by religious and political but not yet by national-policy considerations; they persecuted heretics and rebels, not the Czech nation. Only very recent times have seen attempts at national oppression on a large scale. Russia, Prussia, and Hungary, above all, have been the classical countries of compulsory denationalization. How much success Russianization, Germanization, and Magyarization have achieved is well known. After these experiences, the prognosis that one can make about possible future efforts at Polonization or Czechification is not a favorable one.

13. Cf. Socin, *Schriftsprache und Dialekte im Deutschen nach Zeugnissen alter und neuer Zeit* (Heilbronn: 1888), p. 501.

1   Liberal or Pacifistic Nationalism

That politics should be national is a modern postulate.

In most countries of Europe the princely state had replaced the estate system of the Middle Ages from the beginning of modern times. The political conception of the princely state is the interest of the ruler. The famous maxim of Louis XIV, *L'état c'est moi* ["The State, it is I"], expresses most briefly the conception that was still alive at the three European imperial courts until the recent upheavals. It is no less clear when Quesnay, whose doctrines nevertheless already lead into the new conception of the state, precedes his work with the motto *Pauvre paysan, pauvre royaume; pauvre royaume, pauvre roi* ["Poor countryman, poor realm; poor realm, poor king"]. It is not enough for him to show that on the well-being of the peasant that of the state also depends; he still considers it necessary to show that the king also can be rich only when the peasant is. Only then does the necessity appear proved of taking measures to raise the well-being of the peasants. For the object of the state is precisely the prince.

Against the princely state there then arises in the eighteenth and nineteenth centuries the idea of freedom. It revives the political thought of the republics of antiquity and of the free cities of the Middle Ages; it links up with the monarchomachs' hostility to princes; it patterns itself on the example of England, where the crown had already suffered a decisive defeat in the seventeenth century; it fights with the entire arsenal of philosophy, rationalism, natural law, and history; it wins over the great masses through literature, which puts itself entirely at its service. Absolute kingship succumbs to the attack of the movement for freedom. In its place appears here parliamentary monarchy, there a republic.

The princely state has no natural boundaries. To be an increaser of his family estate is the ideal of the prince; he strives to leave to his successor more land than he inherited from his father. To keep on acquiring new possessions until one encounters an equally strong or stronger adversary—that is the striving of kings. For fundamentally, their greed for lands knows no boundaries; the behavior of individual princes and the views of the literary champions of the princely idea agree on that. This principle threatens, above all, the existence of all smaller and weaker states. That they are nevertheless able to maintain themselves is attributable only to the jealousy of the big ones, which anxiously watch that none should become too strong. That is the conception of European equilibrium, which forms coalitions and breaks them up again. Where it is possible without endangering the equilibrium, smaller states are destroyed; an example: the partition of Poland. Princes regard countries no differently from the way an estate owner regards his forests, meadows, and fields. They sell them, they exchange them (e.g., for "rounding off" boundaries); and each time rule over the inhabitants is transferred also. On this interpretation, republics appear as unowned property that anyone may appropriate if he can. This policy did not reach its high point, by the way, until the nineteenth century, in the Enactment of the Delegates of the Holy Roman Empire of 1803, in Napoleon's establishments of states, and in the decisions of the Congress of Vienna.

Lands and peoples are, in the eyes of princes, nothing but objects of princely ownership; the former form the basis of sovereignty, the latter the appurtenances of landownership. From the people who live in "his" land the prince demands obedience and loyalty; he regards them almost as his property. This bond that binds him with each one of his subjects should, however, also be the only one that joins the individual persons into a unit. The absolute ruler not only regards every other community between his subjects as dangerous, so that he tries to dissolve all traditional comradely relations between them that do not derive their origin from state laws enacted by him and is hostile to every new formation of community, perhaps through clubs; he also will not allow the subjects of his different territories to begin to feel themselves comrades in their role as subjects. But, of course, in seeking to tear apart all class ties to make subjects out of nobles, the bourgeoisie, and peasants, the prince atomizes the social body and thereby creates the precondition for the rise of a new political sentiment. The subject who has grown unaccustomed to feel himself a member of a narrow circle begins to feel himself a person, a member of his nation, and a citizen of the state and of the world. The way opens up for the new outlook on the world.

The liberal theory of the state, hostile to princes, rejects their greed for, and trafficking in, lands. First of all, it finds it a matter of course that state and nation coincide. For so it is in Great Britain, the model country of freedom, so in France, the classical land of the struggle for freedom. That seems such a matter of course that no further word is wasted on it. Since state and nation coincide and there is no need to change this, there is no problem here.

The problem of state boundaries first appeared when the power of the idea of freedom gripped Germany and Italy. Here and in Poland there stands behind the despicable despots of the present day the great shadow of a vanished unified state. All Germans, Poles, and Italians have a great political goal in common: the liberation of their peoples from the rule of princes. That gives them first unity of political thinking and then unity of action. Across state boundaries, guarded by customs guards and gendarmes, the peoples stretch their hands in unity. The alliance of the princes against freedom is confronted by the union of peoples fighting for their freedom.

To the princely principle of subjecting just as much land as obtainable to one's own rule, the doctrine of freedom responds with the principle of the right of self-determination of peoples, which follows necessarily from the principle of the rights of man.[14] No people and no part of a people shall be held against its will in a political association that it does not want. The totality of freedom-minded persons who are intent on forming a state appears as the political nation; *patrie, Vaterland* becomes the designation of the country they inhabit; *patriot* becomes a synonym of *freedom-minded*.[15] In this sense the French begin to feel themselves a nation when they break the despotism of the Bourbons and when they take up the struggle against the coalition of monarchs who threaten their just-won freedom. The Germans, the Italians become nationally minded because foreign princes, joined in the Holy Alliance, hinder them from establishing a free state. This nationalism directs itself not against foreign peoples but against the despot who subjugates foreign peoples also. The Italian hates above all not the Germans but the Bourbons and Habsburgs; the Pole hates not the Germans or Russians but the Czar, the King of Prussia, and the Emperor of Austria. And only because the troops on which the rule of the tyrants rests are foreign does the struggle also adopt a slogan against foreigners. But even in battle the Garibaldians shouted to the Austrian

---

14. Cf. Sorel, *Nouveaux essais d'histoire et de critique* (Paris: 1898), pp. 99 ff.

15. Cf. Michels, "Zur historischen Analyse des Patriotismus," *Archiv für Sozialwissenschaft und Sozialpolitik*, vol. 36, 1913, pp. 38 ff., 402 f.; Pressensé, "L'idée de Patrie," *Revue mensuelle de l'École d'Anthropologie de Paris*, vol. 9, 1899, pp. 91 ff.

soldiers: *Passate l'Alpi e tornerem fratelli* ["Go back across the Alps, and we'll become brothers again"].[16] Among themselves the individual nations fighting for freedom get along marvelously. All peoples hail the struggle for freedom of the Greeks, the Serbs, and the Poles. In "Young Europe" the freedom fighters are united without distinction of nationality.

The nationality principle above all bears no sword against members of other nations. It is directed *in tyrannos*.

Therefore, above all, there is also no opposition between national and citizen-of-the-world attitudes.[17] The idea of freedom is both national and cosmopolitan. It is revolutionary, for it wants to abolish all rule incompatible with its principles, but it is also pacifistic.[18] What basis for war could there still be, once all peoples had been set free? Political liberalism concurs on that point with economic liberalism, which proclaims the solidarity of interests among peoples.

One must also keep that in mind if one wants to understand the original internationalism of the socialist parties since Marx. Liberalism, too, is cosmopolitan in its struggle against the absolutism of the princely state. Just as the princes stand together to defend themselves against the advance of the new spirit, so the peoples also hold together against the princes. If the *Communist Manifesto* calls on the proletarians of all countries to unite in the struggle against capitalism, then that slogan is consistently derived from the asserted fact of the identity of capitalistic exploitation in all countries. It is no antithesis, however, to the liberal demand for the national state. It is no antithesis to the program of the bourgeoisie, for the bourgeoisie, too, is in this sense international. The emphasis lies not on the words "all countries" but on the word "proletarians." That like-thinking classes in the same position in all countries must combine is presupposed as a matter of course. If any point at all can be perceived in this exhortation, it is only the point made against pseudo-national strivings that fight every change in traditional arrangements as an infringement on warranted national individuality.

The new political ideas of freedom and equality triumphed first in the West. England and France thus became the political model countries for the rest of Europe. If, however, the liberals called for adoption of

---

16. Cf. Robert Michels, "Elemente zur Entstehungsgeschichte des Imperialismus in Italien," *Archiv für Sozialwissenschaft*, vol. 34, 1912, p. 57.
17. Cf. Seipel, *Nation und Staat* (Vienna: 1916), pp. 11 f. footnote; Meinecke, loc. cit., pp. 19 f.
18. Cf. Michels, "Patriotismus," loc. cit., p. 403.

foreign institutions, then it was only natural that the resistance mounted by the old forces also made use of the age-old device of xenophobia. German and Russian conservatives also fought against the ideas of freedom with the argument that they were foreign things not suitable for their peoples. Here national values are misused for political purposes.[19] But there is no question of opposition to the foreign nation as a whole or to its individual members.

So far as relations among peoples are concerned, therefore, the national principle is above all thoroughly peaceful. As a political ideal it is just as compatible with the peaceful coexistence of peoples as Herder's nationalism as a cultural ideal was compatible with his cosmopolitanism. Only in the course of time does peaceful nationalism, which is hostile only to princes but not to peoples also, change into a militaristic nationalism. This change takes place, however, only at the moment when the modern principles of the state, in their triumphant march from West to East, reach the territories of mixed population.

The significance of the nationality principle in its older peaceful form becomes especially clear to us when we observe the development of its second postulate. First of all, the nationality principle includes only the rejection of every overlordship and so also of every foreign overlordship; it demands self-determination, autonomy. Then, however, its content expands; not only freedom but also unity is the watchword. But the desire for national unity, too, is above all thoroughly peaceful.

One of its sources, as already mentioned, is historical remembrance. From the dismal present the glance turns back toward a better past. And this past shows a unified state, not in such splendid pictures for every people as for the Germans and the Italians, but, for most, attractive enough.

But the idea of unity is not merely romanticism; it is also important for political reality. In unity strength is sought to overcome the alliance of the oppressors. Unity in a unified state offers the peoples the highest assurance of maintaining their freedom. And there, too, nationalism does not clash with cosmopolitanism, for the unified nation does not want discord with neighboring peoples, but peace and friendship.

19. Cf. Schultze-Gaevernitz, *Volkswirtschaftliche Studien aus Russland* (Leipzig: 1899), pp. 173 ff.; Bauer, *Nationalitätenfrage*, loc. cit., pp. 138 ff.

So we also see, then, that the idea of unity cannot exert its state-destroying and state-creating power where freedom and self-government already prevail and seem assured without it. To this day Switzerland has scarcely been tempted by that idea. The least inclination to secession is shown by the German-Swiss, and very understandably: they could only have exchanged freedom for subjugation in the German authoritarian state. But the French also, and on the whole also the Italians, have felt themselves so free in Switzerland that they felt no desire for political unification with their fellows in nationality.

For the national unified state, however, yet a third consideration is at work. Without doubt the stage of development of the international division of labor already reached today required an extensive unification of law and of communication and transportation facilities in general, and this demand will become all the more pressing the more the economy is further reshaped into a world economy. When economic contacts were still in their earliest stages, on the whole scarcely extending beyond the boundaries of a village, the splitting of the earth's surface into innumerable small legal and administrative districts was the natural form of political organization. Apart from military and foreign-policy interests, which, after all, did not press everywhere for union and for formation of great empires—and even where they were at work in this direction in the age of feudalism and still more in the age of absolutism, they did not always lead to formation of national states—there were no circumstances that demanded unification of law and administration. That became a necessity only to the extent that economic relations began to reach out more and more beyond the boundaries of provinces, of countries, and finally of continents.

Liberalism, which demands full freedom of the economy, seeks to dissolve the difficulties that the diversity of political arrangements pits against the development of trade by separating the economy from the state. It strives for the greatest possible unification of law, in the last analysis for world unity of law. But it does not believe that to reach this goal, great empires or even a world empire must be created. It persists in the position that it adopts for the problem of state boundaries. The peoples themselves may decide how far they want to harmonize their laws; every violation of their will is rejected on principle. Thus a deep chasm separates liberalism from all those views that want forcibly to create a great state for the sake of the economy.

Yet political realism must first still reckon with the existence of states and with the difficulties that they pit against the creation of supranational law and freedom of international transactions. It is with envy, therefore, that the patriots of nations fragmented into many states regard the nationally unified peoples. They want to follow their example. They view things with different eyes than do liberal doctrinaires. In the Germany of the German Confederation, the necessity of unification of law and the administration of justice, of communication and transportation facilities, and of the entire administration was recognized as urgent. A free Germany could also have been created through revolutions within the individual states; for that, unification would not have first been necessary. In favor of the unified state, however, there speaks in the eyes of political realists not only the necessity of setting an alliance of the oppressed against the alliance of the oppressors in order to achieve freedom at all [20] but also the further necessity of holding together in order to find in unity the strength to preserve freedom. Even apart from that, the necessity of trade is pressing for unity. It will no longer do to permit the fragmentation in law, in monetary systems, in communications and transportation, and in many other fields, to continue. In all these fields the times require unification, even beyond national boundaries. Already the peoples are beginning to make preliminary preparations for world unity in all these matters. Does it not seem obvious to achieve in Germany, to begin with, what the other peoples have already achieved — to create a German civil law as precursor of the coming world law, a German penal law as a preliminary stage for world penal law, a German railroad union, a German monetary system, a German postal system? All that, however, the German unified state is to assure. The program of the men of freedom, therefore, cannot limit itself to the "auction of thirty princes' crowns" (Freiligrath [21]); even if only because of the stage of economic development, it must call for the unified state.

Thus the striving for the unified state already contains the kernel of the new interpretation of the nationality principle, which leads from the peaceful liberal nationality principle to militant power-policy nationalism to imperialism.

20. Think of Schleswig-Holstein, the left bank of the Rhine, etc.
21. [Ferdinand Freiligrath (1810–76), German lyric poet and democratic partisan.]

2 Militant or Imperialistic Nationalism

A *The Nationality Question in Territories with Mixed Populations*

The princely state strives restlessly for expansion of its territory and for increase in the number of its subjects. On the one hand it aims at the acquisition of land and fosters immigration; on the other hand it sets the strictest penalties against emigration. The more land and the more subjects, the more revenues and the more soldiers. Only in the size of the state does assurance of its preservation lie. Smaller states are always in danger of being swallowed up by larger ones.

For the free national state, all these arguments do not hold true. Liberalism knows no conquests, no annexations; just as it is indifferent towards the state itself, so the problem of the size of the state is unimportant to it. It forces no one against his will into the structure of the state. Whoever wants to emigrate is not held back. When a part of the people of the state wants to drop out of the union, liberalism does not hinder it from doing so. Colonies that want to become independent need only do so. The nation as an organic entity can be neither increased nor reduced by changes in states; the world as a whole can neither win nor lose from them.

Liberalism has been able to endure only in Western Europe and in America. In Central and Eastern Europe, after flourishing briefly, it was displaced again; its democratic program still lives on there only in the programs and more rarely in the deeds of the socialist parties. State practice has gradually perverted the pacifistic nationality principle of liberalism into its opposite, into the militant, imperialistic nationality principle of oppression. It has set up a new ideal that claims a value of its own, that of the sheer numerical size of the nation.

From the cosmopolitan standpoint, one must describe the splitting of mankind into different peoples as a circumstance that causes much trouble and costs. Much labor is spent on learning foreign languages and is wasted on translations. All cultural progress would make its way more easily, every contact between peoples would proceed better, if there were only *one* language. Even one who appreciates the immeasurable cultural value of diversity of material and intellectual arrangements and of the development of particular individual and national characters must admit this and must not deny that the progress of mankind would be made quite extraordinarily more difficult if there did not exist, besides the small nations numbering only a few hundred thousand or a few million souls, larger nations also.

But even the individual can experience the inconvenience of the multiplicity of languages. He notes it when he travels abroad, when he reads foreign writings, or when he wants to speak with his fellow men or write for them. The ordinary man may not care whether his nation is numerically larger or smaller, but for the intellectual worker this is of the greatest significance. For "for him language is more than a mere means of understanding in social contacts; it is for him one of his chief tools, indeed often his only tool, and one that he can scarcely change." [22] It is decisive for the success of literary work whether the author can make himself directly understood by a larger or a smaller number of persons. No one, therefore, desires a large size for his own nation more ardently than the poet and the scholarly writer, the intellectual leaders of nations. It is easy to understand why they may be enthusiastic about size. But that alone is far from explaining the popularity of this ideal.

For these leaders cannot in the long run even recommend any goals to the nation that the nation has not chosen itself. And there are still other ways to broaden the public for writers; the education of the people can be broadened, creating as many more readers and hearers as through diffusion of the national language abroad. The Scandinavian nations have trod this path. They seek national conquests not abroad but at home.

That the national state could become imperialistic, that, neglecting older principles, it could see a goal of its policy first in maintaining and then in increasing the number of members of the nation, even at the cost of the right of self-determination of individuals and of entire peoples and parts of peoples — for that development, circumstances were decisive that were foreign to the liberalism that had originated in the West and foreign to its pacifistic nationality principle. What was decisive was the fact that the peoples in the East do not have fully distinct areas of settlement but rather live locally mingled in broad territories, as well as the further fact that such mixing of peoples keeps occurring afresh through the migration of peoples. These two problems have brought militant or imperialistic nationalism to maturity. It is of German origin, for the problems out of which it arose first came onto the historical

---

22. Cf. Kautsky, *Nationalität und Internationalität* (Stuttgart: 1908), p. 19; also Paul Rohrbach, *Der deutsche Gedanke in der Welt* (Düsseldorf and Leipzig: Karl Robert Langewiesche Verlag, 1912), copies 108 to 112 thousand, p. 13.

scene when liberalism reached German soil. But it has by no means remained limited to Germany; all peoples in a position to know that these
circumstances are subjecting some of their fellow nationals to national
alienation have followed the German people on the same path or will
do so if history does not first find another solution to the problem.

Every observation of the problems to which we now turn must start
from the fact that the conditions under which people live on particular parts of the earth's surface are different. We would best recognize
the significance of this fact by trying to disregard it. If the conditions of
life were the same everywhere on the earth's surface, then on the whole
there would be no incentive for individuals and for peoples to change
the places where they live.[23]

That the conditions of life are unequal, however, brings it about
that — to use Ségur's[24] formulation — the history of mankind is the striving of peoples to progress from living in worse territories to better ones.
World history is the history of national migrations.

National migrations take place either in forcible military form or in
peaceful forms. The military form used to be the predominant one.
The Goths, Vandals, Lombards, Normans, Huns, Avars, and Tartars
seized their new homes with force and exterminated, drove away, or
subjugated the local populations. Then there were two classes of different nationality in the country, the masters and the subjugated, which
not only confronted each other as political and social classes but also
were foreign to each other in ancestry, culture, and language. In the
course of time these national contrasts disappeared, either because
the conquerers were ethnically absorbed into the conquered or because
the subjugated groups became assimilated to the victors. It has been
centuries since this process took place in Spain and Italy, in Gaul, and
in England.

In Eastern Europe there are still broad territories where this assimilation process has not begun at all or is only just beginning. Between
the Baltic barons and their Estonian and Latvian tenants, between the

---

23. One could object that even if the conditions of life were everywhere the same, there would
have to be migrations when one people grew in size more rapidly than others, for then migrations
would have to take place out of the more densely settled territories into the more thinly settled
ones. The Malthusian law entitles us to assume, however, that growth of population also depends
on the natural conditions of life, so that merely from the assumption of the same external conditions of life there follows equality of increase in population.

24. [Comte Louis Philippe de Ségur (1753–1830), French politician and historian.]

Magyar or Magyarized nobles of Hungary and the Slavic or Rumanian peasants and farm workers, between the German townspeople of the Moravian cities and the Czech proletarians, between the Italian landlords of Dalmatia and the Slavic peasants and farm hands, the deep gap of national differences yawns even today.

The doctrine of the modern state and modern freedom that was developed in Western Europe knows nothing of these conditions. The problem of nationally mixed populations does not exist for it. For it, the formation of nations is a completed historical process. Frenchmen and Englishmen today no longer take any foreign components into their European homelands; they live in compact territories of settlement. If individual foreigners do come to them, then they are easily and painlessly assimilated. No frictions between nationalities could arise from applying the nationality principle on English and French soil in Europe (but things are different in the colonies and in the United States). And so the opinion could also arise that the full application of the nationality principle could assure eternal peace. For since, according to the liberal view, wars of course arise only through kings' lust for conquest, there can be no more war once every people is constituted as a separate state. The older nationality principle is peaceful; it wants no war between peoples and believes that no reason for one exists.

Then it is suddenly discovered that the world does not show the same face everywhere as on the Thames and on the Seine. The movements of the year 1848 first lifted the veil that despotism had spread over the mixture of peoples in the empire of the Habsburgs; the revolutionary movements that later broke out in Russia, in Macedonia and Albania, in Persia and China, revealed the same problems there also. As long as the absolutism of the princely state had oppressed all in the same way, these problems could not be recognized. Now, however, scarcely as the struggle for freedom is beginning, they loom menacingly.[25]

It seemed obvious to work for their solution with the traditional means of the Western doctrine of freedom. The majority principle, whether applied in the form of a referendum or in some other way, was considered suitable for solving all difficulties. That is democracy's answer. But here, was such a solution thinkable and possible at all? Could it have established peace here?

25. Cf. Bernatzik, *Die Ausgestaltung des Nationalgefühls im 19. Jahrhundert* (Hanover: 1912), p. 24.

The basic idea of liberalism and of democracy is the harmony of interests of all sections of a nation and then the harmony of interests of all nations. Since the rightly understood interest of all strata of the population leads to the same political goals and demands, the decision on political questions can be left to the vote of the entire people. It may be that the majority errs. But only through errors that it itself has committed and whose consequences it itself suffers can a people achieve insight and can it become politically mature. Errors once committed will not be repeated; people will recognize where the best in truth is to be found. Liberal theory denies that there are special interests of particular classes or groups opposing the common good. It can therefore see only justice in the decisions of the majority; for the errors that were committed revenge themselves on all, both on those who had supported them and on the outvoted minority, which also must pay for not having understood how to win the majority over to its side.

As soon, however, as one admits the possibility and even the necessity of genuinely opposed interests, the democratic principle also has lost its validity as a "just" principle. If Marxism and Social Democracy see an irreconcilable opposition of conflicting class interests everywhere, then they must, consistently, also reject the democratic principle. This has long been overlooked, since Marxism, precisely among those two nations among whom it had been able to gain the largest number of adherents, the Germans and Russians, has pursued not only socialist but also democratic goals. But that is only a matter of historical accident, the consequence of quite particular circumstances coming together. The Marxists fought for the right to vote, freedom of the press, and the right to form associations and assemblies as long as they were not the ruling party; where they came to power they did nothing more quickly than set these freedoms aside.[26] That quite coincides with the behavior of the Church, which behaves democratically wherever others rule but, where it itself rules, wants nothing of democracy. A majority decision can never be "just" for the Marxists as it is for liberalism; for them it is always only the expression of the will of a particular class. Even seen from this angle alone, therefore, socialism and democracy are irreconcilable contraries; the term Social Democrat contains a *contradictio in adjecto*. For the Marxists, only the triumph of the proletariat, the provisional goal and the end of historical evolution, is good; everything else is bad.

26. Cf. Bucharin, *Das Programm der Kommunisten (Bolschewiki)* (Vienna: 1919), pp. 23 ff.

Like the Marxists, the nationalists also deny the doctrine of the harmony of all interests. Between peoples irreconcilable oppositions are said to exist; here one can never let things depend on the decision of the majority if one has the power to oppose it.

Democracy seeks first to solve the political difficulties that impede the establishment of a national state in territories with nationally mixed populations by those means that have proved themselves in nationally unified countries. The majority should decide; the minority should yield to the majority. That shows, however, that it does not see the problem at all, that it does not have any inkling of where the difficulty lies. Yet belief in the correctness and the all-healing power of the majority principle was so strong that people for a long time would not recognize that nothing could be accomplished with it here. The obvious failure was always attributed to other causes. There were writers and politicians who traced the national disorders in Austria to the fact that there still was no democracy in its territory; if the country should become democratically governed, then all frictions between its peoples would disappear. Precisely the opposite is true. National struggles can arise only on the soil of freedom; where all peoples are subjugated—as in Austria before March 1848—then there can be no dissensions among them.[27] The violence of the struggles between the nationalities grew to the extent that the old Austria approached democracy. They were not ended at all by the dissolution of the state; they are carried on only more bitterly in the new states, where ruling majorities confront national minorities without the mediation of the authoritarian state, which softens much harshness.

To recognize the deeper grounds for the failure of democracy in the nationality struggles of our time, one must first of all strive for clarity about the essence of democratic government.

Democracy is self-determination, self-government, self-rule. In democracy, too, the citizen submits to laws and obeys state authorities and civil servants. But the laws were enacted with his concurrence; the bearers of official power got into office with his indirect or direct concurrence. The laws can be repealed or amended, officeholders can be removed, if the majority of the citizens so wishes. That is the essence of democracy; that is why the citizens in a democracy feel free.

27. For that reason antidemocratic and churchly writers also recommend the return to the absolutism of the princes and of the Pope as a means of avoiding national struggles.

He who is compelled to obey laws on whose enactment he has no influence, he who must endure a government ruling over him in whose formation he can take no part, is, in the political sense, unfree and is politically without rights, even though his personal rights may be protected by law.[28] That does not mean that every minority is politically unfree in the democratic state. Minorities can become the majority, and this possibility influences their position and the way that the majority must behave towards them. The majority parties must always take care that their actions do not strengthen the minority and do not offer it the opportunity to come to power. For the thoughts and programs of the minority affect the entire people as a political entity, whether or not they are able to prevail. The minority is the defeated party, but in the struggle of parties it has had the possibility of winning and, as a rule, despite the defeat, it maintains the hope of winning some time later and becoming the majority.

The members of national minorities that do not hold a ruling position by special privilege, are, however, politically unfree. Their political activity can never lead to success, for the means of political influence on their fellow men, the spoken and written word, are bound up with nationality. In the great national political discussions from which political decisions follow, the citizens of foreign nationality stand aside as mute spectators. They are negotiated about along with others, but they do not join in the negotiations. The German in Prague must pay municipal assessments; he too is affected by every decree of the municipality, but he must stand aside when the political struggle rages over control of the municipality. What he wishes and demands in the municipality is a matter of indifference to his Czech fellow citizens. For he has no means of influencing them unless he gives up the special ways of his people, accommodates himself to the Czechs, learns their language, and adopts their way of thinking and feeling. So long, however, as he does not do this, so long as he remains within his circle of inherited speech and culture, he is excluded from all political effectiveness. Although he also may formally, according to the letter of the law, be a citizen with full rights, although he may, because of his social position, even belong to the politically privileged classes, in truth he is politically without rights, a second-class citizen, a pariah; he is ruled by others without himself having a share in ruling.

28. Frequently, of course, civil rights can also be lost because of political powerlessness.

The political ideas that cause parties to come and go and states to be created and destroyed are bound up with nationality today just as little as any other cultural phenomenon. Like artistic and scientific ideas, they are the common property of all nations; no single nation can escape their influence. Yet every nation develops currents of ideas in its own special way and assimilates them differently. In every people they encounter another national character and another constellation of conditions. The idea of Romanticism was international, but every nation developed it differently, filled it with a particular content, and made something else out of it. We speak rightly, therefore, of German Romanticism as a particular trend in art that we can contrast with the Romanticism of the French or the Russians. And it is no different with political ideas. Socialism had to become something different in Germany, something different in France, something different in Russia. Everywhere, indeed, it met with a particular way of political thinking and feeling, with another social and historical development—in short, with other people and other conditions.

We now recognize the reason why national minorities that hold political power because of special privileges hang on to these privileges and to the ruling position bound up with them incomparably more tenaciously than do other privileged groups. A ruling class not of different nationality from the ruled still retains, even when overthrown, a greater political influence than would accrue to it according to the number of its members among the new rulers. It retains at least the possibility, under the new conditions, of fighting for power anew as the opposition party, of defending its political ideas, and of leading to new victories. The English Tories, as often as they were deprived of their privileges by a reform, have still celebrated a political resurrection every time. The French dynasties have not lost through dethronement all prospect of regaining the crown. They were able to form mighty parties that worked for a restoration; and if their efforts did not lead to success during the Third Republic, this was due to the intransigence and personal wretchedness of the pretender at the time and not to any fact that such efforts were quite hopeless. Rulers of foreign nationality, however, once they have left the scene, can never get power back unless they have the help of foreign arms; and, what is much more important, as soon as they no longer hold power, they not only are deprived of their privileges but are completely powerless politically. Not only are they unable to maintain influence corresponding to their numbers, but, as members of a foreign nationality, they no longer have any possibility at all of even being politically active or of having influence on others. For the political thoughts that now become dominant belong to a cultural circle that is foreign to them and are thought, spoken, and written in a language that they do not understand; they themselves, however, are not in a position to make their political views felt in this environment. From being rulers they become not citizens with equal rights but powerless pariahs who have no say when matters concerning them are being debated. If—without regard to theoretical and antiquarian misgivings that might be raised against it—we want to see a principle of modern democracy in the old postulate of the estates, *nil de nobis sine nobis* [nothing concerning us without us], we also see that it cannot be implemented for national minorities. They are governed; they do not have a hand in governing; they are politically subjugated. Their "treatment" by the national majority may be quite a good one; they may also remain in possession of numerous nonpolitical and even a few political privileges; yet they retain the feeling of being oppressed just because they are "treated" after all and may not take part.

The large German landowners in those Austrian crown lands that had a Slavic majority in the legislature felt themselves—despite their electoral privileges, which assured them a special representation in the provincial chamber and in the provincial committee—nevertheless oppressed, since they were faced by a majority whose political thinking they could not influence. For the same reason, German officeholders and house owners who possessed an electoral privilege that assured them a third of the seats on the municipal council in a municipality with a Slavic council majority still felt oppressed.

No less politically powerless are national minorities that never have possessed political dominance. They need to be especially mentioned even as do members of historyless nations who have lived as political inferiors for centuries under foreign rulers and immigrants into colonial settlement areas overseas. Accidental circumstances may temporarily give them the possibility of political influence; in the long run this is out of the question. If they do not want to remain politically without influence, then they must adapt their political thinking to that of their environment; they must give up their special national characteristics and their language.

In polyglot territories, therefore, the introduction of a democratic constitution does not mean the same thing at all as introduction of democratic autonomy. Majority rule signifies something quite different here than in nationally uniform territories; here, for a part of the people, it is not popular rule but foreign rule.[29] If national minorities oppose democratic arrangements, if, according to circumstances, they prefer princely absolutism, an authoritarian regime, or an oligarchic constitution, they do so because they well know that democracy means the same thing for them as subjugation under the rule of others. That holds true everywhere and also, so far, for all times. The often cited example of Switzerland is not relevant here. Swiss democratic local administration is possible without frictions under the nationality circumstances of Switzerland only because internal migrations between the individual nationalities have long since had no significance there. If, say, migrations of French Swiss to the east should lead to stronger foreign national minorities in the German cantons, then the national peace of Switzerland would already have vanished long ago.

For all friends of democracy, for all those who see the political remedy only in the self-administration and self-government of a people, this must cause severe distress. The German democrats of Austria were in this position, above all, as well as the few honorable democrats that the Hungarian people counted in their midst. It was they who were looking for new forms of democracy to make democracy possible even in polyglot countries.

Furthermore, people tend to recommend proportional representation as a remedy for the defects of the majority system. For nationally mixed territories, however, proportional representation is no way out of these difficulties. A system of proportional representation is applicable only to elections but not also to decisions about acts of legislation, administration, and jurisprudence. Proportional representation makes it impossible, on the one hand, that one party, through gerrymandering, be represented less in the representative body than corresponds to its strength; on the other hand it assures the minority of representation in the bodies of elected representatives and so offers it the possibility of exercising a check on the majority and of making its own voice heard. All that does not operate for a national minority. Being an actual minority in the people, it can never hope to obtain a majority in the

29. On the point that the majority principle appears applicable only where it is a question of settlement of differences within a homogenous mass, cf. Simmel, *Soziologie* (Leipzig: 1908), pp. 192 ff.

representative body through proportional representation. There remains to it, therefore, only the second significance of proportional representation. But the mere possibility of having some seats in the representative body is of little value for the national minority. Even when its representatives can sit in the representative body and take a part in deliberations, speeches, and decisions, the national minority still remains excluded from collaboration in political life. A minority is politically collaborating in the true sense of the word only if its voice is heard because it has prospects of coming to the helm some time. For a national minority, however, that is ruled out. Thus the activity of its deputies remains limited from the beginning to fruitless criticism. The words that they speak have no significance because they can lead to no political goal. In voting, their votes can be decisive only when nationally unimportant questions are on the agenda; in all other questions — and these are most of them — the national majority stands against it united like a phalanx. To realize this, one need only think of the roles that the Danes, Poles, and Alsatians played in the German Reichstag and the Croats in the Hungarian parliament or of the position that the Germans had in the Bohemian provincial legislature. If things were different in the Austrian Chamber of Deputies, if here, because no nation had an absolute majority, it was possible for the "delegation" of every single nation to become part of the majority, well, this proves nothing to the contrary because, after all, Austria was an authoritarian state in which not parliament but the government held all the cards. Precisely the Austrian Chamber of Deputies, in which the formation of parties was conditioned above all by tensions among nationalities, has shown how slightly a parliamentary collaboration of different peoples is possible.

It is therefore understandable why the principle of proportional representation also cannot be regarded as a usable means of overcoming the difficulties that arise from different nations living together. Where it has been introduced, experience has shown that it is admittedly quite usable for certain purposes, that it overcomes many frictions, but that it is far from being the remedy for national controversies that well-meaning utopians have considered it.

In Austria, the classical land of the nationality struggle, the proposal emerged in the first decade of the twentieth century for overcoming national difficulties by introducing national autonomy on the basis of the personality principle. These proposals, which came from the Social

Democrats Karl Renner[30] and Otto Bauer,[31] envisaged transformation of the Austrian authoritarian state into a democratic people's state. Legislation and administration of the entire state and the local administration of the autonomous areas should not extend to nationally disputed affairs; these should be administered in the local administrations by the members of the nations themselves, organized according to the personality principle, over whom, then, there should stand national councils as highest authorities of the individual nations. The educational system and the promotion of art and science, above all, were to be regarded as national issues.

Here we are not speaking of the significance that the program of national autonomy had in the historical development of the nationality program of the German-Austrians or of the basic presuppositions from which it proceeded. Here we must face only the question whether this program could have provided a satisfying solution to the fundamental difficulty that arises when different peoples live together. We can only reply "no" to this question. As before, those facts would still remain that exclude a national minority from participation in power and that, despite the letter of the law, which calls on them to join in governing, allow them to be not corulers but only the ruled. It is quite unthinkable from the start to split up all matters by nationality. It is impossible in a nationality-mixed city to create two police forces, perhaps a German and a Czech, each of which could take action only against members of its own nationality. It is impossible to create a double railroad administration in a bilingual country, one under the control only of Germans, a second only of Czechs. If that is not done, however, then the above-mentioned difficulties remain. The situation is not as though handling political problems directly connected with language was all that caused national difficulties; rather, these difficulties permeate all of public life.

National autonomy would have offered national minorities the possibility of administering and arranging their school systems independently. They had this possibility to a certain degree, however, even without the implementation of this program, though at their own cost. National autonomy would have allowed them a special right of taxation for these purposes and, on the other hand, relieved them from

---

30. Cf. Renner, *Das Selbstbestimmungsrecht der Nationen in seiner Anwendung auf Österreich* (Vienna: 1918), and numerous older writings of the same author.
31. Cf. Bauer, *Nationalitätenfrage*, loc. cit., pp. 324 ff.

contributing to the schools of other nationalities. That alone, however, is not worth as much as the authors of the program of national autonomy thought.

The position that the national minority would have obtained from the grant of national autonomy would have approximated the position of those privileged colonies of foreigners that the estate system established and that the princely state then established on models bequeathed by the estate system, perhaps like the position of the Saxons in Transylvania. This would not have been satisfactory in modern democracy. Generally speaking, the whole line of thought about national autonomy looks back more to the medieval conditions of the estate system than to the conditions of modern democracy. Given the impossibility of creating modern democracy in a multinational state, its champions, when as democrats they rejected the princely state, necessarily had to turn back to the ideals of the estate system.

If one looks for a model of national autonomy in certain problems of organization of minority churches, then this is only quite superficially a correct comparison. It is overlooked that since the force of faith no longer can, as it once could, determine the entire lifestyle of the individual, there no longer exists between members of different churches today that impossibility of political understanding that does indeed exist between different peoples because of differences of language and the resulting differences in styles of thinking and of outlook.

The personality principle can bring no solution to the difficulties of our problem because it indulges in extreme self-deception about the scope of the questions at issue. If only language questions, so called in the narrower sense, were the object of the national struggle, then one could think of paving the way for peace between peoples by special treatment of those questions. But the national struggle is not at all limited to schools and educational institutions and to the official language of the courts and authorities. It embraces all of political life, even all that which, as Renner and many others with him believe, ties a unifying bond around the nations, the so-called economic aspect. It is astonishing that this could be misunderstood precisely by Austrians, who, after all, were bound to see every day how everything became a national bone of contention — road construction and tax reforms, bank charters and public purveyances, customs tariffs and expositions, factories and hospitals. And purely political questions above all. Every foreign-policy question is the object of national struggle in the multinational state, and never did this show up more clearly in Austria-Hungary than during the World War. Every report from the battlefield was received differently by the different nationalities: some celebrated when others grieved; some felt downcast when others were happy. All these questions are controversial by nationality; and if they are not included in the solution of the nationality question, then the solution just is not complete.

The problem that the national question poses is precisely that the state and administration are inevitably constructed on a territorial basis in the present stage of economic development and so inevitably must embrace the members of different nationalities in territories of mixed language.

The great multinational states, Russia, Austria, Hungary, and Turkey, have now fallen apart. But that too is no solution to the constitutional problem in polyglot territories. The dissolution of the multinational state gets rid of many superfluous complications because it separates territories from each other that are compactly inhabited by the members of one people.[32] The dissolution of Austria solves the national question for the interior of Bohemia, for Western Galicia, and for the greater part of Carniola. But, as before, it remains a problem in the isolated German cities and villages that are sprinkled in the Czech-language territory of Bohemia, in Moravia, in Eastern Galicia, in the Gottschee [Kočevje] district, etc.

In polyglot territories the application of the majority principle leads not to the freedom of all but to the rule of the majority over the minority. The situation is made no better by the fact that the majority, in inner recognition of its injustice, shows itself anxious to assimilate the minorities nationally by compulsion. That attitude of course also implies — as a keen writer has noted — an expression of the nationality principle, an acknowledgement of the demand that state boundaries should not stretch beyond the boundaries of peoples.[33] Still the tormented peoples wait for the Theseus who shall overcome this modern Procrustes.

A way must be found out of these difficulties, however. It is not a question only of small minorities (for example, remnants of migrations that have long since come to a standstill), as one would tend to think if

32. The abuse of the compactly settled territories of the Germans in Bohemia is disregarded here; the national question would be soluble there, only people do not want to solve it.
33. Cf. Kjellén, loc. cit., p. 131.

one assessed this situation only from the point of view of a few German cities in Moravia or Hungary or of the Italian colonies on the east coast of the Adriatic. The great present-day migrations of peoples have given all these questions a heightened importance. Every day new migrations create new polyglot territories; and the problem that a few decades ago was visible only in Austria has long since become a world problem, although in another form.

The catastrophe of the World War has shown to what abyss that problem has led mankind. And all the streams of blood that have flowed in this war have not brought it a hair's-breadth closer to solution. In polyglot territories, democracy seems like oppression to the minority. Where only the choice is open either oneself to suppress or to be suppressed, one easily decides for the former. Liberal nationalism gives way to militant antidemocratic imperialism.

B   The Migration Problem and Nationalism

The variety of conditions of life in the individual parts of the earth's surface touches off migrations of individual persons and entire peoples. If the world economy were managed by the decree of an authority that surveyed everything and ordered what was most appropriate, then only the absolutely most favorable conditions of production would be utilized. Nowhere would a less productive mine or a less productive field be in use if more productive mines or fields lay unused elsewhere. Before a less productive condition of production is put to use, one must always first consider whether there do not exist more productive ones. Less productive conditions of production that might be in use would be discarded at once if others should be found whose yield would be so much greater that an increased yield would be attained from discarding the old and introducing the new sources of production, even despite the loss to be expected because the immovably invested capital would become useless. Since the workers have to settle in places of production or in their immediate neighborhood, the consequences for the conditions of settlement follow automatically.

The natural conditions of production are by no means unchangeable. In the course of history they have undergone great changes. Changes can take place in nature itself, for example, through changes of climate, volcanic catastrophes, and other elemental events. Then there are the changes that occur from human activity, for example, exhaustion of mines and of the fertility of the soil. More important, however, are changes in human knowledge, which overturn traditional views about the productivity of the factors of production. New needs are awakened, either from the development of the human character or because the discovery of new materials or forces has stimulated them. Previously unknown production possibilities are discovered, either through the discovery of hitherto unknown natural forces and putting them to use or through the progress of productive techniques, which makes it possible to tap natural forces that had been unusable or less usable before. It follows that it would not be enough for the director of the world economy to determine the locations of production once and for all; he would continually have to make changes in them according to changing circumstances, and every change would have to go hand in hand with a resettlement of workers.

What would happen under ideal world socialism by order of the general director of the world economy is achieved in the ideal of the free world economy by the reign of competition. The less productive enterprises succumb to the competition of the more productive. Primary production and industry migrate from places of lower-yielding conditions of production to places of higher-yielding ones; and with them migrate workers and also capital, so far as it is mobile. The result for the movement of peoples is thus the same in either case: the stream of population goes from the less fruitful territories to the more fruitful.

That is the basic law of migrations of persons and peoples. It holds true in the same degree for the socialist and the free world economy; it is identical with the law under whose operation the distribution of population takes place in every smaller territory cut off from the outside world. It always holds true, even though its effectiveness may be disturbed in greater or lesser degree by extra-economic factors also, perhaps by ignorance of conditions, by sentiments that we are accustomed to calling love of home, or by intervention of an external power that hinders migration.

The law of migration and location makes it possible for us to form an exact concept of relative overpopulation. The world, or an isolated country from which emigration is impossible, is to be regarded as overpopulated in the absolute sense when the optimum of population — that point beyond which an increase in the number of people would mean not an increase but a decrease of welfare — is exceeded.[34] A country is relatively overpopulated where, because of the large size of the

34. Compare Wicksell, *Vorlesungen über Nationalökonomie auf Grundlage des Marginalprinzipes* (Jena: 1913), vol. 1, p. 50.

population, work must go on under less favorable conditions of production than in other countries, so that, *ceteris paribus*, the same application of capital and labor yields a smaller output there. With complete mobility of persons and goods, relatively overpopulated territories would give up their population surplus to other territories until this disproportion had disappeared.

The principles of freedom, which have gradually been gaining ground everywhere since the eighteenth century, gave people freedom of movement. The growing security of law facilitates capital movements, improvement of transportation facilities, and the location of production away from the points of consumption. That coincides — not by chance — with a great revolution in the entire technique of production and with drawing the entire earth's surface into world trade. The world is gradually approaching a condition of free movement of persons and capital goods. A great migration movement sets in. Many millions left Europe in the nineteenth century to find new homes in the New World, and sometimes in the Old World also. No less important is the migration of the means of production: capital export. Capital and labor move from territories of less favorable conditions of production to territories of more favorable conditions of production.

Now, however — as a result of a historical process of the past — the earth is divided up among nations. Each nation possesses definite territories that are inhabited exclusively or predominantly by its own members. Only a part of these territories has just that population which, in conformity with the conditions of production, it would also have under complete freedom of movement, so that neither an inflow nor an outflow of people would take place. The remaining territories are settled in such a way that under complete freedom of movement they would have either to give up or to gain population.

Migrations thus bring members of some nations into the territories of other nations. That gives rise to particularly characteristic conflicts between peoples.

In that connection we are not thinking of conflicts arising out of the purely economic side effects of migrations. In territories of emigration, emigration drives up the wage rate; in territories of immigration, immigration depresses the wage rate. That is a necessary side effect of migration of workers and not, say, as Social Democratic doctrine wants to have believed, an accidental consequence of the fact that the emigrants stem from territories of low culture and low wages. The motive of the emigrant is precisely the fact that in his old homeland, because of its relative overpopulation, he can get no higher wage. If this reason were absent, if there were no difference in the productivity of labor between Galicia and Massachusetts, then no Galician would emigrate. If one wants to raise the European territories of emigration to the level of development of the eastern states of the Union, then there is just nothing else to do than let the emigration proceed to the point that the relative overpopulation of the former and the relative underpopulation of the latter have disappeared. Clearly, American workers view this immigration just as unhappily as European employers view the emigration. Indeed, the Junker east of the Elbe thinks no differently about the flight of workers from the land when his tenant goes to West Germany than when he goes to America; the unionized worker of the Rhineland is disturbed by immigration from the lands east of the Elbe no less than members of a Pennsylvania trade union. But that in the one case the possibility exists of forbidding the emigration and immigration, or at least of impeding it, while in the other case such measures could be thought of by at most a few eccentrics born a couple of centuries too late, is only to be attributed to the fact that, besides damage to the interests of individuals in the case of international migration, other interests also are damaged.

Emigrants who settle in previously uninhabited territories can preserve and further cultivate their national character in the new home also. Spatial separation can lead over time to the emigrants' developing a new independent nationality. Such development of independence was in any case easier in times when transport and communication still had to struggle with great difficulties and when the written transmission of the national culture was greatly impeded by the slight diffusion of literacy. With the present-day development of the means of transportation and communication, with the relatively high degree of popular education and the wide dissemination of the monuments of national literature, such national splitting off and the formation of new national cultures is far more difficult. The trend of the times works rather toward convergence of the cultures of peoples living far apart, if not even toward a blending of nations. The bond of common language and culture that links England with its faraway dominions and with the United States of America, which now will soon have been politically independent for one and a half centuries, has become not looser but closer. A people that today sends out colonists into an uninhabited territory can count on the emigrants' keeping their national character.

If, however, the emigration is directed to already inhabited territories, then various possibilities are conceivable. It may be that the immigrants come in such masses or possess such superiority through their physical, moral, or intellectual constitution that they either entirely displace the original inhabitants, as the Indians of the prairies were displaced by the palefaces and were driven to destruction, or that they at least achieve domination in their new home, as would perhaps have been the case with the Chinese in the western states of the Union if legislation had not restricted their immigration in time or as could be the case in the future with the European immigrants into North America and Australia. Things are different if immigration takes place into a country whose inhabitants, because of their numbers and their cultural and political organization, are superior to the immigrants. Then it is the immigrants who sooner or later must take on the nationality of the majority.[35]

The great discoveries had made the whole surface of the earth known to Europeans since the end of the Middle Ages. Now all traditional views about the inhabitability of the earth gradually had to change; the New World, with its excellent conditions of production, was bound to attract settlers from old and now relatively overpopulated Europe. At first, of course, it was only adventurers and political malcontents who moved far away to find a new home. Reports of their successes then drew others after them, at first only a few, then ever more and more, until finally in the nineteenth century, after improvement of the means of ocean transportation and the removal of limitations on freedom of movement in Europe, millions went migrating.

Here is not the place to investigate how it happened that all colonial land suitable for settlement by white Europeans was colonized by the English, Spanish, and Portuguese. Here it is enough for us to recognize the outcome that the best parts of the earth's surface inhabitable by whites thereby became English national property and that not even the Spaniards and Portuguese in America, and scarcely also the Dutch in South Africa and the French in Canada, enter into consideration. And this outcome is extremely important. It made the Anglo-Saxons the most numerous nation among the white civilized peoples. This, coupled

35. The assimilation is furthered if the immigrants come not all at once but little by little, so that the assimilation process among the early immigrants is already completed or at least already under way when the newcomers arrive.

with the circumstance that the English possess the largest merchant fleet in the world and that they administer the best territories of the tropics as political rulers, had led to the fact that the world today wears an English face. The English language and English culture have impressed their stamp on our times.

For England this means above all that Englishmen who leave the island of Great Britain because of its relative overpopulation can almost always settle in territories where the English language and English culture prevail. When a Briton goes abroad, whether to Canada or to the United States or to South Africa or to Australia, he does cease to be a Briton, but he does not cease to be an Anglo-Saxon. It is true that the English, until quite recently, did not appreciate this circumstance, that they paid no special attention to emigration, that they faced the dominions and the United States indifferently, coldly, and sometimes even with hostility, and that only under the influence of Germany's efforts directed against them did they begin to seek closer economic and political relations first with the dominions and then with the United States. It is just as true that the other nations, which had been less successful in acquiring overseas possessions, also long paid just as little attention to this development of affairs as the English themselves and that they envied the English more for their rich tropical colonies, for their trade and seaport colonies, and for shipping, industry, and trade than for possession of territories of settlement, which were less appreciated.

Only as the stream of emigrants, flowing abundantly at first only from England, also came to be fed more from other European territories did people begin to concern themselves with the national fate of the emigrants. People noticed that while the English emigrants could maintain their mother tongue and national culture, home customs, and usages of their fathers in their new homes, the other European emigrants overseas gradually ceased to be Dutchmen, Swedes, Norwegians, etc., and adapted themselves to the nationality of their environment. People saw that this alienation was unavoidable, that it occurred quicker here, slower there, but that it never failed to occur and that the emigrants—at the latest in the third generation, most already in the second, and not seldom even in the first—became members of Anglo-Saxon culture. The nationalists who dreamed about the size of their nation viewed this with sorrow, but it seemed to them that nothing could be done about it. They founded associations that endowed schools, libraries, and newspapers for the colonists to check the emigrants' national alienation; but what they achieved thereby was not much. People had no illusions about the fact that the reasons for emigration were of compelling economic nature and that the emigration as such could not be impeded. Only a poet like Freiligrath could ask the emigrants:

> Oh sprecht! warum zogt ihr von dannen?
> Das Neckartal hat Wein und Korn.
> [Oh speak! Why are you moving away?
> The Neckar Valley has wine and grain.]

The statesman and the economist well knew that there were more wine and more grain overseas than at home.

As late as the beginning of the nineteenth century people could scarcely suspect the significance of this problem. Ricardo's theory of foreign trade still started with the assumption that the free mobility of capital and labor exists only within the boundaries of a country. In the home country all local differences in the profit rate and the wage rate are evened out by movements of capital and workers. Not so for differences between several countries. Lacking there was that free mobility which would ultimately be bound to cause capital and labor to flow from the country offering less favorable conditions of production to the country of more favorable conditions. A range of emotional factors ("which I should be sorry to see weakened," the patriot and politician Ricardo interjects here into the exposition of the theorist) resists that. Capital and workers remain in the country, even though they thereby suffer a loss of income, and turn to those branches of production having, while not absolutely, still relatively more favorable conditions.[36] The basis of the free-trade theory is thus the fact that noneconomic reasons keep capital and labor from moving across national boundaries, even if this seems advantageous for economic motives. This may have been true on the whole in the days of Ricardo, but for a long time it has no longer been true.

But if the basic assumption of Ricardo's doctrine of the effects of free trade falls, then this doctrine must also fall along with it. There is no basis for seeking a fundamental difference between the effects of freedom

---

36. Cf. Ricardo, *Principles of Political Economy and Taxation* in *The Works of D. Ricardo*, edited by McCulloch, second edition (London: 1852), pp. 76 ff.

in domestic trade and in foreign trade. If the mobility of capital and labor internally differs only in degree from their mobility between countries, then economic theory can also make no fundamental distinction between the two. Rather, it must necessarily reach the conclusion that the tendency inheres in free trade to draw labor forces and capital to the locations of the most favorable natural conditions of production without regard to political and national boundaries. In the last analysis, therefore, unrestricted free trade must lead to a change in the conditions of settlement on the entire surface of the earth — from the countries with less favorable conditions of production capital and labor flow to the countries with more favorable conditions of production.

The free-trade theory modified in this way, just like the doctrine of Ricardo, also reaches the conclusion that from the purely economic point of view nothing speaks against free trade and everything against protectionism. But since it leads to quite different results regarding the effect of free trade on locational shifts of capital and labor, it presents a quite changed point of departure for testing the extraeconomic reasons for and against the protective system.

If one sticks with the Ricardian assumption that capital and labor are not impelled to move abroad even by more favorable conditions of production, then it turns out that the same applications of capital and labor lead to different results in the individual countries. There are richer and poorer nations. Trade-policy interventions can change nothing about that. They cannot make the poorer nations richer. The protectionism of the richer nations, however, appears completely senseless. If one drops that Ricardian assumption, then one sees a tendency prevail over the entire earth toward equalization of the rate of return on capital and of the wage of labor. Then, finally, there no longer are poorer and richer nations but only more densely and less densely settled and cultivated countries.

There can be no doubt that, even then, Ricardo and his school would have advocated nothing other than the policy of free trade, since they could not have avoided recognizing that protective tariffs are not the way out of these difficulties. For England, however, this problem never existed. Its rich holdings of territories for settlement lets emigration appear a matter of national indifference. The British emigrants can maintain their national character even far away; they cease to be Englishmen and Scots, but they remain Anglo-Saxons, and the war showed anew what that means politically.

For the German people, though, things are different. For reasons that go far back, the German nation has no territories for settlement at its disposal where emigrants can maintain their German character. Germany is relatively overpopulated; it must sooner or later yield up its surplus population, and if for some reason or other it could not or would not do this, then the standard of living of the Germans would have to sink to a lower level. If, however, Germans do emigrate, then they lose their national character, if not in the first generation, then in the second, third, or at the latest the fourth.

That was the problem that German policy saw posed for it after the establishment of the empire of the Hohenzollerns. The German people faced one of those great decisions that a nation does not have to make every century. It was fateful that the solution to this great problem became urgent before another, no less great, problem was solved, that of the establishment of the German national state. Even only to comprehend a question of this significance and of this historical gravity in its full scope would have required a generation that could decide its fate fearlessly and freely. That, however, was not allowed to the German people of the Great Prussian Reich, the subjects of the twenty-two federated princes. In these questions, also, it did not take its fate into its own hands; it left the most important decision to the generals and diplomats; it followed its leaders blindly without noticing that it was being led to the precipice. The end was defeat.

As early as the beginning of the thirties of the nineteenth century, people in Germany had begun to concern themselves with the problem of emigration. Now it was the emigrants themselves who made the unsuccessful attempt to establish a German state in North America; now again it was the Germans at home who sought to take the organization of emigration into their hands. That these efforts could lead to no success is not surprising. How could the attempt to establish a new state succeed for the Germans, who in their own country were not even able to transform the pitiable multiplicity of several dozen patrimonial principalities, with their enclaves, their hereditary affiliations, and their family laws, into a national state? How could Germans have found the strength to assert themselves out there in the wide world among Yankees and Creoles when at home they were not even able to put an end to the farcical rule of the miniature thrones of the Rusin and Schwarzburg princes? Where was the German subject to get the political insight that politics on the grand scale requires when it was forbidden to him at home "to judge to the extent of his limited intellect the actions of the supreme state authority?"[37]

In the middle of the seventies of the last century the problem of emigration had acquired such significance that its solution could no longer be dragged out. The decisive thing was not that emigration was steadily growing. According to data of the United States, the immigration of Germans there (not counting Austrians) had risen from 6,761 in the decade 1821 to 1830 to 822,007 in the decade 1861 to 1870; then, right after 1874, a dropoff—although at first only temporary—occurred in the German emigration to the United States. Far more important was that it was becoming ever clearer that the conditions of production in Germany for agriculture and for the most important branches of industry were so unfavorable that competition with foreign countries was no longer possible. The extension of the railroad net in the countries of Eastern Europe and the development of ocean and river shipping made it possible to import agricultural products into Germany in such quantity and at such low prices that the continued existence of the bulk of German agricultural units was most seriously threatened. Already from the fifties Germany was a rye-importing country; since 1875 it has also been a wheat-importing country. A number of branches of industry, particularly the iron industry, also had to struggle with growing difficulties.

It is clear where the causes lay, even though people of the time may have felt it only vaguely. The superiority of the natural conditions of production of foreign countries made itself all the more strongly evident as the continuing development of means of transportation cheapened freight rates. People did try to explain the lesser competitive capacity of German production in another way; and in that connection, as indeed is generally characteristic of the discussion of problems of economic policy in Germany during the last few decades, people concerned themselves predominantly with nonessential side issues and so quite overlooked the great significance of the principles of the problem.

If people had recognized the fundamental significance of these problems and had grasped the deeper interconnection of things, then they would have had to say that Germany was relatively overpopulated and that to restore a distribution of population over the entire surface

37. Cf. the decree of 15 January 1838 of the Prussian Minister of the Interior, v. Rochow, reprinted in Prince-Smith's *Gesammelte Schriften* (Berlin: 1880), vol. 3, p. 230.

of the earth corresponding to the conditions of production, part of the Germans had to emigrate. Whoever did not share misgivings of national policy about a decline in the size of population or even about an end to the growth of population in Germany would have been content with this judgment. In any case he would have consoled himself with the fact that individual branches of production would move abroad partially in such a way that German entrepreneurs would establish enterprises abroad so that the consumption of the entrepreneurs' incomes would take place in the German Reich and would thereby expand the food-supply margin of the German people.

The patriot who sees his ideal in a large number of people would have had to recognize that his goal could not be reached without reduction of the standard of living of the nation unless the possibility were created, through acquiring colonies for settlement, of retaining part of the surplus population within the nation despite its emigration from the mother country. He would then have had to turn all his strength to acquisition of land for settlement. In the middle of the seventies of the nineteenth century, and even a decade later, conditions were not yet such that it would not have been possible to reach this goal. In any case it could have been reached only in association with England. England was at that time and for long afterwards still troubled by a great concern, by anxiety that its Indian possession could be seriously threatened by Russia. For that reason it needed an ally who would have been in a position to hold Russia in check. Only the German Reich might have done that. Germany was strong enough to guarantee England the possession of India; Russia could never have thought of attacking India as long as it was not sure of Germany on its western border.[38] England could have given a great compensation for this guarantee, and surely would have given it. Perhaps it would have let Germany have its extensive South African possession, which at that time had only a very thin Anglo-Saxon settlement; perhaps it also would have helped Germany obtain a large territory for settlement in Brazil or Argentina or in western Canada. Whether this was attainable

---

38. To rule out any misunderstanding, let it be expressly noted that there is no intention here of taking a position on the question that was much discussed in Germany whether the "western" or "eastern" orientation for German policy was to be preferred. Both orientations were imperialist-minded, i.e., the question ran whether Germany should attack Russia or England. Germany should have allied itself with England to stand by it in a *defensive* war against Russia. There is no doubt, however, that then this war would never have occurred.

may be doubted after all.[39] But it is certain that if Germany could have attained anything along this line at that time, it could have done so only in association with England. The great Prussian Reich of the Junkers east of the Elbe, however, wanted no alliance with liberal England. For reasons of domestic politics, the Three Emperors' League,[40] the continuation of the Holy Alliance,[41] seemed to it to be the sole suitable association that it could enter into. When this alliance finally showed itself untenable and the German Reich, faced with the choice either of siding with Russia against Austria-Hungary or with Austria-Hungary against Russia, decided for the alliance with Austria, as Bismarck still sought repeatedly to maintain a friendly relationship with Russia. So, then, this opportunity of acquiring a great territory for settlement for Germany remained unused.

Instead of seeking, in association with England, to acquire a colony for settlement, the German Reich made the transition to protective tariffs from 1879 on. As ever at great turning points of policy, here, too, people saw neither the deeper significance of the problem nor the meaning of the new policy being adopted. To the liberals the protective tariff seemed a temporary backsliding into a superseded system. The practitioners of political realism, that hodgepodge of cynicism, lack of conscience, and unvarnished selfishness, evaluated the policy merely from the standpoint of their own interests as an increase in the incomes of landowners and entrepreneurs. The Social Democrats trotted out their faded recollections of Ricardo; as for a deeper knowledge of things, which surely would not have been difficult with the help of this guide, they were hindered by their doctrinaire clinging to Marxist theory. Only much later, and even then only hesitantly, was the great significance grasped that that policy shift had, not only for the German people, but for all peoples.[42]

The most remarkable thing about the protective tariff policy of the German Empire is that it lacked any deeper foundation. For the

39. But let it be noted that England, until the outbreak of the World War, repeatedly made attempts to have peaceful negotiations with Germany and was ready to buy peace even at the price of giving up some land.
40. [Germany, Austria-Hungary, and Russia]
41. [The post-Napoleonic league of the sovereigns of Russia, Prussia, and Austria]
42. When Lensch (*Drei Jahre Weltrevolution* [Berlin: 1917], pp. 28 ff.) designates the shift in trade policy of 1879 as one of the deepest grounds of today's world revolution, then he is certainly to be agreed with, but for quite other reasons than those he adduces. In view of the events that have taken place in the meanwhile, it is no longer worthwhile to refute his further discussions.

political realist it was sufficiently justified by its finding a majority in the German Reichstag. Any theoretical foundation for the protective tariff theory, however, looked very bad. The appeal to List's theory of an infant-industry tariff just did not hold water. It is no refutation of the free-trade argument to assert that the protective system puts idle productive forces to use. That they do not come into use without protection proves that their use is less productive than that of the productive forces used in their place. The infant-industry tariff also cannot be economically justified. Old industries have an advantage over young ones in many respects. But the rise of new industries is to be deemed productive from the overall point of view only when their lesser productivity at the start is at least made up for by greater productivity later. Then, however, the new enterprises are not only productive from the point of view of the whole economy but also privately profitable; they would be brought into existence even without special encouragement. Every newly established firm reckons with such initial costs that should be recovered later. It is untenable to cite, in opposition, the fact that almost all states have supported the rise of industry by protective tariffs and other protectionistic measures. The question remains open whether the development of viable industries would have proceeded even without such encouragement. Within the territories of states, changes of location occur without any external help. In territories that lacked industry before, we see industries arise that not only maintain themselves successfully alongside those of older industrial territories but not seldom drive those quite out of the market.

None of the German tariff rates, moreover, could be called an infant-industry tariff; neither the grain tariffs nor the iron tariffs nor any one of the several hundred other protective tariffs may be given this name. And tariffs other than infant-industry tariffs were never advocated by List; he was fundamentally a free-trader.

Moreover, the presentation of a protective-tariff theory in Germany has never once been attempted at all.[43] The long-winded and self-contradictory discussions about the necessity of protection for all national labor and of a gap-free tariff cannot lay claim to this name. They

---

43. Schuller, in *Schutzzoll und Freihandel* (Vienna: 1905), gives a theory of the setting of tariff rates; on his arguments for the protective tariff, cf. Mises, "Vom Ziel der Handelspolitik," *Archiv für Sozialwissenschaft und Sozialpolitik*, vol. 42, 1916/1917, p. 562, and Philippovich, *Grundriss der politischen Ökonomie*, vol. 2, 1st part, seventh ed. (Tübingen: 1914), pp. 359 f.

do indicate the direction in which reasons for the protective tariff policy had to be sought; they could not be suitable, however — and precisely because they renounced any economic line of thinking in advance and were oriented purely by power politics — for examining the question whether the goals being sought could also really be attained by this means.

Of the arguments of the protective-tariff advocates, we must at first leave aside the military one — or, as people now commonly say, the "war-economy" one — regarding autarky in case of war; that one will be discussed later. All other arguments start from the fact that the natural conditions for great and important branches of production are more unfavorable in Germany than in other territories and that the natural disadvantages must be compensated for by protective tariffs if production is to take place in Germany at all. For agriculture it could only be a question of thereby maintaining the internal market, for industry only of maintaining foreign markets, a goal that could be reached only by dumping by branches of production cartelized under the protection of the tariff. Germany, as a relatively overpopulated country working under more unfavorable conditions than foreign countries in a number of branches of production, had to export either goods or people. It decided for the former. It overlooked the fact, however, that export of goods is possible only if one competes with countries of more favorable conditions of production, that is, if, despite higher costs of production, one delivers just as cheaply as the countries producing at lower costs. That means, however, pressing down workers' wages and the standard of living of the whole people.

For years people in Germany could indulge in extreme illusions about that. To understand this interconnection of things, it would have been necessary to think economically and not in terms of statism and power politics. But someday it was nevertheless bound to impress itself on everyone with irrefutable logic that the protective tariff system was bound to fail in the end. One could deceive oneself about the fact that it was damaging the relative well-being of the German people as long as an absolute growth of national wealth could still be observed. But attentive observers of world economic development could not help but express misgivings about the future development of German foreign trade. What would happen to German commodity exports once an independent industry had become developed in the countries that still formed the market for German industry and had been in a position to produce under more favorable conditions?[44]

From this situation the desire finally arose among the German people for great colonies for settlement and for tropical territories that could supply Germany with raw materials. Because England stood in the way of the realization of these intentions, because England had broad territories at its disposal in which Germans could have settled, and because England possessed great tropical colonies, the desire arose to attack England and defeat it in war. That was the idea that led to construction of the German battle fleet.

England recognized the danger in time. First it strove for a peaceful settlement with Germany; it was ready to pay a high price for that. When this intention was wrecked on the resistance of German policy, England prepared itself accordingly. It was firmly resolved not to wait until Germany had a fleet superior to the English; it was resolved to wage war earlier, and it enlisted allies against Germany. When Germany got into war with Russia and France in 1914 over Balkan affairs, England fought also because it knew that in case of a German victory it would have to wage war alone with Germany in a few years. The construction of the German battle fleet had to lead to war with England before the German fleet had achieved superiority over the English. For the English knew that the German ships could be used in no other way than to attack England's fleet and its coast. The pretext with which Germany sought to conceal the ultimate intentions that it was pursuing by constructing the fleet was that it needed a mighty fleet to protect its expanded ocean trade. The English knew what to make of that. Once, when there still were pirates, merchant ships did need protection by cruisers on endangered seas. Since the establishment of security on the sea (approximately since 1860) that had no longer been necessary. It was quite impossible to explain the construction of a battle fleet usable only in European waters by a desire to protect trade.

It is also immediately understandable why, from the beginning, almost all states of the world sympathized with England against Germany. Most had to fear Germany's hunger for colonies. Only a few nations of Europe are in a situation similar to that of Germany in being able to feed their populations within their own borders only under

44. Cf., out of a large literature, Wagner, *Agrar- und Industriestaat*, second ed.

more unfavorable conditions than are found in the rest of the world. To these belong the Italians in the first place, and also the Czechs. That these two nations also were on the side of our [Germany's and Austria's] adversaries was Austria's doing.[45]

Now the war has been fought, and we have lost it. The German economy has been quite shattered by the long "war economy"; in addition, it will have to bear heavy reparations burdens. But far worse than these direct consequences of the war must appear the repercussion on Germany's world economic position. Germany has paid for the raw-material supplies on which it depends partly by export of manufactures, partly from the yield of its foreign enterprises and capital investments. That will no longer be possible in the future. During the war the foreign investments of the Germans were expropriated or used up in payment for the import of various goods. The export of manufactures, however, will encounter extreme difficulties. Many markets have been lost during the war and will not be easy to win back. Here, too, the war has created no new situation but has only hastened a development that would have occurred without it. The impediment to trade caused by the war has brought new industries to life in Germany's former markets. They would have arisen even without the war, but later. Now, once they are there and are operating under more favorable conditions of production than German enterprises, they will pose severe competition to German exports. The German people will be compelled to shrink their consumption. They will have to work more cheaply, that is, live worse, than other peoples. The entire level of German culture will thereby be depressed. After all, culture is wealth. Without well-being, without wealth, there never has been culture.

True, emigration might still remain open. But the inhabitants of the territories that might be considered do not want to admit any German immigrants. They fear being outnumbered by the German elements; they fear the pressure that immigration would be bound to exert on wages. Even long before the war, Wagner could already refer to the fact

45. That Japan and China were also against us is to be ascribed to the disastrous Chiao-chou policy. [At the time of the 1914–18 war, both China and Japan harbored ill feelings toward Germany. After two German missionaries were killed in 1897 by a mob in the port city of Chiao-chou, Germany had sent her navy, seized Chiao-chou, and imposed on China a ninety-nine-year lease for the port and the bay. Shortly after Japan had acquired the Liaodong peninsula, with the ports of Dairen and Port Arthur, by defeating China in the 1894–95 Sino-Japanese War, she had been forced by Germany, Russia, and France to return it to China.]

that, except for the Jews, only the German people, "who are scattered over almost the entire earth's surface, are fragmented among so many peoples, with individuals scattered among other civilized peoples and nations. They often form a very capable element, even a sort of cultural fertilizer, though seldom are they in leading positions, more frequently they are little men and little women in middle to lower positions." And he added that "this German diaspora" is not much more liked, even though more respected, than that of the Jews and Armenians, and it is often subject to just as strong an aversion on the part of the native population.[46] How will things be now, after the war?

Only now can one fully survey the damage that the departure from the principles of liberal policy has caused for the German people. How very different a position Germany and Austria would be in today if they had not undertaken the fateful return to the protective tariff! Of course, the size of the population would not be as large as it is today. But the smaller population could be living and working under conditions just as favorable as those of the other countries of the world. The German people would be richer and happier than it is today; it would have no enemies and no enviers. Hunger and anarchy — that is the result of the protectionist policy.

The outcome of German imperialism, which cast the German people into bitter misery and made it into a pariah people, shows that those whose leadership it followed in the last generation were not on the right path. Neither fame nor honor nor wealth nor happiness was to be found on this path. The [pre–French Revolution liberal] ideas of 1789 would not have brought the German people to its position today. Did not the men of the Enlightenment, who today are reproached for lack of state feeling,[47] better understand what is good for the German people and the entire world? More clearly than all theories could do, the course of history shows that properly understood patriotism leads to cosmopolitanism, that the welfare of a people lies not in casting other peoples down but in peaceful collaboration. Everything that the German people possessed, its intellectual and material culture, it has uselessly sacrificed to a phantom, to no one's benefit and to its own harm.

---

46. Cf. Wagner, loc. cit., p. 81.
47. Cf. Sprengel, *Das Staatsbewusstsein in der deutschen Dichtung seit Heinrich von Kleist* (Leipzig: 1918), pp. 8 ff.

A nation that believes in itself and its future, a nation that means to stress the sure feeling that its members are bound to one another not merely by accident of birth but also by the common possession of a culture that is valuable above all to each of them, would necessarily be able to remain unperturbed when it saw individual persons shift to other nations. A people conscious of its own worth would refrain from forcibly detaining those who wanted to move away and from forcibly incorporating into the national community those who were not joining it of their own free will. To let the attractive force of its own culture prove itself in free competition with other peoples—that alone is worthy of a proud nation, that alone would be true national and cultural policy. The means of power and of political rule were in no way necessary for that.

That nations favored by fate possess wide territories of settlement could provide no cogent grounds for adopting another policy. It is true that those colonies were not taken with smooth talk, and one can think only with shudders and anger of the fearful mass murders that prepared the basis for many of the colonial settlements flourishing today. But all other pages of world history were also written in blood, and nothing is more stupid than efforts to justify today's imperialism, with all of its brutalities, by reference to atrocities of generations long since gone. It must be recognized that the time for expeditions of conquest is past, that today it is at least no longer acceptable to use force on peoples of the white race. Whoever wanted to contradict this principle of modern political world law, an expression of the liberal ideas of the time of the Enlightenment, would have to set himself against all other nations of the world. It was a fateful error to want to undertake a new partition of the earth with cannons and armored ships.

The nations suffering from relative overpopulation in their homelands can no longer use those means of relief today that were usual at the time of national migrations. Full freedom of emigration and immigration and unlimited free mobility of capital must be their demand. Only in this way can they attain the most favorable economic conditions for their fellow nationals.

Of course, the struggle of nationalities over the state and government cannot disappear completely from polyglot territories. But it will lose sharpness to the extent that the functions of the state are restricted and the freedom of the individual is extended. Whoever wishes peace among peoples must fight statism.

C   *The Roots of Imperialism*

It is usual to seek the roots of modern imperialism in the desire for territories to settle and colonies to exploit. This interpretation represents imperialism as an economic necessity. We best recognize that this interpretation is inadequate if we consider how liberalism stands on the same problem. Its watchword is freedom of movement; at the same time, it is averse to all colonial undertakings. The proof that the liberal school has provided is irrefutable: that free trade and only free trade appears justified from the purely economic point of view, that only it guarantees the best provisioning of all persons, the greatest yield of labor with the smallest expenditure of costs.

This liberal dogma cannot be shaken, either, by the assertion — on whose correctness we offer no opinion — that there are peoples who are not ready for self-government and never will be ready. These lower races supposedly must be politically governed by the higher races, without economic freedom being in any way limited thereby. Thus have the English long interpreted their rule in India, thus was the Congo Free State conceived: the open door for economic activity of all nations in free competition both with the members of the ruling nation and with the natives. That the practice of colonial policy deviates from this ideal, that it again, as formerly, regards the natives only as a means, not as an end in their own right, that it — above all the French, with their trade-policy assimilation system — excludes from the colonial territories all who do not belong to the ruling nation, is only a consequence of imperialistic lines of thinking. But where do these come from?

An individualistic justification for imperialism can also be found. That is the one based on the conditions of territories with mixed population. There the consequences of the application of the democratic principle were bound by themselves alone to lead to militant aggressive nationalism. Things are no different in those territories to which the stream of immigration is directed today. There the problem of mixed languages arises ever anew, there imperialistic nationalism must also arise ever anew. Thus we see efforts growing in America and in Australia for limitation of undesired — foreign-nationality — immigration, efforts that were bound to arise out of the fear of being outnumbered by foreigners in one's own country at the same time that the fear arose that the immigrants of foreign national origin could no longer be fully assimilated.

Doubtless this was the point from which the rebirth of imperialistic thinking proceeded. From here the spirit of imperialism gradually undermined the entire thought structure of liberalism, until finally it could also replace the individualistic basis from which it had originated with a collectivistic one. The idea of liberalism starts with the freedom of the individual; it rejects all rule of some persons over others; it knows no master peoples and no subject peoples, just as within the nation itself it distinguishes between no masters and no serfs. For fully developed imperialism, the individual no longer has value. He is valuable to it only as a member of the whole, as a soldier of an army. For the liberal, the number of fellow members of his nationality is no unduly important matter. It is otherwise for imperialism. It strives for the numerical greatness of the nation. To make conquests and hold them, one must have the upper hand militarily, and military importance always depends on the number of combatants at one's disposal. Attaining and maintaining a large population thus becomes a special goal of policy. The democrat strives for the unified national state because he believes that this is the will of the nation. The imperialist wants a state as large as possible; he does not care whether that corresponds to the desire of the peoples.[48]

The imperialistic people's state scarcely differs from the old princely state in its interpretation of sovereignty and its boundaries. Like the latter, it knows no other limits to the expansion of its rule than those drawn by the opposition of an equally strong power. Even its lust for conquest is unlimited. It wants to hear nothing of the right of peoples. If it "needs" a territory, then it simply takes it and, where possible, demands further from the subjugated peoples that they find this just and reasonable. Foreign peoples are in its eyes not subjects but objects of policy. They are — quite as the princely state once thought — appurtenances of the country where they live. Expressions also recur in the modern imperialistic manner of speaking, therefore, that were believed to be already forgotten. People speak again of geographic boundaries,[49] of the

48. We have seen how the striving for the unified national state originates from the desire of the peoples. Imperialism interprets the matter otherwise. For it, the idea of the unified state is a legal title for annexations. Thus the Pan-Germans wanted to annex the German cantons of Switzerland and even the Netherlands against their will.
49. The answer of the nationality principle to the theory of natural geographic boundaries was given by Arndt when he explained that "the single most valid natural boundary is made by language" (*Der Rhein. Deutschlands Strom aber nicht Deutschlands Grenze*, 1813, p. 7) and then was aptly formulated by J. Grimm when he speaks of the "natural law . . . that not rivers and not mountains form the boundary lines of peoples and that for a people that has moved over mountains and

necessity of using a piece of land as a "buffer zone"; territories are again rounded off; they are exchanged and sold for money.

These imperialistic doctrines are common to all peoples today. Englishmen, Frenchmen, and Americans who marched off to fight imperialism are no less imperialistic than the Germans. Of course, their imperialism differed from the German variety before November 1918 in one important point. While the other nations brought their imperialistic efforts to bear only against the peoples of the tropics and subtropics and treated the peoples of the white race in conformity with the principles of modern democracy, the Germans, precisely because of their position in the polyglot territories in Europe, directed their imperialistic policy against European peoples also.[50] The great colonial powers have held fast to the democratic-pacifistic nationality principle in Europe and America and have practiced imperialism only against the African and Asiatic peoples. They have therefore not come into conflict with the nationality principle of the white peoples, as has the German people, which even in Europe has sought to practice imperialism everywhere.

To justify the application of imperialistic principles in Europe, the German theory saw itself compelled to fight the nationality principle and replace it with the doctrine of the unified state. Small states are said no longer to have any justification for their existence nowadays. They are said to be too small and too weak to form an independent economic territory. They supposedly must therefore necessarily seek links with larger states in order to form an "economic and protectionist community."[51]

If this means no more than that small states are scarcely able to mount sufficient resistance to the lust for conquest of their more powerful neighbors, well, one cannot contradict that. Small states cannot in fact compete with large ones on the battlefield; if it comes to war

rivers, its own language alone can set the boundary" (loc. cit., p. 557). How one can manage to derive from the nationality principle the demand for annexation of the territories "of the small, unviable peoples, specifically, those incapable of having their own state" may be seen in Hasse, *Deutsche Politik*, vol. 1, third part (Munich: 1906), pp. 12 f.

50. Only in impeding immigration does imperialism on the part of the Anglo-Saxons operate against the whites also.

51. Cf. Naumann, *Mitteleuropa* (Berlin: Georg Reimer, 1915), pp. 164 ff. (*Central Europe*, trans. by Christabel M. Meredith [New York: Knopf, 1917], pp. 179 ff.); Mitscherlich, *Nationalstaat und Nationalwirtschaft und ihre Zukunft* (Leipzig: 1916), pp. 26 ff.; on other writers of the same orientation, cf. Zurlinden, *Der Weltkreig. Vorläufige Orientierung von einem schweizerischen Standpunkt aus*, vol. 1 (Zurich: 1917), pp. 393 ff.

between them and a great power, then they must succumb unless help comes to them from outside. This help seldom is lacking. It is provided by large and small states, not from sympathy or on principle but in their own interest. In fact, we see that small states have maintained themselves for centuries just as well as the great powers. The course of the World War shows that even nowadays small states do not always prove weakest in the end. If one seeks to prod the small states by threats into association with a larger state or if one compels them into subjugation through force of arms, well, this is no proof of the assertion that "time is working against small state sovereignties." [52] This proposition is no less correct or false today than in the days of Alexander the Great, Tamerlane, or Napoleon. The political ideas of modern times allow the continued existence of a small state to appear rather more secure today than in earlier centuries. That the Central Powers won military victories over a number of small states during the World War in no way justifies our declaring that "a small-scale state" is just as out of date today as a small-scale ironworks. When Renner, with reference to military victories that German and Austrian troops won over the Serbs, thinks he can dispose of the nationality principle with the Marxist expression "the materialistic conditions of statehood are in rebellion against the idealistic—a conceptual contradiction that in practice has a tragic consequence for people and state," [53] he is thereby overlooking the fact that military weakness could be fatal for small states thousands of years ago also.

The assertion that all small states have had their day is further supported by Naumann, Renner, and their followers by the remark that a state must at least possess enough territory for a self-sufficient economy. That this is not true is already clear from what was said earlier. There can be no question of a test of economic self-sufficiency in the formation of states at a time when the division of labor embraces broad stretches of land, whole continents, indeed the whole world. It does not matter whether the inhabitants of a state meet their needs directly or indirectly by production at home; what is important is only that they can meet them at all. When Renner confronted the individual Austrian nations striving for political independence with the question of where they then would obtain this or that article once they had been detached

52. Cf. Renner, *Österreichs Erneuerung*, vol. 3 (Vienna: 1916), p. 65.
53. Ibid., p. 66.

from the whole of the Austro-Hungarian state, well, that was an absurd question. Even when the state structure was unified, they did not obtain these goods for nothing, but only in exchange for something of equivalent value, and this equivalent value does not become any larger if the political community falls apart. This objection would have made sense only if we were living at a time when trade between states was impossible.

The size of a state's territory therefore does not matter. It is another question whether a state is viable when its population is small. Now, it is to be noted that the costs of many state activities are greater in small states than in large ones. The dwarf states, of which we still have a number in Europe, like Liechtenstein, Andorra, and Monaco, can organize their court systems by levels of jurisdiction, for example, only if they link up with a neighboring state. It is clear that it would be financially quite impossible for such a state to set up as comprehensive a court system as that which a larger state makes available to its citizens, for example, by establishing courts of appeal. One can say that, seen from this point of view, states encompassing a smaller number of people than the administrative units of the larger states are viable only in exceptional cases, namely, only when they have especially rich populations. The smaller states for which this precondition does not hold will, for reasons of state finance, have to link their administrations with a larger neighboring state.[54] Nations so small in number of people that they do not satisfy these conditions do not exist at all and cannot exist at all, since the development of an independent standard language presupposes, after all, the existence of several hundred thousand speakers.

When Naumann, Renner, and their numerous disciples recommended to the small peoples of Europe an association with a Central Europe under German leadership, they completely misunderstood the essence of the protective-tariff policy. On political or military grounds, an alliance with the German nation assuring independence to all participants could be desirable for the small nations of Eastern and Southeastern Europe. In no case, however, could an alliance that would be serviceable exclusively to German interests appear welcome to them. That was the only kind, however, that the advocates of Central Europe had in view. They wanted an alliance that would enable Germany to

54. Cf. also the speech of Bismarck in the session of the Prussian House of Deputies of 11 December 1867 on Prussia's treaty of accession with the principality of Waldeck-Pyrmont. (*Fürst Bismarcks Reden*, edited by Stein, vol. 3, pp. 235 ff.)

compete militarily with the world's great powers for colonial possessions, possessions whose advantages could have benefited the German
nation alone. They conceived of the Central European world empire,
furthermore, as a protective-tariff community. Just that, however, is
what all these smaller nations do not want. They do not want to be mere
markets for German industrial products; they do not want to forgo developing at home those branches of industry that have their natural locations there and importing from outside Germany the goods produced
more cheaply there. It was thought that the rise in prices of agricultural
products that was infallibly bound to occur in consequence of incorpo-
ration into the Central European tariff territory would, even by itself
alone, be attractive to the predominantly agrarian states whose incor-
poration into the Central European empire was being sought. It was
overlooked, however, that this argument could make an impression
only on economically untrained persons. It is not to be denied that
Rumania, say, on joining a German-Austrian-Hungarian customs community, would have experienced a rise in the prices of agricultural products. It is overlooked, however, that industrial products would have risen
in price, on the other hand, since then Rumania would have had to pay
the higher German domestic prices, while if it is not joined in a customs
community with Germany, it pays the lower world-market prices. What
it would have lost from joining the German customs community would
have been greater than what it would have gained thereby. At present
Rumania is a relatively underpopulated or at least a not overpopulated
country; that means that the bulk of its export goods can at present and
in the foreseeable future be exported without any dumping. Rumania
has no enterprises in primary production and only a few in industry
whose location would not be natural. Things are different for Germany,
which, precisely in the most important branches of production, works
under more unfavorable conditions than foreign countries.

The imperialistic way of thinking, which comes forward with the
claim to be helping modern economic development to its rightful condition, is in truth gripped by barter-economy and feudal preconcep-
tions. In the age of the world economy it is downright nonsensical to represent the demand for creation of large autarkic economic territories as
an *economic* demand. In peacetime it is a matter of indifference whether
one produces foodstuffs and raw materials at home oneself or, if it seems
more economic, obtains them from abroad in exchange for other products that one has produced. When a medieval prince acquired a piece

of land where ore was mined, then he had a right to call this mine his own. But if a modern state annexes a mining property, these mines still have not thereby become those of its citizens. They must buy their products by transferring products of their own labor just as they did before, and that changes have occurred in the political order remains without significance for ownership of them. If the prince is happy about the annexation of a new province, if he is proud about the size of his realm, that is immediately understandable. If, however, the common man is happy that "our" realm has become larger, that "we" have acquired a new province, well, that is a joy that does not arise from the satisfaction of economic needs.

In economic policy, imperialism in no way suits the stage of world economic development reached in 1914. When the Huns slashed through Europe killing and burning, they harmed their enemies by the destruction that they left behind, but not themselves also. But when German troops destroyed coal mines and factories, then they also worsened the provisioning of the German consumer. That coal and various manufactured products can be produced in the future only in smaller quantities or only with higher costs will be felt by everyone involved in world economic transactions.

Once that has been recognized, however, then only the military argument can still be adduced in favor of the policy of national expansion. The nation must be populous to field many soldiers. Soldiers are needed, however, to acquire land on which soldiers can be raised. That is the circle that the imperialistic way of thinking does not escape.

D   Pacifism

Dreamers and humanitarians have long campaigned for the idea of general and eternal peace. Out of the misery and distress that wars have brought to individuals and peoples, the deep longing arose for peace that should never again be disturbed. Utopians paint the advantages of freedom from war in the most splendid colors and call on states to unite in an enduring alliance for peace embracing the entire world. They appeal to the highmindedness of emperors and kings; they refer to divine commands and promise whoever would realize their ideals undying fame far exceeding even that of the great war heroes.

History has omitted these peace proposals from its agenda. They have never been anything more than literary curiosities that no one took seriously. The powerful have never thought of renouncing their power; it has never occurred to them to subordinate their interests to the interests of humanity, as the naive dreamers demanded.

To be judged quite differently from this older pacifism, which was carried along by general considerations of humanitarianism and horror of bloodshed, is the pacifism of the Enlightenment philosophy of natural law, of economic liberalism, and of political democracy, which has been cultivated since the eighteenth century. It does not arise from a sentiment that calls on the individual and the state to renounce the pursuit of their earthly interests out of thirst for fame or in hope of reward in the beyond; nor does it stand as a separate postulate without organic connection with other moral demands. Rather, pacifism here follows with logical necessity from the entire system of social life. He who, from the utilitarian standpoint, rejects the rule of some over others and demands the full right of self-determination for individuals and peoples has thereby rejected war also. He who has made the harmony of the rightly understood interests of all strata within a nation and of all nations among each other the basis of his worldview can no longer find any rational basis for warfare. He to whom even protective tariffs and occupational prohibitions appear as measures harmful to everyone can still less understand how one could regard war as anything other than a destroyer and annihilator, in short, as an evil that strikes all, victor as well as vanquished. Liberal pacifism demands peace because it considers war useless. That is a view understandable only from the standpoint of the free-trade doctrine as developed in the classical theory of Hume, Smith, and Ricardo. He who wants to prepare a lasting peace must, like Bentham, be a free-trader and a democrat and work with decisiveness for the removal of all political rule over colonies by a mother country and fight for the full freedom of movement of persons and goods.[55] Those and no others are the preconditions of eternal peace. If one wants to make peace, then one must get rid of the possibility of conflicts between peoples. Only the ideas of liberalism and democracy have the power to do that.[56]

Once one has abandoned this standpoint, however, one can make no sound argument against war and conflict. If one holds the view that

55. Cf. Bentham, *Grundsätze für ein zukünftiges Völkerrecht und für einen dauernden Frieden,* translated by Klatscher (Halle: 1915), pp. 100 ff.
56. Today people have managed to hold liberalism responsible for the outbreak of the World War. Compare, on the other hand, Bernstein, *Sozialdemokratische Völkerpolitik* (Leipzig: 1917), pp. 170 ff., where the close connection of free trade with the peace movement is mentioned. Spann, an opponent of pacifism, expressly emphasizes the "dislike and dread of war which today characterizes the capitalist community" (loc. cit., p. 137).

there are irreconcilable class antagonisms between the individual strata of society that cannot be resolved except by the forcible victory of one class over others, if one believes that no contacts between individual nations are possible except those whereby one wins what the other loses, then, of course, one must admit that revolutions at home and wars abroad cannot be avoided. The Marxian socialist rejects war abroad because he sees the enemy not in foreign nations but in the possessing classes of his own nation. The nationalistic imperialist rejects revolution because he is convinced of the solidarity of interests of all strata of his nation in the fight against the foreign enemy. Neither is a principled opponent of armed intervention, neither a principled opponent of bloodshed, as the liberals are, who sanction only defensive war. Nothing, therefore, is in such bad taste for Marxian socialists as to fume over war, nothing in such bad taste for chauvinists as to fume over revolution, out of philanthropic concern for the innocent blood thereby shed. *Quis tulerit Gracchos de seditione querentes?* [Who could endure the Gracchi complaining of sedition?]

Liberalism rejects aggressive war not on philanthropic grounds but from the standpoint of utility. It rejects aggressive war because it regards victory as harmful, and it wants no conquests because it sees them as an unsuitable means for reaching the ultimate goals for which it strives. Not through war and victory but only through work can a nation create the preconditions for the well-being of its members. Conquering nations finally perish, either because they are annihilated by strong ones or because the ruling class is culturally overwhelmed by the subjugated. Once already the Germanic peoples conquered the world, yet were finally defeated. East Goths and Vandals went down fighting; West Goths, Franks and Lombards, Normans and Varangians remained victors in battle, but they were culturally defeated by the subjugated; they, the victors, adopted the language of the defeated and were absorbed into them. One or the other is the fate of all ruling peoples. The landlords pass away, the peasants remain; as the chorus in the *Bride of Messina* expresses it: "The foreign conquerers come and go, and we obey but we remain." The sword proves in the long run not to be the most suitable means of gaining broad diffusion for a people. That is the "impotence of victory" of which Hegel speaks.[57]

57. Compare Hegel, *Werke*, third edition, vol. 9 (Berlin: 1848), p. 540.
   One could raise the question of what, then, the distinction between pacifism and militarism really consists, since the pacifist, too, is fundamentally not for maintaining peace at any price;

Philanthropic pacifism wants to abolish war without getting at the causes of war.

It has been proposed to have disputes between nations settled by courts of arbitration. Just as in relations between individuals self-help is no longer permitted and, apart from special exceptional cases, the harmed person has only the right to call on the courts, so must things also become in relations between nations. Here also force would have to give way to law. It is supposedly no harder to settle disputes between nations peacefully than those among individual members of a nation. The opponents of arbitration in disputes between nations were to be judged no differently than the medieval feudal lords and brawlers, who also resisted the jurisdiction of the state as far as they could. Such resistances must simply be abolished. If this had already been done years ago, then the World War, with all of its sad consequences, could have been avoided. Other advocates of arbitration between states go less far with their demands. They desire the obligatory introduction of arbitration, at least for the near future, not for all disputes but only for those touching on neither the honor nor the conditions of existence of nations, that is, only for the lesser cases, while for the others the old method of decision on the field of battle could still be retained.

It is a delusion to assume that the number of wars can thereby be reduced. For many decades already, wars have still been possible only for

---

rather, under certain conditions he prefers war to an unbearable state of peace; and conversely, the militarist, too, does not want to wage perpetual war but only to restore a definite condition that he regards as desirable. Both supposedly stand, therefore, in fundamental opposition to the absolute life-renouncing passivity that the Gospel proclaims and that many Christian sects practice; between the two themselves, however, there exists only a difference of degree. In fact, however, the contrast is so great that it becomes a fundamental one. It lies, on the one hand, in assessment of the size and difficulty of the impediment barring us from peace and, on the other hand, in assessment of the disadvantages connected with conflict. Pacifism believes that we are barred from eternal peace only by a thin partition whose removal must lead at once to the state of peace, while militarism sets such remote goals for itself that their attainment in the foreseeable future cannot be expected, so that a long era of war still lies ahead. Liberalism believed that eternal peace could be lastingly established merely by the abolition of princely absolutism. German militarism, however, was clear about the fact that achieving and maintaining the German supremacy being sought would continually entail wars for a long time yet. Furthermore, pacifism always has an eye open to the damages and disadvantages of war, while militarism considers them slight. From that there then follows in pacifism its outspoken preference for the state of peace and in militarism its constant glorification of war and, in its socialist form, of revolution. A further fundamental distinction between pacifism and militarism is possible according to their positions on the theory of power. Militarism sees the basis of rule in material power (Lassalle, Lasson), liberalism in the power of the mind (Hume).

weighty reasons. That requires neither confirmation by citing historical examples nor even a long explanation. The princely states waged
war as often as required by the interests of princes aiming at extending
their power. In the calculation of the prince and his counsellors, war
was a means just like any other; free from any sentimental regard for the
human lives that were thereby put at stake, they coolly weighed the advantages and disadvantages of military intervention as a chess player
considers his moves. The path of kings led literally over corpses. Wars
were not perhaps begun, as people are accustomed to saying, for "triv-
ial reasons." The cause of war was always the same: the princes' greed
for power. What superficially looked like the cause of war was only a
pretext. (Remember, say, the Silesian wars of Frederick the Great.) The
age of democracy knows no more cabinet wars. Even the three European imperial powers, which were the last representatives of the old ab-
solutist idea of the state, had for a long time already no longer possessed
the power to instigate such wars. The democratic opposition at home
was already much too strong for that. From the moment when the
triumph of the liberal idea of the state had brought the nationality principle to the fore, wars were possible only for national reasons. That
could be changed neither by the fact that liberalism soon was seriously
endangered by the advance of socialism nor by the fact that the old military powers still remained at the helm in Central and Eastern Europe.
That is a success of liberal thinking that can no longer be undone, and
that should not be forgotten by anyone who undertakes to revile liberalism and the Enlightenment.

Whether the arbitration procedure should now be chosen for less
important disputes arising in relations among nations or whether their
settlement should be left to negotiations between the parties is a question that interests us less here, however important it may otherwise be.
It must be noted only that all arbitration treaties discussed in recent
years seem suitable only for settlement of such less important matters
of dispute and that up to now all attempts further to extend the range
of international arbitration have failed.

If it is asserted that utterly *all* disputes between peoples can be settled
through courts of arbitration, so that decision by war can be quite elim-
inated, then the fact must be noted that every administration of justice
first presupposes the existence of a generally recognized law and then
the possibility of applying the legal maxims to the individual case. Neither applies to those disputes between nations of which we speak. All

attempts to create a substantive international law through whose application disputes among nations could be decided have miscarried. A
hundred years ago the Holy Alliance sought to elevate the principle of
legitimacy to the basis of international law. The possessions of the
princes at that time were to be protected and guaranteed both against
other princes and also, in line with the political thinking of the time,
against the demands of revolutionary subjects. The causes of the failure of this attempt need not be investigated at length; they are obvious.
And yet today people seem inclined to renew the same attempt again
and to create a new Holy Alliance in Wilson's League of Nations. That
it is not princes but nations that are guaranteeing their possessions today is a distinction that does not affect the essence of things. The decisive thing is that possessions are ensured at all. It is again, as a hundred
years ago, a division of the world that presumes to be an eternal and
final one. It will be no more enduring than the earlier one, however,
and will, no less than that one, bring blood and misery to mankind.

As the legitimacy principle as understood by the Holy Alliance was
already shaken, liberalism proclaimed a new principle for regulating
relations among nations. The nationality principle seemed to signify
the end of all disputes between nations; it was to be the norm by which
all conflict should be peacefully solved. The League of Nations of Versailles adopts this principle also, though, to be sure, only for the nations
of Europe. Yet in doing so it overlooks the fact that applying this principle wherever the members of different peoples live mingled together
only ignites conflict among peoples all the more. It is still more serious
that the League of Nations does not recognize the freedom of movement of the person, that the United States and Australia are still allowed to block themselves off from unwanted immigrants. Such a
League of Nations endures so long as it has the power to hold down its
adversaries; its authority and the effectiveness of its principles are built
on force to which the disadvantaged must yield but which they will
never recognize as right. Never can Germans, Italians, Czechs, Japa-
nese, Chinese, and others regard it as just that the immeasurable
landed wealth of North America, Australia, and East India should remain the exclusive property of the Anglo-Saxon nation and that the
French be allowed to hedge in millions of square kilometers of the best
land like a private park.

Socialist doctrine hopes for establishment of eternal peace through
the realization of socialism. "Those migrations of individuals," says

Otto Bauer, "that are dominated by the blindly prevailing laws of capitalist competition and are almost fully exempt from the application of deliberate rules then cease. Into their place steps the deliberate regulation of migrations by the socialist community. They will draw immigrants to where a larger number of people at work increases the productivity of labor; where the land bestows a declining yield to a growing number of persons, they will induce part of the population to emigrate. With emigration and immigration thus being consciously regulated by society, the power over its language boundaries falls for the first time into the hands of each nation. Thus, no longer can social migrations against the will of the nation repeatedly violate the nationality principle."[58]

We can imagine the realization of socialism in two ways. First, in its highest fulfillment as a socialist world state, as unified world socialism. In such a state the office responsible for the overall control of production will determine the location of each unit of production and thereby also regulate migrations of workers and thus perform the same tasks that fall to the competition of producers in the — so far not even approximately implemented — free economy. This office will resettle workers from the territories with more unfavorable conditions of production into those with more favorable conditions. Then, however, nationality problems will still turn up in the socialist world community. If spinning and iron production are to be cut back in Germany and expanded in the United States, then German workers will have to be resettled in Anglo-Saxon territory. It is precisely such resettlements that, as Bauer says, repeatedly violate the nationality principle against the will of the nation; but they violate it not only in the capitalist economic order, as he thinks, but also in the socialist order. That they are governed in the liberal economic order by the "blindly ruling" laws of capitalist competition but in the socialist community are "deliberately" regulated by society is incidental. If the deliberate regulation of the migrations of workers is guided by the rational point of view of pure economic efficiency — which of course Bauer too, and with him every Marxist, takes for granted — then it must lead to the same result that free competition also leads to, namely, that workers, without regard to historically inherited national conditions of settlement, are resettled where they are needed for exploitation of the most favorable conditions of production.

58. Cf. Bauer, loc. cit., p. 515.

Therein, however, lies the root of all national frictions. To assume that migrations of workers transcending the boundaries of national territories of settlement would not lead to the same conflicts in the socialist community as in the free community would of course be a downright utopian way of thinking. If, though, one wants to conceive of the socialist community as a nondemocratic one, then such an assumption is permissible; for, as we have seen, all national frictions first arise under democracy. World socialism, conceived of as a world empire of general servitude of peoples, would admittedly bring national peace also.

The realization of socialism is also possible, however, otherwise than through a world state. We can imagine a series of independent socialist political systems — perhaps nationally unified states — existing side by side without there being a common management of world production. The individual communities, which then are owners of the natural and produced means of production located in their territories, are connected with each other only in the exchange of goods. In a socialism of that kind, national antagonisms will not only not be made milder in comparison with the situation in the liberal economic order but they will be considerably sharpened. The migration problem would lose nothing of its capacity to create conflicts between peoples. The individual states would perhaps not completely shut themselves off from immigration, but they would not allow immigrants to acquire resident status and to acquire a full share of the fruits of national production. A kind of international migrant-worker system would arise. Since each one of these socialist communities would have the product of the natural resources found in its territory at its disposal, so that the income of the residents of the individual territories would be different in size — larger for some nations, smaller for others — people would resist the inflow of foreign nations for this reason alone. In the liberal economic order it is possible for members of all nations to acquire private ownership of the means of production of the entire world so that, e.g., Germans also can assure themselves a part of the land resources of India and, on the other hand, again, German capital can move to India to help exploit the more favorable conditions of production there. In a socialist order of society, that sort of thing would not be possible, since political sovereignty and economic exploitation must coincide in it. The European peoples would be excluded from ownership in foreign continents. They would have to endure calmly the fact that the immeasurable riches of overseas territories redound to the advantage of the local inhabitants only and would have to observe how a part of this landed wealth remains unexploited because capital for its use cannot be obtained.

All pacifism not based on a liberal economic order built on private ownership of the means of production always remains utopian. Whoever wants peace among nations must seek to limit the state and its influence most strictly.

It is no accident that the basic ideas of modern imperialism can already be found in the writings of two fathers of German socialism and of modern socialism in general, namely, in the works of Engels and Rodbertus. From the statist outlook of a socialist it seems obvious, because of geographic and commercial necessities, that a state must not let itself be shut off from the sea.[59] The question of access to the sea, which has always directed the Russian policy of conquest in Europe and in Asia and has dominated the behavior of the German and Austrian states regarding Trieste and of the Hungarian state regarding the South Slavs and which has led to the infamous "corridor" theories to which people want to sacrifice the German city of Danzig, does not exist at all for the liberal. He cannot understand how persons may be used as a "corridor," since he takes the position from the first that persons and peoples should never serve as means but always are ends and because he never regards persons as appurtenances of the land on which they dwell. The free-trader, who advocates complete freedom of movement, cannot understand what sort of advantage it offers to a people if it can send its export goods to the coast over its own state territory. If the old Russia of Czarism had acquired a Norwegian seaport and in addition a corridor across Scandinavia to this seaport, it could not thereby have shortened the distance of the individual parts of the Russian interior from the sea. What the Russian economy feels as disadvantageous is that the Russian production sites are located far from the sea and therefore lack those advantages in the transport system that ease of ocean freight transport assures. But none of that would be changed by acquisition of a Scandinavian seaport; if free trade prevails, it is quite a matter of indifference whether the nearest seaports are administered by Russian or other officials. Imperialism needs seaports because it needs naval stations and because it wants to wage economic wars. It needs them not to use them but to exclude others from them.

59. Cf. Rodbertus, *Schriften*, edited by Wirth, new edition, vol. 4 (Berlin: 1899), p. 282.

The nonstatist economy of trade free of the state does not recognize this argumentation.

Rodbertus and Engels both oppose the political demands of the non-German peoples of Austria. Engels reproaches the Pan-Slavists for not having understood that the Germans and Magyars, at the time when the great monarchies really became a historical necessity in Europe, "put all these small, stunted, impotent nationlets together into a great empire and thereby made them capable of taking part in a historical development to which they, left to themselves, would have remained quite foreign." He admits that such an empire cannot prevail "without forcibly crushing many a tender flowerlet of a nation. But without force and without iron ruthlessness, nothing is accomplished in history; and if Alexander, Caesar, and Napoleon had possessed the same capacity for compassion to which Pan-Slavism now appeals for the sake of its decayed clients, what then would have become of history! And are the Persians, Celts, and Christian Germans not worth the Czechs and the people of Ogulin and Sereth?"[60] These sentences could have come quite well from a Pan-German writer or *mutatis mutandis* from a Czech or Polish chauvinist. Engels then continues: "Now, however, in consequence of the great progress of industry, trade, and communications, political centralization has become a much more pressing need than back in the fifteenth and sixteenth centuries. What still must be centralized becomes centralized. And now the Pan-Slavists come and demand that we should 'set free' these half-Germanized Slavs, we should undo a centralization that is imposed on these Slavs by all their material interests?" That is in essence nothing but Renner's doctrine of the tendency toward concentration in political life and of the economic necessity of the multinational state. We see that the orthodox Marxists did Renner an injustice in accusing him of heresy as a "revisionist."

The way to eternal peace does not lead through strengthening state and central power, as socialism strives for. The greater the scope the state claims in the life of the individual and the more important politics becomes for him, the more areas of friction are thereby created in territories with mixed population. Limiting state power to a minimum, as liberalism sought, would considerably soften the antagonisms among different nations that live side by side in the same territory. The only

60. Cf. Mehring, *Aus dem literarischen Nachlass von Marx, Engels und Lassalle*, vol. 3 (Stuttgart: 1902), pp. 255 f.

true national autonomy is the freedom of the individual against the state and society. The "nationalization" of life and of the economy by the state leads with necessity to the struggle of nations.

Full freedom of movement of persons and goods, the most comprehensive protection of the property and freedom of each individual, removal of all state compulsion in the school system, in short, the most exact and complete application of the ideas of 1789, are the prerequisites of peaceful conditions. If wars then cease, "then peace has proceeded from the inner forces of things, then people and indeed free people have become peaceful."[61]

Never have we been further from this ideal than today.

3   On the History of German Democracy

A   *Prussia*

Among the most notable phenomena of the history of the last hundred years is the fact that the modern political ideas of freedom and self-government could not prevail among the German people, while elsewhere they could make themselves influential almost everywhere on earth. Everywhere democracy has been able to overcome the old princely state; everywhere the revolutionary forces have triumphed. Only precisely in Germany and in Austria—and besides there only in Russia—has the democratic revolution been defeated again and again. While every nation of Europe and America has experienced an age of liberalism in constitutional and economic policy, in Germany and Austria only slight successes have been accorded to liberalism. In the political sector, the old princely state, as represented at its purest in the constitution of Prussia under Frederick the Great, did indeed have to grant some concessions, but it was far from transforming itself into a parliamentary monarchy of, say, the English or Italian sort; as a result of the great political movements of the nineteenth century the authoritarian state appears here.

The democratic state, as we see it realized almost everywhere at the beginning of the twentieth century, rests on the identity of the rulers and

61. Cf. W. Humboldt, *Ideen zu einem Versuch, die Grenzen der Wirksamkeit des Staats zu bestimmen*, edition of the "Deutsche Bibliothek," (Berlin), p. 66.

the ruled, of the state and of the people. In it no government is possible against the will of the majority of the people. In it government and the governed, state and people, are one. Not so in the authoritarian state. Here on the one side stand the state-preserving elements, which regard themselves and themselves alone as the state; the government proceeds from them and identifies itself with them. On the other side stands the people, who appear only as object, not as subject, of government actions, who address the state sometimes pleadingly, sometimes demandingly, but who never identify themselves with it. This antithesis found its most eloquent expression in former Austrian parliamentary language in the contrast of "state necessities" with "people's necessities." The former were understood to include what the state sought and the latter what the people sought from the financial expenditures of the budget. And the deputies were at pains to be compensated for the granting of state necessities by the granting of people's necessities — which sometimes were necessities of the individual political parties or even of individual deputies. These contradistinctions could never have been made understandable to an English or French politician; he would not have been able to understand how something could be necessary for the state without at the same time being necessary for the people, and conversely.

The contrast between authorities and people which characterizes the authoritarian state is not quite identical with the one between prince and people that characterizes the princely state; still less is it identical with the contrast between the prince and the estates in the old estate system. In their contrast with the modern democratic state, with its fundamental unity of government and people, however, all these dualistic state forms do share a common characteristic.

Attempts have not been lacking to explain the origin and basis of this peculiarity of German history. Those writers made it easiest for themselves who believed they understood the authoritarian state as the emanation of a special type of German spirit and sought to portray the democratic national state as "un-German," as not suitable for the soul of the German.[62] Then, again, the attempt has been made to draw the special political position of Germany into an explanation. A state that seems endangered by external enemies, in such a way as the German

62. Max Weber provided a destructive critique of these theories in *Parlament und Regierung im neugeordneten Deutschland* (Munich: 1918).

state supposedly was, cannot tolerate a freedom-oriented constitution at home. "The measure of political freedom that can be permitted in governmental institutions must rationally be inversely proportional to the military-political pressure bearing on the borders of the state."[63] That an intimate connection must exist between the political position and the constitution of a people will be conceded without further ado. But it is striking that efforts were made to bring only the foreign political position, but not the domestic political position, into explaining constitutional conditions. In what follows the converse procedure will be followed. An attempt will be made to explain that much-discussed peculiarity of German constitutional life by domestic political conditions, namely, by the position of the Germans of Prussia and Austria in the polyglot territories.

When the subjects of the German princes began to awake from their centuries-long political slumber, they found their fatherland torn to shreds, divided as patrimonial estates among a number of families whose external impotence was but poorly cloaked by their ruthless internal tyranny. Only two territorial princes were strong enough to stand on their own feet; their means of power rested, however, not on their German position but on their possessions outside Germany. For Austria this assertion needs no further justification; the fact was never disputed. It was otherwise for Prussia. It is common to overlook the fact that the position of Prussia in Germany and in Europe always remained insecure until the Hohenzollerns succeeded in building a rather large contiguous state territory, first by the annexation of Silesia, which at the time was half Slavic, and then by the acquisition of Posen and West Prussia. Precisely those deeds of Prussia on which its power rested—its participation in the victory over the Napoleonic system, the crushing of the revolution of 1848, and the war of 1866—could not have been accomplished without the non-German subjects of its eastern provinces. Even the acquisition of German land accomplished by the struggles waged from 1813 to 1866 with the help of its non-German subjects in no way shifted the center of gravity of the Prussian state from the east to the west. Still, as before, the undiminished maintenance of its possessions east of the Elbe remained a condition of existence for Prussia.

63. Cf. Hintze in the collective work *Deutschland und der Weltkrieg* (Leipzig: 1915), p. 6. A penetrating critique of these views, which rest on a proposition of the English historian Seeley, appears in Preuss, *Obrigkeitsstaat und grossdeutscher Gedanke* (Jena: 1916), pp. 7 ff.

The political thinking of the German mind, which was slowly maturing for public life, could be modeled on none of the states existing on German soil. What the patriotic German saw before him was only the ruins of the old imperial magnificence and the disgraceful and slovenly administration of the German petty princes. The way to the German state would have to involve the overthrow of these small despots. All agreed on that. What, however, should happen to the two German powers, i.e., Germany and Austria?

The difficulty inherent in the problem may best be recognized from a comparison with Italy. Conditions in Italy were similar to those in Germany. Blocking the modern national state were a number of petty princes and the great power Austria. The Italians would have gotten rid of the former quickly, but of the latter—by themselves—never. And Austria not only held fast to a large part of Italy directly, it also protected the sovereignty of the individual princes in the remaining territories. Without Austria's intervention, Joachim Murat or General Pepe would long since probably have established an Italian national state. But the Italians had to wait until Austria's relations with the other powers offered them the opportunity to reach their goal. Italy owes its freedom and unity to French and Prussian help, and in a certain sense to English help also; to unite Trentino, too, with the kingdom of Italy required the help of the entire world. The Italians themselves lost all the battles they fought against Austria.

In Germany conditions were different. How were the German people to succeed in overcoming Austria and Prussia, the two mighty military monarchies? Foreign help, as given in Italy, could not be counted on. The most natural course would probably have been for the German national idea to acquire so much power over the Germans in Prussia and Austria that they strove for a united Germany. If the Germans, who were the majority by far in the Prussian army and represented the most important element in the Austrian army, had proved true as Germans the way the Magyars did in 1849 as Magyars, then there would have arisen out of the confusions of the revolution of 1848 a German Reich free and united from the Belt to the Etsch. The non-German elements in the armies of Austria and Prussia would hardly have been in a position to mount successful resistance to the assault of the entire German people.

The Germans in Austria and Prussia, however, were also opponents or at least only limited adherents of the German strivings for unity— and that is what was decisive. The efforts of the men of St. Paul's

Church[64] suffered shipwreck, not, as legends have it, because of doctrinairism, idealism, and professorial ignorance of the ways of the world but rather because of the fact that the majority of Germans supported the cause of the German nation only halfheartedly. What they desired was not the German state alone but rather the Austrian or the Prussian state as well at the same time — and this is not to mention those who actually considered themselves *only* Austrians or Prussians and not at all Germans.

We who today are accustomed to seeing the pure Prussian and the pure Austrian only in the conservative east of the Elbe and the Alpine clerical, we who in the appeal to Prussia or Austria can always see only the pretexts of enemies of the national state — we can only with difficulty concede even mere good faith to the black-and-yellow and black-and-white patriots of that time. This not only does a serious injustice to men about whose honorable striving there should be no doubt; this lack of historical perspective also blocks our path to knowledge of the most important events of German history.

Every German knows the passage in Goethe's *Dichtung und Wahrheit* in which the aging poet portrays the deep impression that the figure of Frederick the Great made on his contemporaries.[65] It is true that the state of the Hohenzollerns, too, which Prussian court historiography lauded as the implementation of all utopias, was not a whit better than the other German states; and Frederick William I or Frederick II were no less hateful despots than any Württemberg or Hessian lord. But one thing distinguished Brandenburg-Prussia from the other German territories: the state was not ridiculous; its policy was purposeful, steady, and power-seeking. This state could be hated, it might be feared, but it could not be overlooked.

If, thus, the political thoughts of even the non-Prussian Germans secretly strayed toward Prussia out of the narrowness of their political existence, if even foreigners judged this state not totally unfavorably, was it any wonder that the beginnings of political thought in the Prussian provinces clung more often to the Prussian state, which, with all its faults, still had the advantage of actual existence, than to the dream of

64. [St. Paul's Church (Paulskirche) was the site of the Frankfurt Parliament, the liberal and democratic factions of which were seeking to unify Germany and the German-speaking sections of Austria (see p. xviii, above).]

65. The criticism that Mehring makes (*Die Lessing-Legende*, third edition [Stuttgart: 1909], pp. 12 ff.) does not weaken the force of this passage as evidence for the views of the old Goethe.

a German state, which was unmasked every day by the wretchedness of the Holy Roman Empire? Thus a Prussian state-consciousness was formed in Prussia. And these feelings were shared not only by the salaried champions of the Prussian state apparatus and its beneficiaries but also by men of undoubtedly democratic sentiments like Waldeck[66] and hundreds of thousands like him.

It is common to describe the German question much too narrowly as the opposition of great-German and small-German. In truth the problem was larger and broader. It was first of all the gap that yawned between German national sentiment on the one side and Austrian and Prussian state-consciousness on the other.

The German unified state could have been built only on the ruins of the German states; whoever wanted to construct it therefore first had to root out those sentiments that were striving to maintain the Prussian and Austrian states. In March 1848 that seemed easy to do. At that time it could be expected that the Prussian and Austrian democrats, faced with the need to decide, would, even if perhaps after inner struggles, join the side of a great and unified Germany. Yet in both great German states, democracy was defeated sooner than one would have thought possible. Its sway lasted scarcely a few weeks in Vienna and Berlin; then the authoritarian state embarked on the plan that pulled the reins tight. What was the cause? The turnaround did come extraordinarily quickly. Right after the complete victory of democracy in March, the power of the new spirit began to crumble; and after a short time the Prussian army, led by the Prince of Prussia, who had fled the country only shortly before, could already take the offensive against the revolution.

There should be general agreement that the position of the eastern provinces of Prussia was decisive here.[67] If this is remembered, it will not be too hard to understand clearly the causes of the turnaround. There in the East the Germans were in the minority amidst a numerically superior population speaking foreign languages; there they had to fear that the implementation and application of democratic principles would cost them the ruling position that they had so far possessed. They would have become a minority that could never have expected to

66. Cf. Oppenheim, *Benedikt Franz Leo Waldeck* (Berlin: 1880), pp. 41 ff.
67. Cf. Bismarck, *Gedanken und Erinnerungen* (Stuttgart: 1898), vol. 1, p. 56 [*The Man and the Statesman*, 2 vols. (London, 1898)].

acquire power; they would have had to taste that lack of political rights that is the fate of minorities of foreign nationality.

The Germans of the provinces of Prussia, Posen, and Silesia could hope for nothing good from democracy. That, however, determined the positions of the Germans of Prussia on the whole, for the Germans of the polyglot territories had much greater political importance than corresponded to their numbers. These Germans included, after all, almost all members of the higher strata of the population of those provinces — the officials, teachers, merchants, estate owners, and larger industrialists. In the upper strata of the Germans of Prussia, the members of the threatened borderlands therefore formed a numerically far larger part than the German borderland inhabitants formed on the whole in the total German population of Prussia. The solid mass of inhabitants of the borderlands joined with the parties supporting the state and thereby gave them preponderance. The idea of the German state could win no power over the non-German subjects of Prussia, and its German subjects feared German democracy. That was the tragedy of the democratic idea in Germany.

Here lie the roots of the peculiar political-intellectual constitution of the German people. It was the threatened position of the Germans in the borderlands that caused the ideal of democracy in Germany to fade quickly away and the subjects of Prussia, after a short honeymoon of revolution, to return penitently to the military state. They knew now what lay ahead for them in democracy. However much they might despise Potsdam's despotism, they had to bow to it if they did not want to fall under the rule of Poles and Lithuanians. From then on they were the faithful guard of the authoritarian state. With their help the Prussian military state triumphed over the men of freedom. All Prussia's political questions were now judged exclusively according to the position in the East. It was what determined the feeble position of the Prussian liberals in the constitutional conflict. It was what caused Prussia to seek Russian friendship, so long as that could be done at all, and thereby thwarted the natural alliance with England.

It now occurred to the Prussian authoritarian state to apply its methods of gaining and maintaining its position in Germany to the solution of the greater German national problem also. The weapons of the Junkers had triumphed in Germany. They had crushed the German bourgeoisie; they had excluded the Habsburg influence and elevated the Hohenzollerns high above the smaller and middle princes. Prussian military power suppressed the non-German elements in the Slavic eastern provinces of Prussia, in North Schleswig, and in Alsace-Lorraine. The bright splendor of the victories won in three wars shone on Prussian militarism. As it had crushed with power everything trying to hinder it on its way, so it believed it should also use armed force to solve all newly arising problems. By the power of weapons the hard-pressed position of the Habsburgs and the Germans in the Danube monarchy should be sustained and conquests made in the East and West and overseas.

The liberal theory of the state had long since exposed the error in this reasoning. The theorists and practitioners of power politics should have remembered Hume's famous arguments that all rule rests on power over minds; the government is always only a minority and can govern the majority only because the latter either is convinced of the legitimacy of the rulers or considers their rule desirable in its own interests.[68] Then they could not have overlooked the fact that the German authoritarian state, even in Germany, rested in the last analysis not on the power of bayonets but precisely on a particular disposition of the German mind, which was caused by the national conditions of settlement of the Germans in the East. They should not have deceived themselves over the fact that the defeat of German liberalism was attributable solely to the conditions of settlement in the German East: the rule of democracy there would have led to driving the Germans out and depriving them of rights; hence a predisposition toward antidemocratic currents had been created in wide circles of the German people. They would have had to recognize that even the German authoritarian state, like any other state, rested not on victories of weapons but on victories of the spirit, on victories won by dynastic-authoritarian sentiment over liberal sentiment. These relationships could not be misinterpreted worse than they were by that German school of political realists that denied the influence of every intellectual current in the life of nations and wanted to trace everything back to "real power relations." When Bismarck said that his successes rested only on the power of the Prussian army and had only derision and scorn for the pro-liberal ideals of St. Paul's Church, then he overlooked the fact that the power of the Prussian state was grounded on ideals also, although on the opposite ideals, and that it would have had to collapse immediately if liberal thought

68. Cf. Hume, *Of the First Principles of Government* (*Essays*, edited by Frowde), pp. 29 ff.

had penetrated the Prussian army further than it actually did. Those circles that were anxiously striving to keep the "modern spirit of demoralization" away from the army were better informed in this respect.

The Prussian authoritarian state could not defeat the world. Such a victory could have been achieved by a nation hopelessly in the minority only through ideas, through public opinion, but never with weapons. But the German authoritarian state, filled with a boundless contempt for the press and for all "literature," scorned ideas as a means of struggle. For its adversaries, however, the democratic idea made propaganda. Not until the middle of the war, when it was already too late, was it recognized in Germany what power lay in this propaganda and how vain it is to fight with the sword against the spirit.

If the German people found the allotment of territories of settlement on the earth unjust, then they should have sought to convert the public opinion of the world, which did not see the injustice of this allotment. Whether this would have been possible is another question. It is not wholly improbable that allies for this struggle could have been found, united with whom much, perhaps even everything, could have been attained. It is certain, however, that the undertaking of a nation of eighty million to fight against the whole remaining world was hopeless if it was not pursued with intellectual means. Not with weapons but only with the spirit can a minority overcome the majority. True practical politics is only the kind that knows how to enlist ideas in its service.

B   Austria

The teleological interpretation of history, by which all historical events appear as realization of definite goals set for human development, has assigned many kinds of tasks to the Danube state of the Habsburgs, which for four hundred years has maintained its position among the European powers. Now it should be the shield of the West against the threat from Islam, now the stronghold and refuge of Catholicism against the heretics; others wanted to see it as the support of the conservative element in general, still others as the state summoned by its nationally polychromatic character to promote peace among peoples by way of example.[69] One sees that the tasks were multifarious; according

69. A compendium of the various tasks that people have sought to assign to Austria is given by Seipel, loc. cit., pp. 18 ff.

to the shape of political affairs, people favored now the one and now the other interpretation. History goes its course, however, without regard to such chimeras. Princes and peoples bother themselves very little over what missions the philosophy of history assigns to them.

Causal historiography does not look for the "mission" or the "idea" that nations and states have to realize; it seeks the political concept that forms states out of nations and parts of nations. The political concept at the basis of almost all state structures of the last centuries of the Middle Ages and the first centuries of modern times was princely dominion. The state existed for the sake of the king and his house. That holds true of the state of the Austrian Habsburgs, from the Ferdinand who as German emperor was called the First to the Ferdinand who as Austrian emperor was the only one of that name, just as it holds true of all other states of that time. In that respect the Austrian state was no different from the other states of its time. The hereditary lands of Leopold I were fundamentally no different from the state of Louis XIV or Peter the Great. But then came other times. The princely state succumbed to the attack of the freedom movement; in its place appeared the free national state. The nationality principle became the bearer of state coherence and the concept of the state. Not all states could take part in this development without change in their geographical extent; many had to submit to changes in their territory. For the Danube monarchy, however, the nationality principle actually signified the negation of its justification for existence.

Farseeing Italian patriots passed the death sentence on the state of the House of Habsburg-Lorraine as early as 1815; no later than 1848 there already were men among all peoples forming the Empire who agreed with this opinion, and for more than a generation one could easily say that the entire thinking youth of the Monarchy—perhaps aside from part of the Alpine Germans educated in Catholic schools—were hostile to the state. All non-Germans in the country longingly awaited the day that would bring them freedom and their own national state. They strove to get out of the "married-together" state. Many of them made compromises. They saw with open eyes how things stood in Europe and in the world; they had no illusions about the impediments that initially still stood in the way of realization of their ideals, and they were therefore ready to moderate their claims in the meanwhile. They came to terms with the provisional continuation of the Austrian and Hungarian states; indeed, even more, they used the Dual

Monarchy as a counter in their own game. The Poles, the South Slavs, the Ukrainians, and in a certain sense the Czechs also, sought to make the weight of this great state, which despite everything was still powerful, serviceable for their own purposes. Superficial critics have sought to conclude from that fact that these peoples had reconciled themselves to the existence of the state, that they even desired it. Nothing was more wrong than this view. Never did irredentism[70] seriously disappear from the program of any of the non-German parties. It was tolerated that official circles did not openly show the ultimate goals of their national strivings in Vienna; at home, however, people thought and spoke, with formal attention to the limits drawn by the paragraphs on high treason of the penal law, of nothing other than liberation and shaking off the yoke of the foreign dynasty. The Czech and Polish ministers, and even the numerous South Slav generals, never forgot that they were sons of subjugated peoples; never did they feel themselves in their court positions as other than pacemakers of the freedom movement that wanted to get out of this state.

Only the Germans took a different position toward the state of the Habsburgs. It is true that there was also a German irredentism in Austria, even if one may not interpret in this sense every hurrah for the Hohenzollerns or for Bismarck shouted at solstice festivals, student assemblages, and gatherings of voters. But although the Austrian government in the last forty years of the existence of the Empire was, with a few transitory exceptions, more or less anti-German and often draconically persecuted relatively harmless utterances of German national sentiments, while far sharper speeches and deeds of the other nationalities enjoyed benevolent toleration, the state-supporting parties among the Germans always kept the upper hand. Up to the last days of the Empire the Germans felt themselves the real champions of the state idea, citizens of a German state. Was that a delusion, was it political immaturity?

To be sure, a large part, even the largest part, of the German people in Austria was, and today still is, politically backward. But this explanation cannot satisfy us. We just are not satisfied with the assumption of an innate political inferiority of the German; we seek precisely the causes that made the Germans march politically behind the Ruthenians and Serbs. We ask ourselves how it then happened that all other peoples inhabiting the imperial state readily adopted the modern ideas

70. [The desire of a national group for union or reunification with others of the same nationality.]

of freedom and national independence but that the German-Austrians so much identified themselves with the state of the Habsburgs that, for the sake of its continuation, they finally readily incurred the immense sacrifices of goods and blood that a war of more than four years imposed on them.

It was German writers who expounded the theory that the Austro-Hungarian dual state was no artificial construction, as the doctrine misled by the nationality principle announced, but rather a natural geographic unit. The arbitrariness of such interpretations of course needed no special refutation. With this method one can just as well prove that Hungary and Bohemia had to form *one* state as the opposite. What is a geographic unit, what are "natural" boundaries? No one can say. With this method Napoleon I once argued France's claim to Holland, for the Netherlands are an alluvial deposit of French rivers; with the same method Austrian writers sought, before the fulfillment of Italian strivings for unity, to support the right of Austria to the lowlands of upper Italy.[71]

Another interpretation is that of the state as an economic territory, which was urged above all by Renner, who, besides that, also considered the geographic interpretation of the state valid. For Renner the state is an "economic community," an "organized economic territory." Unified economic territories should not be torn apart; thus it was foolish to want to destroy the continued territorial existence of the Austro-Hungarian Monarchy.[72] But this unified economic territory is just what the non-German peoples of Austria did not want; they did not let themselves be influenced by Renner's arguments either. Why did the Germans, precisely the Germans of Austria, create such doctrines, which were supposed to prove the necessity of this state, and sometimes even consider them right?

That the Germans always cared somewhat for the Austrian state, although this state was not at all a German state and, when it suited it, oppressed the Germans just the same as or even more than its other

---

71. Cf. pp. 65–66 above; further, the criticism in Justus, "Sozialismus und Geographie," *Der Kampf*, vol. 11, pp. 469 ff. Today the Czechs apply this theory to justify the annexation of German Bohemia.

72. Cf. Renner, *Österreichs Erneuerung*; *Marxismus, Krieg und Internationale* (Stuttgart: 1917); on the other hand, Mises, "Vom Ziel der Handelspolitik," op. cit., pp. 579 ff. (during the writing of this essay only the first volume of *Österreichs Erneuerung* was available to me), further, Justus, loc. cit.; Emil Lederer, "Zeitgemässe Wandlungen der sozialistischen Idee und Theorie," *Archiv für Sozialwissenschaft*, vol. 45, 1918/1919, pp. 261 ff.

peoples — we must try to understand that fact by the same principle that explains the development of the Prussian-German political spirit of conservatism and militarism.

The political thinking of the Germans in Austria suffered from a double orientation toward the German and toward the Austrian state. After they had awakened from the centuries-long sleep into which the Counter-Reformation had sunk them and when they began, in the second half of the eighteenth century, timidly to concern themselves with public questions, the Germans in Austria turned their thoughts to the Reich also; many a bold person dreamed, even before March 1848, of a unified German state. But never did they make it clear to themselves that they had to choose between being German and being Austrian and that they could not desire the German and the Austrian state at the same time. They did not or would not see that a free Germany was possible only if Austria was destroyed first and that Austria could endure only if it withdrew part of its best sons from the German Reich. They did not see that the goals they sought were incompatible and that what they wanted was an absurdity. They were not at all conscious of their halfheartedness, that halfheartedness that caused the whole pitiable irresoluteness of their policy, that halfheartedness that brought failure to all and everything they undertook.

Since Königgrätz it has become the fashion in North Germany to doubt the German sentiment of the German-Austrians. Since people equated German and Reichs-German without further ado and, moreover, true to the generally prevailing statist way of thinking, also identified all Austrians with the policy of the Vienna court, it was not hard to find a basis for this interpretation. It was nevertheless thoroughly wrong. Never did the Germans of Austria forget their national character; never, not even in the first years following the defeat in the Bohemian campaign, did they lose for even a minute the feeling of belonging together with the Germans on the other side of the black-and-yellow border posts. They were German and also wanted to remain so; least of all should they be blamed for also wanting to be Austrians at the same time by those who subordinated the German idea to the Prussian.

No less wrong, however, is the opinion that was widespread in Austrian court circles that the German-Austrians were not serious about their Austrianism. Catholic-oriented historians sadly lamented the decline of the old Austria, that Austrian princely state which, from Ferdinand II until the outbreak of the revolution of March 1848, had been the protector of Catholicism and of the legitimist idea of the state in Europe. Their complete lack of understanding of everything that had been thought and written since Rousseau, their aversion to all political changes that had taken place in the world since the French Revolution, caused them to believe that that esteemed old state of the Habsburgs could have endured if the "Jews and Freemasons" had not brought on its downfall. Their entire grudge was directed against the Germans in Austria and among them above all against the German Liberal Party, to which they attributed responsibility for the decline of the old empire. They saw how the Austrian state was more and more falling apart internally; and they dumped the guilt precisely onto those who alone were the champions of the Austrian state idea, who alone affirmed the state, who alone desired it.

From the moment when the modern ideas of freedom also crossed the boundaries of Austria, which had been anxiously guarded by Metternich and Sedlnitzky, the old Habsburg family state was done for. That it did not fall apart as early as 1848, that it could maintain itself for seventy years more — that was solely the work of the Austrian state idea of the German-Austrians, that was solely the service of the German freedom parties, of precisely those who were more hated and persecuted by the court than all others, more hated even than those who openly threatened and fought the continuation of the state.

The material basis of the Austrian political thought of the German-Austrians was the fact of German settlements strewn over the entire extent of the Habsburg lands. As a result of centuries-long colonization, the urban bourgeoisie and the urban intelligentsia were German everywhere in Austria and Hungary, large landownership was in great part Germanized, and everywhere, even in the middle of foreign-language territory, there were German peasant settlements. All Austria outwardly bore a German stamp; everywhere German education and German literature were to be found. Everywhere in the Empire the Germans were also represented among the petty bourgeoisie, among the workers, and among the peasants, even though in many districts, especially in Galicia, in many parts of Hungary, and in the coastal territories, the German minority among the members of the lower strata of the people was quite small. But in the entire Empire (upper Italy excepted) the percentage of Germans among the educated and among the members of the higher strata was quite considerable, and all those educated persons and prosperous bourgeois who were not themselves

German and did not want to acknowledge belonging to the German nation were German by their education, spoke German, read German, and appeared at least outwardly to be German. That part of the Austrian population that most strongly felt the intolerableness of the tyranny of the Vienna government and alone seemed capable of replacing the court circles in governing were the upper middle class and the members of the free professions and educated persons — just those strata that are commonly called the bourgeoisie and the intellectuals. But they were German in the entire Empire, at least in lands belonging to the German Federation. Thus Austria no doubt was not German, but politically it wore a German face. Every Austrian who wanted to take any interest at all in public affairs had to master the German language. For the members of the Czech and of the Slovene peoples, however, education and social ascent could be achieved only through Germanness. They still had no literature of their own that would have made it possible for them to do without the treasures of German culture. Whoever rose became German because precisely the members of the higher strata were German.

The Germans saw that and believed that it had to be so. They were far from wanting to Germanize all non-Germans compulsorily, but they thought that this would take place on its own. They believed that every Czech and South Slav would try, even in his own interest, to adopt German culture. They believed that it would remain so forever, that for the Slav the way to culture was Germanness, and that social ascent was bound up with Germanization. That these peoples also could develop independent cultures and independent literatures, that from their midst they could also bring forth independent national characters — they did not think of that at all. Thus the naive belief could arise among them that all Austria felt and thought politically as they did, that all had to share their ideal of the great, mighty, unified state of Austria, which could bear only a German stamp.

Those were the political ideas with which the German-Austrians went into the revolution. The disappointment that they experienced was abrupt and painful.

Today, as we look back in review over the development of the last seven decades, it is easy to say what position the Germans should have taken in view of the new state of affairs; it is easy to show how they could and should have done better. Today one can clearly show how much better the German nation in Austria would have fared if it had adopted in 1848 that program that it in 1918 then perforce made its own. The share that would have fallen to the German people in a splitting up of Austria into independent national states in the year 1848 was bound to have been far larger than the one that it acquired in 1918 after the terrible defeat in the World War. What held the Germans back at that time from undertaking a clean separation between German and non-German? Why did they not make the proposal themselves; why did they reject it when the Slavs brought it forth?

It has already been mentioned that the Germans then held the widespread opinion that the Germanization of the Slavs was only a question of time, that it would take place without external compulsion by the necessity of development. Even this interpretation alone was bound to influence the entire choice of positions on the problem of nationalities. The decisive factor, however, was different. It was that the Germans could not and did not want to give up the national minorities sprinkled in the contiguous territories of settlement of the other peoples. They had blood brothers living everywhere in Slavic territory; all cities there were either entirely or at least in large part German. Of course, it was only a fraction of the whole German people in Austria that they would have given up in this way. But the numerical significance of this enclaved population in relation to all the rest of the German people in Austria hardly expresses the significance of the loss that they would thereby have suffered. These enclaved people belonged in greatest part to the higher strata of the nation. To give them up signified, therefore, a far heavier loss than the mere numbers indicated. To give them up meant to give up the best parts of the German people in Austria; it meant to sacrifice the University of Prague and the merchants and factory owners of Prague, Brünn [Brno], Pilsen [Plzeň], Budweis [Česke Budějovice], Olmütz [Olomouc], of Trieste, Laibach [Ljubljana], of Lemberg [Lwów, Lvov], Czernowitz [Cernăuți, Chernovtsy], of Pest, Pressburg [Bratislava], Temesvar [Timişoara], etc., who were very significant for Austrian conditions. To give them up meant to wipe out the colonizing work of centuries; it meant to deprive German peasants in all parts of the broad empire and German officers and officials of their rights.

One now understands the tragic position of the Germans in Austria. With a bold, defiant spirit of rebellion the Germans had risen up to break the despotism and take the government of the state into their own hands; they wanted to create a free, great Austria out of the hereditary estate of the dynasty. Then they had to recognize all at once that the great majority of the people did not at all desire their free German Austria, that they even preferred to remain subjects of the Habsburgs rather than be citizens of an Austria bearing a German stamp. Then they discovered to their dismay that the application of democratic principles was bound to lead to the dissolution of this empire, in which, after all, they had been the leading elements intellectually and wished to remain the leading elements. Then they had to recognize that democracy was bound to deprive German citizens of their political rights in territories inhabited predominantly by Slavs. They had to recognize that the Germans of Prague and Brünn [Brno] were indeed in a position to take the scepter away from the Habsburgs and establish a parliamentary form of government but that they not only had nothing to win thereby but much to lose. Under the despotism of the sovereign's officials, they could still live as Germans; although they might also be subjects, they were still subjects enjoying the same rights as other subjects. But in a free state they would have become second-class citizens; for others, foreigners, whose language they did not understand, whose train of thought was foreign to them, on whose politics they could have had no influence, would have harvested the fruits of their struggle for freedom. They recognized that they were without power against the crown, for the crown could always call up peoples against them to whom their voice could not penetrate; they recognized and had to feel it as painful, when Slavic regiments subdued the uprising of German citizens and students, that they had no prospect of shaking off the yoke that oppressed them. At the same time, however, they recognized that the victory of the old reactionary Austria still had to be more welcome to them than victory of the new freedom-oriented state; for under the scepter of the Habsburgs they still could live as Germans; under the dominion of the Slavs, however, there was for them only political death.

Scarcely a people has ever found itself in a more difficult political position than the German-Austrians after the first bloody days of the March 1848 revolution. Their dream of a free German Austria had suddenly come to naught. In view of their national comrades scattered about in foreign territories of settlement, they could not desire the dissolution of Austria into national states; they had to desire the continued existence of the state, and then there remained nothing else for them than to support the authoritarian state. The Habsburgs and their adherents, however, did not desire an alliance with the anticlerical liberals.

They would rather have seen the state collapse than share it with the German freedom party. They recognized only too soon that the Germans in Austria must support the state whether they wanted to or not, that one could rule without danger in Austria without the Germans and even against them, because the Germans were not in a position to form a serious opposition; and they oriented their policy accordingly.

Thus every straightforward policy was made impossible for the Germans of Austria. They could not work seriously for democracy, for that would have been national suicide; they could not renounce the Austrian state because, despite everything, it still offered protection against the most extreme oppression. From this division the divided German policy developed.

The essence of the policy was maintaining the national patrimony, as it was called, that is, the effort to hold back the gradually occurring annihilation of the German minorities strewn about in territory of foreign settlement. From the beginning that was a hopeless undertaking, for these minorities were fated to disappear.

Only the peasant settlements had the possibility, where the German settlers were living together in self-contained villages, of still preserving their German character. Of course, even here the process of de-Germanization goes on uninterruptedly. Even mere economic contact with neighbors of foreign nationality, which becomes all the more active as economic development proceeds, wears away at their special character and makes it difficult for a small colony far removed from the main stem of its people to preserve its mother tongue. The effect of the school is added; even the German school in foreign land must include the language of the country in the curriculum if it is not to make the later advancement of the children all too difficult. Once the youth learns the language of the country, however, there begins that process of adaptation to the environment that finally leads to complete assimilation. What is decisive, however, is that a locality in the modern economic organism in which constant migrations must take place cannot long exist without immigration from the outside or without loss of population to the outside. In the first case the locality is exposed to being inundated by members of foreign nationalities and, in further consequence, to the native population's also losing its original national character; in the second case, the leftover part of the population remaining behind may well preserve its original nationality, but the emigrants become nationally alienated. Of the numerous peasant settlements that had arisen, strewn about and isolated, in the Habsburg lands, only those where modern industry or mining developed did become alienated from German character. In the remaining ones immigration from outside was lacking. But the better, more energetic elements are gradually moving away; they may gain economically thereby, but they lose their nationality. The ones remaining behind can preserve their national character but often suffer from inbreeding.

In short, the German minorities in cities strewn about in Slavic land were hopelessly fated to decline. With the emancipation from the pre-1848 feudal system of land tenure, the migration movement set in in Austria also. Internal migrations took place on a large scale. Thousands moved from the countryside into the cities and industrial centers, and the immigrants were Slavs, who quickly pushed the Germans into the numerical minority.[73]

Thus the Germans of the cities saw the Slavic tide rising all around them. Around the old center of the city, where German townspeople had dwelt for centuries, a garland of suburbs developed where no German sound was heard. Within the old city everything still bore a German stamp: the schools were German, German was the language of the city administration, and the Germans still held all municipal offices. But day by day their number dwindled. First the German petty bourgeoisie disappeared. Bad times had come for the crafts and trades, on whose golden base the German colonization of these lands had once grown up; they declined uninterruptedly, for they were not capable of competing with factory industry, just that industry that was attracting the Slavic workers. The German master craftsman sank into the proletariat; and his children, who went into the factory along with the Slavic immigrants, became Slavs through contact with their new comrades. But the German patrician families also became ever smaller in number. They became poor because they could not adapt to the new conditions, or they died out. Replacements did not come. Earlier, those who had risen from below became German. This was now no longer true. Slavs who had become rich were no longer ashamed of their national character. If the old German families shut themselves off from the upstarts, the upstarts formed a new Slavic society of the upper strata.

73. On the causes of the faster population growth of the Slavs, to which is to be ascribed the fact that the movement into the cities in Austria had a predominantly Slavic character, cf. Hainisch, *Die Zukunft der Deutschösterreicher* (Vienna: 1892), pp. 68 ff.

The German policy in Austria, which was based on maintaining the political power position of these minorities, became in this way a conservative—a reactionary—policy. Every conservative policy, however, is fated from the start to fail; after all, its essence is to stop something unstoppable, to resist a development that cannot be impeded. What it can gain at best is time, but it is questionable whether this success is worth the cost. Every reactionary lacks intellectual independence. If one wanted to apply here metaphors taken over from military thinking, as is usual for all lines of political thought in Germany, then one could say that conservatism is defense and, like every defense, lets the terms be dictated to it by its adversary, while the attacker dictates the terms of action to the defender.

The essence of German policy in Austria had become that of holding lost positions as long as possible. Here one struggled over the seats in the administration of a municipality, there over a chamber of commerce, there again over a savings bank or even over only a government job. Little questions were puffed up to great significance. It was bad enough that the Germans thereby put themselves repeatedly in the wrong when, for example, they denied the Slavs the establishment of schools or when they sought with the means of power available to them to make forming clubs or holding meetings more difficult. But it was still worse that in these struggles they always suffered and were bound to suffer defeats and that they thereby became accustomed to being always in retreat and being always defeated. The history of the German policy in Austria is a chain of uninterrupted failures.

These conditions had a devastating effect on the German spirit. People gradually grew accustomed to looking at every measure, every political matter, exclusively from the viewpoint of its local significance. Every reform in public life, every economic measure, every construction of a road, every establishment of a factory, became a question of national patrimony. To be sure, the Slavs also looked at everything from this point of view, but the effect on the political character of the nation was different with them. For through these ways of thinking the Germans became reactionaries, enemies of every innovation, opponents of every democratic arrangement. They left to the Slavs the dubious honor of being fighters for the modern European spirit in Austria and took it upon themselves again and again to support and defend what was out of date. All economic and cultural progress and especially every democratic reform that was carried through in Austria was bound to work against the German minorities in the polyglot territories. It was therefore resisted by the Germans; and if it finally triumphed, then this victory was a defeat for the Germans.

This policy also deprived the Germans of every freedom against the Crown. In the revolution of 1848 the Germans of Austria had risen against the Habsburgs and their absolutism. But the German Liberal Party, which had written the principles of 1848 on its banner, was not in a position to lead the struggle against the Dynasty and against the Court with vigor. It had no firm ground under its feet in the polyglot lands; it was dependent on the favor and disfavor of the government there. If the Court wanted, it could annihilate it; and it did so too.

The empire of the Habsburgs was erected by Ferdinand II on the ruins of the freedoms of the estates and the ruins of Protestantism. It was not only the Bohemian estates that he had to fight against, but also the Styrian and Austrian. The Bohemian rebels fought against the Emperor in alliance with those of Lower and Upper Austria; and the Battle on the White Mountain established the absolute rule of the Habsburgs not only over Bohemia, Moravia, and Silesia but also over the Austrian lands. From the beginning the Habsburg Empire was neither German nor Czech; and when in 1848 it had to fight for its existence anew, Czech and German freedom movements alike were against it. After the establishment of sham constitutionalism in the sixties, the Court would much rather have relied on the Slavs than on the Germans. For years the government was carried on with the Slavs against the Germans; for nothing was more hateful to the Court than the German element, which could not be forgiven for the loss of political position in the German Reich. But all the concessions of the Court could not hold the Czechs and South Slavs firm to the authoritarian state. Among all other peoples of Austria the democratic idea triumphed over the authoritarian idea; it was not possible for the authoritarian state to work with them in the long run. Only with the Germans was it otherwise. Against their will they could not get loose from the Austrian state. When the state called them, they were always at its service. In the Empire's final hour the Germans stood loyal to the Habsburgs.

A turning point in the history of the German-Austrians was the Peace of Prague, which brought about the dissolution of the German Confederation. Now the naive belief was done that Germanness and Austrianness could be reconciled. Now it seemed that one had to choose between being German and being Austrian. But the Germans in Austria did not want to see the necessity of this decision; they wanted, as long as they could, to remain both Germans and Austrians at the same time.

The pain that the German-Austrians felt in 1866 over the turn of events went deep; they never were able to recover from the blow. So quickly had the decision broken over them, so quickly had the events played themselves out on the battlefield, that they had scarcely become conscious of what was going on. Only slowly did they grasp the meaning of what had happened. The German fatherland had expelled them. Were they then not also Germans? Did they not remain Germans, even if there was no place for them in the new political structure being erected on the ruins of the German Confederation?

No one has given better expression to this pain than the aged Grillparzer. He who put into the mouth of Ottokar von Horneck the praise of the "rosy-cheeked youth" Austria and made Libussa proclaim a great future to the Slavs in obscure words,[74] he, who was totally an Austrian and totally a German, finds his equilibrium again in the proud verses:

Als Deutscher ward ich geboren,
Bin ich noch einer?
Nur was ich deutsch geschrieben,
Das nimmt mir keiner.
[As a German I was born,
Am I one still?
Only what I have written in German
No one takes away from me.]

But the German-Austrians had to come to terms with the fact that no Germany still existed, only a Great Prussia. From then on they no longer existed for the Germans in the Reich; they no longer bothered themselves about them, and every day the facts belied the pretty words spoken at gymnastic and shooting festivals. The Great Prussian policy prepared to travel those paths on which it finally wound up at the Marne. It no longer cared about the Germans in Austria. The treaties that bound the Austro-Hungarian Monarchy with the German Reich from 1879 on were concluded by the Great Prussian authoritarian government with the Emperor of Austria and the Magyar oligarchy in

---

74. "You who have long served will finally rule" (*Libussa*, fifth act).

Hungary. Precisely they took away from the Germans in Austria the hope of being able to count on the help of the Germans in the Reich with regard to irredentist strivings.

The defeat that the Great German idea had suffered at Königgrätz was at first papered over by the fact that precisely because of the unfortunate outcome of the war the German Liberal Party for a short time acquired a certain, if limited, influence on state affairs. For a dozen years it could furnish ministers to the government; during this time it repeatedly furnished ministers, even the Prime Minister, and pushed through many important reforms against the will of the Crown, the feudal nobility, and the Church. With extreme exaggeration, that has been called the rule of the Liberal Party in Austria. In truth, the Liberal Party never ruled in Austria; it could not rule. The majority of the people never followed its banners. How could non-Germans also have joined this German party? Among the Germans it always, even when it was flourishing, met strong opposition from the Alpine peasants blindly following the clergy. Its position in the House of Deputies rested not on having the majority of the people behind it but on the electoral system, which in a subtle manner favored the upper middle class and the intelligentsia but withheld the right to vote from the masses. Every extension of the right to vote, every change in the arrangement of electoral districts or of the manner of voting, had to be and was damaging to it. It was a democratic party, but it had to fear the consistent application of democratic principles. That was the inner contradiction from which it suffered and from which it was finally bound to be ruined; it resulted with compelling necessity from that *proton pseudos* [basic fallacy] of its program, which sought to reconcile Germanness with Austrianness.

The German Liberal Party could exert a certain influence on the government as long as this was allowed to it from above. The military and political defeats that the old Austrian princely state had repeatedly suffered compelled the Court to yield temporarily. The Liberals were needed; they were summoned into the ministries not, as it were, because they could no longer be resisted but rather because only they could be expected to put state finances in order and carry through the defense reform. Since no one knew where else to turn, they were entrusted with the reconstruction as the only party that affirmed Austria. They were dismissed in disfavor when they were thought to be no longer needed. When they tried to resist, they were annihilated.

Then Austria gave up on itself. After all, the German Liberal Party had been the only one that had affirmed this state, that sincerely desired it and acted accordingly. The parties that the later governments depended on did not desire Austria. The Poles and Czechs who held ministerial portfolios were frequently competent as specialists and even sometimes pursued a policy that benefited the Austrian state and its peoples. But all their thinking and efforts always concerned only the national plans for the future of their own peoples. Their relation to Austria was always guided only by regard to their peoples' strivings for independence. To their own consciences and to the fellow members of their nationality, their administration of office seemed valuable only for the successes that they obtained in the national emancipation struggle. They were given credit by their fellow countrymen, on whose opinion alone they as parliamentarians laid weight, not because they had administered their offices well, but because they had done much for national separatism.

Besides being filled by Czechs, Poles, and occasional South Slavs and clerical Germans, the highest positions of the Austrian authoritarian government were almost always filled by officials whose only political goal was the maintenance of the authoritarian government and whose only political means was *divide et impera*. Here and there an old Liberal still turns up in between, usually a professor seeking in vain to swim against the current, only finally, after many disappointments, to disappear again from the political scene.

The point at which the interests of the Dynasty and of the Germans seemed to meet was their aversion to democracy. The Germans of Austria had to fear every step on the way to democratization because they were thereby being driven into the minority and delivered up to a ruthless arbitrary rule of majorities of foreign nationality. The German Liberal Party recognized that fact and turned energetically against all efforts for democratization. The contradiction with its liberal program into which it thereby fell caused its ruin. Faced with a historic decision in which it had to choose between the wretched muddling along of the Austrian state for a few decades at the price of giving up the freedom-oriented principles of its program and the immediate annihilation of this state with sacrifice of the German minorities in the territories of foreign language, it undoubtedly made the wrong choice. It may be blamed for that. Yet nothing is more certain than that in the position it found itself in, it could not choose freely. It simply could not sacrifice the minorities any more than the German parties that succeeded it in Austria could do so.

No reproach is less justified, therefore, than that the German Liberals had been poor politicians. This judgment is usually based on their position on the question of the occupation of Bosnia and Herzegovina. That the German Liberal Party had spoken out against the imperialist tendencies of Habsburg militarism was much held against it, especially by Bismarck. Today one will judge otherwise about that. What was previously a matter of reproach against the German Liberal Party—that it had sought to resist militarism and that it went into opposition right at the beginning of the expansion policy that finally led to the Empire's downfall—will in the future redound to its praise and not to its blame.

The German Liberal Party had in any case a much deeper insight into the conditions of existence of the Austrian state than all other powers and parties operating in this country. The Dynasty, especially, had done its utmost to hasten the destruction of the Empire. Its policy was guided less by rational considerations than by resentment. It persecuted the German Liberal Party in blind rage with its hate, even beyond the grave. Since the German Liberals had become antidemocratic, the Dynasty, which always wanted only to restore the old princely state and to which even the authoritarian state seemed too modern a form of state constitution, thought it could indulge in democratic antics from time to time. Thus it repeatedly pushed through the extension of the right to vote against the will of the Germans, each time with the result that the German elements in the House of Deputies lost ground and the radical-national elements of the non-Germans won ever greater influence. Austrian parliamentarianism was thereby finally blown apart. With Badeni's electoral reform of the year 1896 the Empire entered a state of open crisis. The House of Deputies became a place in which the deputies no longer pursued any goal other than to demonstrate the impossibility of the continued existence of this state. Everyone who observed party relations in the Austrian House of Deputies was bound to recognize immediately that this state could still drag out its existence only because European diplomacy was at pains to postpone the danger of war as long as possible. Already twenty years before the end of the war, the domestic political conditions of Austria were more than ripe for collapse.

The German parties that succeeded the German Liberals also showed much less insight into political conditions than the much-reviled German Liberals. The German Nationalist factions, which energetically fought the German Liberals, behaved like democrats at the beginnings of their party activity, when they were still concerned with overcoming the German Liberals. Very soon, however, they had to recognize that democratization in Austria was identical with de-Germanization, and from this recognition they then became just as antidemocratic as the German Liberals had once become. If one disregards the resonant words with which they sought in vain to conceal the paltriness of their program, as well as their anti-Semitic tendencies, which from the standpoint of maintenance of German character in Austria had to be called downright suicidal, then the German Nationalists really differed from the German Liberals only on one single point. In the Linz Program they gave up German claims to Galicia and Dalmatia and contented themselves with claiming for Germanism the lands of the former German Confederation. In raising this claim, however, they clung to the same error that the German Liberals had committed, namely, underrating the capacity for development and the prospects for the future of Slavs of western Austria. They had no more decided than had the German Liberals to sacrifice the German minorities scattered in foreign-language lands, so that their policy incorporated the same irresolution as that of the old German Liberals. They did indeed play with irredentist thoughts more often than the Liberals, but they never had anything seriously in mind other than maintaining the Austrian state under German leadership and German predominance. Faced with the same choice that the German Liberals had been faced with, they trod the same path that the Liberals had already embarked on before them. They decided for the maintenance of the Empire and against democracy. Thus their fate also became the same as that of the old German Liberals. They were used by the Dynasty in the same way as the Liberals. The Dynasty could treat them as badly as possible and yet knew that it could always count on them.

The greatest error that the German Liberals committed in judging their fellow citizens of foreign language was that they saw in all non-Germans nothing but enemies of progress and allies of the Court, of the Church, and of the feudal nobility. Nothing is easier to understand than that this interpretation could arise. The non-German peoples of Austria were equally averse to Great-Austrian and Great-German aspirations; they had recognized earlier than all others, earlier even than the German Liberal Party, that Austria's support was to be sought only in the party association of the German Liberals. To annihilate the German Liberal Party therefore became the most important and at first the only goal of their policy, and in so doing they sought and found as allies all those who, like them, were fighting this party to the death. Thus the serious error for which they paid dearly could arise among the Liberals. They misunderstood the democratic element in the fight of the Slavic nations against the Empire. They saw in the Czechs nothing other than the allies and willing servants of the Schwarzenbergs and Clam-Martinics. The Slavic movement was compromised in their eyes by its alliance with the Church and the Court. How, also, could those men who had fought on the barricades in 1848 forget that the uprising of the German bourgeoisie had been put down by Slavic soldiers?

The mistaken position of the German Liberal Party on national problems resulted from this misunderstanding of the democratic content of the nationality movements. Just as they did not doubt the final victory of light over darkness, of the Enlightenment over clericalism, so they also did not doubt the final victory of progressive Germanism over the reactionary Slavic masses. In every concession to Slavic demands it saw nothing other than concessions to clericalism and militarism.[75]

That the position of the Germans on the political problems of Austria was determined by the force of the conditions into which history had placed them is best shown by the development of the nationality program of German Social Democracy in Austria. Social Democracy had first won ground in Austria among the Germans, and for long years it was and remained no more than a German party, with a few fellow travelers among the intellectuals of the other nationalities. At this time when, because of the electoral system, it was scarcely possible for it to play a role in Parliament, it could regard itself as uninvolved in the national struggles. It could take the position that all national quarrels were nothing more than an internal concern of the bourgeoisie. On the vital questions of Germanism in Austria, it took no position other than that of its brother party in the German Empire toward the foreign policy of the Junkers, of the National Liberals, or even of the Pan-Germans. If those German parties that were waging the national struggle reproached it, like the German clericals and the Christian Socialists, for harming its own people by its behavior, well, this was thoroughly justified at the

---

75. Note that Marx and Engels had also fallen into the same error; quite like the Austrian-German Liberals, they too saw reactionary doings in the national movements of the nations without history and were convinced that with the unavoidable victory of democracy, Germanism would triumph over these dying nationalities. Cf. Marx, *Revolution und Kontrerevolution in Deutschland*, German translation by Kautsky, third edition (Stuttgart: 1913), pp. 61 ff.; Engels (Mehring, loc. cit.), pp. 246 ff. Cf. in addition Bauer, "Nationalitätenfrage," loc. cit., pp. 271 f.

time, even though the extent of this damage was only slight precisely because of the also slight political significance of Social Democracy at the time. The more, however, the significance of Social Democracy in Austria grew — and it grew above all because in Austrian conditions Social Democracy was the only democratic party among the Germans of Austria — it was all the more bound to acquire the responsibility that was incumbent on every German party in Austria in national questions. It began to become German-nationalist; then, no more than the two older German parties of Austria, could it get around the conditions that had brought Germanism and democracy into contradiction in Austria. Just as the German Liberal Party finally had to drop its democratic principles because following them was bound to lead to harming Germanism in Austria, just as the German Nationalist Party had done the same, so Social Democracy too would have had to do this if history had not forestalled it and shattered the Austrian state before this turn of events was fully completed.

After a series of programmatic declarations of merely academic value had been overtaken by the facts, Social Democracy at first made a try with the program of national autonomy.[76]

There is no doubt that this program rests on a deeper grasp of nationality problems than the Linz Program, on which, though, the flower of German Austria at the time had also collaborated. In the decades between these two programs, much had taken place that was bound to open the eyes of the Germans of Austria also. But there, too, they could not escape the constraint that historical necessity had placed on them. The program of national autonomy, even if it spoke of democracy and self-government, was also basically nothing but what the nationality programs of the German Liberals and the German Nationalists had really been in essence: namely, a program for saving the Austrian state of Habsburg-Lorraine dominion over the Imperial and Royal hereditary lands. It claimed to be much more modern that the older programs, but it was in essence nothing else. One cannot even say that it was more democratic than the earlier ones, for democracy is an absolute concept, not a concept of degree.

The most important difference between the program of national autonomy and the older German nationality programs is that it feels the necessity of justifying the existence and demonstrating the necessity of the existence of the Austrian state not only from the standpoint of the

76. Cf. above, pp. 42 ff.

Dynasty and from the standpoint of the Germans but also from that of the other nationalities. And it does not content itself, moreover, with those showy phrases that were usual among the so-called black-and-yellow writers, as, for example, with a reference to the maxim of Palacký that one would have had to invent Austria if it had not already existed. But this argument, which was worked out particularly by Renner, is totally untenable. It starts with the idea that maintaining the Austro-Hungarian customs territory as a distinct economic territory is in the interest of all the peoples of Austria and that each one, therefore, has an interest in creating an order that maintains the viability of the state. That this argument is not correct has already been shown; when one has recognized the faultiness of the program of national autonomy, then one sees immediately that it contains nothing but an attempt to find a way out of the nationality struggles without destroying the Habsburg state. Not quite unjustifiably, therefore, the Social Democrats have occasionally been called Imperial and Royal Social Democrats; they did appear as the only pro-state party in Austria, especially at those moments of the kaleidoscopically changing party constellation in Austria when the German Nationalists temporarily set aside their Austrian sentiment and behaved irredentistically.

The collapse of Austria saved Social Democracy from going too far in this direction. In the first years of the World War, Renner, in particular, did everything in this respect that was at all possible with his doctrines that opponents called social imperialism. That the majority of his party did not unconditionally follow him on this path was not a merit of its own but rather the consequence of growing dissatisfaction with a policy that was imposing the most extreme bloody sacrifices on the population and condemning it to hunger and misery.

The German and German-Austrian Social Democrats could represent themselves as democratic because they were opposition parties without responsibility as long as the German people could not fully accept democratic principles, fearing that their application would harm the Germans in the polyglot territories of the East. With the outbreak of the World War, when a part, perhaps the largest part, of the responsibility for the fate of the German people fell to them, too, they also took the path taken before them by the other democratic parties in Germany and Austria. With Scheidemann in the Reich and with Renner in Austria they made the change that was bound to take them away from democracy. That Social Democracy did not proceed further on this path, that it did not become a new guard of the authoritarian state which, with regard to democracy, would scarcely have been different from the National Liberals in the Reich and the German Nationalists in Austria—that was due to the sudden change in conditions.

Now, with defeat in the World War and its consequences for the position of German-speaking people in the territories with mixed population, the circumstances have been removed that previously forced all German parties away from democracy. The German people can today seek salvation only in democracy, in the right of self-determination both of individuals and of nations.[77]

77. The same causes that held the German people back from democracy were at work in Russia, Poland, and Hungary also. One will have to draw them into the explanation if one wants to understand the development of the Russian Constitutional Democrats or of the Polish club in the Austrian Imperial Council or of the Hungarian party of 1848.

War and the Economy

1   The Economic Position of the Central Powers in the War

The economic aspects of the World War are unique in history in kind and in degree; nothing similar ever existed before nor ever will exist again. This combination of developments was in general conditioned both by the contemporary stage of development of the division of labor and state of war technique, but in particular by both the grouping of the belligerent powers and the particular features of their territories as far as geography and technique of production were concerned. Only the conjunction of a large number of preconditions could lead to the situation that was quite unsuitably summarized in Germany and Austria under the catchword "war economy." No opinion need be expressed whether this war will be the last one or whether still others will follow. But a war which puts one side in an economic position similar to that in which the Central Powers found themselves in this war will never be waged again. The reason is not only that the configuration of economic history of 1914 cannot return but also that no people can ever again experience the political and psychological preconditions that made a war of several years' duration under such circumstances still seem promising to the German people.

The economic side of the World War can scarcely be worse misunderstood than in saying that in any case "the understanding of most of these phenomena will not be furthered by a good knowledge of the conditions of the peacetime economies of 1913 but rather by adducing those of the peacetime economies of the fourteenth to eighteenth centuries or the war economy of Napoleonic times."[1] We can best see how

1. Cf. Otto Neurath, "Aufgabe, Methode und Leistungsfähigkeit der Kriegswirtschaftslehre," *Archiv für Sozialwissenschaft und Sozialpolitik*, vol. 44, 1917/1918, p. 765; cf., on the contrary, the discussion of Eulenburg, "Die wissenschaftliche Behandlung der Kriegswirtschaft," ibid., pp. 775–85.

much such an interpretation focuses on superficialities and how little it enables us to grasp the essence of the phenomena if we imagine, say, that the World War had been waged *ceteris paribus* at the stage of the international division of labor reached one hundred years before. It could not have become a war of starving out then; yet that was precisely its essence. Another grouping of the belligerent powers would also have resulted in quite a different picture.

The economic aspects of the World War can only be understood if one first keeps in view their dependence on the contemporary development of world economic relations of the individual national economies, in the first place of Germany's and Austria-Hungary's and then of England's also.

Economic history is the development of the division of labor. It starts with the self-contained household economy of the family, which is self-sufficient, which itself produces everything that it uses or consumes. The individual households are not economically differentiated. Each one serves only itself. No economic contact, no exchange of economic goods, occurs.

Recognition that work performed under the division of labor is more productive than work performed without the division of labor puts an end to the isolation of the individual economies. The trade principle, exchange, links the individual proprietors together. From a concern of individuals, the economy becomes a social matter. The division of labor advances step by step. First limited to only a narrow sphere, it extends itself more and more. The age of liberalism brought the greatest advances of this sort. In the first half of the nineteenth century the largest part of the population of the European countryside, in general, still lived in economic self-sufficiency. The peasant consumed only foodstuffs that he himself had grown; he wore clothes of wool or linen for which he himself had produced the raw material, which was then spun, woven, and sewn in his household. He had built a house and farm buildings and maintained them himself, perhaps with the help of neighbors, whom he repaid with similar services. In the out-of-the-way valleys of the Carpathians, in Albania, and in Macedonia, cut off from the world, similar conditions still existed at the outbreak of the World War. How little this economic structure corresponds, however, to what exists today in the rest of Europe is too well known to require more detailed description.

The locational development of the division of labor leads toward a full world economy, that is, toward a situation in which each productive activity moves to those places that are most favorable for productivity; and in doing so, comparisons are made with all the production possibilities of the earth's surface. Such relocations of production go on continually, as, for example, when sheep-raising declines in Central Europe and expands in Australia or when the linen production of Europe is displaced by the cotton production of America, Asia, and Africa.

No less important than the spatial division of labor is the personal kind. It is in part conditioned by the spatial division of labor. When branches of production are differentiated by locality, then personal differentiation of producers must also occur. If we wear Australian wool on our bodies and consume Siberian butter, then it is naturally not possible that the producer of the wool and of the butter are one and the same person, as once was the case. Indeed, the personal division of labor also develops independently of the spatial, as every walk through our cities or even only through the halls of a factory teaches us.

The dependence of the conduct of war on the stage of development of the spatial division of labor reached at the time does not in itself, even today, make every war impossible. Individual states can find themselves at war without their world economic relations being essentially affected thereby. A German-French war would have been bound to lead or could have led to an economic collapse of Germany just as little in 1914 as in 1870–71. But today it must seem utterly impossible for one or several states cut off from world trade to wage war against an opponent enjoying free trade with the outside world.

This development of spatial division of labor is also what makes local uprisings appear quite hopeless from the start. As late as the year 1882, the people around the Gulf of Kotor and the Herzegovinians could successfully rebel against the Austrian government for weeks and months without suffering shortages in their economic system, composed of autarkic households. In Westphalia or Silesia, an uprising that stretched only over so small a territory could already at that time have been suppressed in a few days by blocking shipments into it. Centuries ago, cities could wage war against the countryside; for a long time now that has no longer been possible. The development of the spatial division of labor, its progress toward a world economy, works more effectively for peace than all the efforts of the pacifists. Mere recognition of the worldwide economic linkage of material interests would have shown the German militarists the danger, indeed impossibility, of their efforts. They were so much caught up in their power-policy ideas, however, that they were never able to pronounce the peaceful term "world economy" otherwise than in warlike lines of thought. Global policy was for them synonymous with war policy, naval construction, and hatred of England.[2]

That economic dependence on world trade must be of decisive significance for the outcome of a campaign could naturally not also escape those who had occupied themselves for decades with preparation for war in the German Reich. If they still did not realize that Germany, even if only because of its economic position, could not successfully wage a great war with several great powers, well, two factors were decisive for that, one political and one military. Helfferich summarized the former in the following words: "The very position of Germany's borders as good as rules out the possibility of lengthy stoppage of grain imports. We have so many neighbors—first the high seas, then Holland, Belgium, France, Switzerland, Austria, Russia—that it seems quite inconceivable that the many routes of grain import by water and by land could all be blocked to us at once. The whole world would have to be in alliance against us; however, to consider such a possibility seriously, even for a minute, means having a boundless mistrust in our foreign policy."[3] Militarily, however, recalling the experiences of the European wars of 1859, 1866, and 1870–71, people believed that they had to reckon with a war lasting only a few months, even weeks. All German war plans were based on the idea of success in completely defeating France within a few weeks. Anyone who might have considered that the war would last long enough for the English and even the Americans to appear on the European continent with armies of millions would have been laughed down in Berlin. That the war would become a war of emplacements was not understood at all; despite the experiences of the

2. Especially characteristic of this tendency are the speeches and essays published by Schmoller, Sering, and Wagner under the auspices of the "Free Association for Naval Treaties" under the title *Handels- und Machtpolitik* (Stuttgart: 1900), 2 volumes.

3. Cf. Helfferich, *Handelspolitik* (Leipzig: 1901), p. 197; similarly Dietzel, "Weltwirtschaft und Volkswirtschaft," *Jahrbuch der Gehe-Stiftung*, vol. 5 (Dresden: 1900), pp. 46 f.; Riesser, *Finanzielle Kriegsbereitschaft und Kriegsführung* (Jena: 1909), pp. 73 f. Bernhardi speaks of the necessity of taking measures to prepare ways during a German-English war "by which we can obtain the most necessary imports of foods and raw materials and at the same time export the surplus of our industrial products at least partially" (*Deutschland und der nächste Krieg* [Stuttgart: 1912], pp. 179 f.). He proposes making provisions for "a kind of commercial mobilization." What illusions about the political situation he thereby indulged in can best be seen from his thinking that in a fight against England (and France allied with it), we would "not stand spiritually alone, but rather all on the wide earthly sphere who think and feel freedom-oriented and self-confident will be united with us" (ibid., p. 187).

Russo-Japanese war, people believed that they could end the European war in a short time by rapid offensive strikes.[4] The military calculations of the General Staff were just as false as its economic and political ones.

The assertion is not true, therefore, that the German Empire had neglected to make the necessary economic preparations for war. It simply had counted on a war of only short duration; for a short war, however, no economic provisions had to be made beyond those of finance and credit policy. Before the outbreak of the war the idea would no doubt have been called absurd that Germany could ever be forced to fight almost the whole rest of the world for many years in alliance only with Austria-Hungary (or more exactly in alliance with the German-Austrians and the Magyars, for the Slavs and Rumanians of the Monarchy stood with their hearts — and many of them also with weapons — on the side of the enemy), Turkey, and Bulgaria. And in any case one would have had to

4. Modern war theory started with the view that attack is the superior method of waging war. It corresponds to the spirit of conquest-hungry militarism when Bernhardi argues for this: "Only attack achieves positive results; mere defense always delivers only negative ones." (Cf. Bernhardi, *Vom heutigen Krieg* [Berlin: 1912], vol. 2, p. 223.) The argumentation for the attack theory was not merely political, however, but was also based on military science. Attack appears as the superior form of fighting because the attacker has free choice of the direction, of the goal, and of the place of the operations, because he, as the active party, determines the conditions under which the fight is carried out, in short, because he dictates to the party under attack the rules of action. Since, however, the defense is tactically stronger in the front than the offense, the attacker must strive to get around the flank of the defender. That was old war theory, newly proved by the victories of Frederick II, Napoleon I, and Moltke and by the defeats of Mack, Gyulai, and Benedek. It determined the behavior of the French at the beginning of the war (Mulhouse). It was what impelled the German army administration to embark on the march through neutral Belgium in order to hit the French on the flank because they were unattackable in the front. His remembering the many Austrian commanders for whom the defensive had become misfortune drove Conrad in 1914 to open the campaign with goalless and purposeless offensives in which the flower of the Austrian army was uselessly sacrificed. But the time of battles of the old style, which permitted getting around the opponent's flank, was past on the great European theaters of war, since the massiveness of the armies and the tactics that had been reshaped by modern weapons and means of communication offered the possibility of arranging the armies in such a way that a flank attack was no longer possible. Flanks that rest on the sea or on neutral territory cannot be gotten around. Only frontal attack still remains, but it fails against an equally well-armed opponent. The great breakthrough offensives in this war succeeded only against badly armed opponents, as especially the Russians were in 1915 and in many respects also the Germans in 1918. Against inferior troops a frontal attack could of course succeed even against equally good, even superior, weapons and armaments of the defender (twelfth battle of the Isonzo). Otherwise, the old tactics could be applied only in the battles of mobile warfare (Tannenberg and the Masurian Lakes in 1914 and individual battles in Galicia). To have misunderstood this has been the tragic fate of German militarism. The whole German policy was built on the theorem of the military superiority of attack; in war of emplacements the policy broke down with the theorem.

recognize, after calm reflection, that such a war neither could have been waged nor should have been waged and that if an unspeakably bad policy had let it break out, then one should have tried to conclude peace as quickly as possible, even at the price of great sacrifices. For, indeed, there never could be any doubt that the end could be only a fearful defeat that would deliver the German people defenseless to the harshest terms of its opponents. Under such circumstances a quick peace would at least have spared goods and blood.

That should have been recognized at once even in the first weeks of the war and the only possible implications then drawn. From the first days of the war—at the latest, however, after the defeats on the Marne and in Galicia in September 1914—there was only *one* rational goal for German policy: peace, even if at the price of heavy sacrifices. Let us quite disregard the fact that until the summer of 1918 it was repeatedly possible to obtain peace under halfway acceptable conditions, that the Germans of Alsace, the South Tyrol, the Sudetenland, and the eastern provinces of Prussia could probably have been protected from foreign rule in that way; even then, if continuation of the war might have afforded a slightly more favorable peace, the incomparably great sacrifices that continuation of the war required should not have been made. That this did not happen, that the hopeless, suicidal fight was continued for years, political considerations and grave errors in the military assessment of events were primarily responsible.[5] But delusions about economic policy also contributed much.

Right at the beginning of the war a catchword turned up whose unfortunate consequences cannot be completely overlooked even today: the verbal fetish "war economy." With this term all considerations were beaten down that could have led to a conclusion advising against continuing the war. With this one term all economic thought was put aside; ideas carried over from the "peacetime economy" were said not to hold for the "war economy," which obeyed other laws. Armed with this catchword, a few bureaucrats and officers who had gained full power by exceptional decrees substituted "war socialism" for what state socialism and militarism had still left of the free economy. And when the hungry people began to grumble, they were calmed again by reference to the

5. It was an incomprehensible delusion to speak of the possibility of a victorious peace when German failure had already been settled from the time of the battle of the Marne. But the Junker party preferred to let the German people be entirely ruined rather than give up its rule even one day earlier.

"war economy." If an English cabinet minister had voiced the watchword "business as usual" at the beginning of the war, which, however, could not be continued in England as the war went on, well, people in Germany and Austria took pride in traveling paths as new as possible. They "organized" and did not notice that what they were doing was organizing defeat.

The greatest economic achievement that the German people accomplished during the war, the conversion of industry to war needs, was not the work of state intervention; it was the result of the free economy. If, also, what was accomplished in the Reich in this respect was much more significant in absolute quantity than what was done in Austria, it should not be overlooked that the task which Austrian industry had to solve was still greater in relation to its powers. Austrian industry not only had to deliver what the war required beyond peacetime provisions; it also had to catch up on what had been neglected in peacetime. The guns with which the Austro-Hungarian field artillery went to war were inferior; the heavy and light field howitzers and the mountain cannons were already out of date at the time of their introduction and scarcely satisfied the most modest demands. These guns came from state factories; and now private industry, which in peacetime had been excluded from supplying field and mountain guns and could supply such material only to China and Turkey, had to produce not only the material for expanding the artillery, but also to replace the unusable models of the old batteries with better ones. Things were not much different with the clothing and shoeing of the Austro-Hungarian troops. The so-called bluish-gray — more correctly, light blue — fabrics proved to be unusable in the field and had to be replaced as rapidly as possible by gray ones. Supplying the army with boots, which in peacetime had been carried out exclusively by the market-oriented mechanized shoe industry, had to be turned over to the management of factories which had previously been avoided.

The great technical superiority that the armies of the Central Powers had achieved in the spring and summer of 1915 in the eastern theater of the war and that formed the chief basis of the victorious campaign from Tarnów and Gorlice to deep into Volhynia was likewise the work of free industry, as were the astonishing achievements of German and also of Austrian labor in the delivery of war material of all kinds for the western and the Italian theaters of war. The army administrations of Germany and Austro-Hungary knew very well why they did not give in to the pressure for state ownership of the war-supplying enterprises. They put aside their outspoken preference for state enterprises oriented toward power policy and state omnipotence, which would have better suited their worldview, because they knew quite well that the great industrial tasks to be accomplished in this area could be accomplished only by entrepreneurs operating on their own responsibility and with their own resources. War socialism knew very well why it had not been entrusted with the armaments enterprises right in the first years of the war.

2   War Socialism

So-called war socialism has been regarded as sufficiently argued for and justified with reference mostly to the emergency created by the war. In war, the inadequate free economy supposedly cannot be allowed to exist any longer; into its place must step something more perfect, the administered economy. Whether or not one should return after the war to the "un-German" system of individualism was said to be another question that could be answered in different ways.

This argumentation for war socialism is just as inadequate as it is characteristic of the political thinking of a people that was hampered in every free expression of views by the despotism of the war party. It is inadequate because it could really be a powerful argument only if it had been established that the organized economy is capable of yielding higher outputs than the free economy; that, however, would first have to be proved. For the socialists, who advocate the socialization of the means of production anyway and want to abolish the anarchy of production thereby, a state of war is not first required to justify socializing measures. For the opponents of socialism, however, the reference to the war and its economic consequences is also no circumstance that could recommend such measures. For anyone of the opinion that the free economy is the superior form of economic activity, precisely the need created by the war had to be a new reason demanding that all obstacles standing in the way of free competition be set aside. War as such does not demand a [centrally] organized economy, even though it may set certain limits in several directions to the pursuit of economic interests. In the age of liberalism, even a war of the extent of the World War (so far as such a war would have been thinkable at all in a liberal and therefore pacifistic age) would in no way have furthered tendencies toward socialization.

The most usual argument for the necessity of socialist measures was the argument about being besieged. Germany and its allies were said to be in the position of a besieged fortress that the enemy was trying to conquer by starving it out. Against such a danger, all measures usual in a besieged city had to be applied. All stocks had to be regarded as a mass under the control of a unified administration that could be drawn on for equally meeting the needs of all, and so consumption had to be rationed.

This line of argument starts from indisputable facts. It is clear that starving out (in the broadest sense of the term), which in the history of warfare had generally been used only as a tactical means, was used in this war as a strategic means.[6] But the conclusions drawn from the facts were mistaken. Once one thought that the position of the Central Powers was comparable to that of a besieged fortress, one would have had to draw the only conclusions that could be drawn from the military point of view. One would have had to remember that a besieged place, by all experience of military history, was bound to be starved out and that its fall could be prevented only by help from outside. The program of "hanging on" would then have made sense only if one could count on time's working for the besieged side. Since, however, help from outside could not be expected, one should not have shut one's eyes to the knowledge that the position of the Central Powers was becoming worse from day to day and that it was therefore necessary to make peace, even if making peace would have imposed sacrifices that did not seem justified by the tactical position of the moment. For the opponents would still have been ready to make concessions if they, for their part, had received something in return for the shortening of the war.

It cannot be assumed that the German General Staff had overlooked this. If it nevertheless clung to the slogan about "hanging on," that reflected not so much a misunderstanding of the military position as the hope for a particular psychic disposition of the opponent. The Anglo-Saxon nation of shopkeepers would get tired sooner than the peoples of the Central Powers, who were used to war. Once the English, also, felt the war, once they felt the satisfaction of their needs being limited, they

6. One war in which starving the opponent out was used as a strategic means was the Herero uprising in German Southwest Africa in 1904; in a certain sense the Civil War in North America and the last Boer War can also count here.

would turn out to be much more sensitive than the Central Europeans. This grave error, this misunderstanding of the psyche of the English people, also led to adoption first of limited and then of unlimited submarine warfare. The submarine war rested on still other false calculations, on an overestimation of one's own effectiveness and on an underestimation of the opponent's defense measures, and finally on a complete misunderstanding of the political preconditions of waging war and of what is permitted in war. But it is not the task of this book to discuss these questions. Settling accounts with the forces that pushed the German people into this suicidal adventure may be left to more qualified persons.

But quite apart from these deficiencies, which more concern the generally military side of the question, the theory of siege socialism also suffers from serious defects concerning economic policy.

When Germany was compared with a besieged city, it was overlooked that this comparison was applicable only with regard to those goods that were not produced at home and also could not be replaced by goods producible at home. For these goods, apart from luxury articles, the rationing of consumption was in any case indicated at the moment when, with the tightening of the blockade and with the entry of Italy and Rumania into the war, all import possibilities were cut off. Until then it would have been better, of course, to allow full free trade, at least for the quantities imported from abroad, in order not to reduce the incentive to obtain them in indirect ways. It was mistaken in any case, as happened at the beginning of the war, especially in Austria, to resist price rises of these goods by penal measures. If the traders had held the goods back with speculative intent to achieve price increases, this would have limited consumption effectively right at the beginning of the war. The limitation of price increases was bound, therefore, to have downright harmful consequences. For those goods that could in no way be produced at home and also could not be replaced by substitutes producible at home, the state would better have set minimum rather than maximum prices to limit consumption as much as possible.

Speculation anticipates future price changes; its economic function consists in evening out price differences between different places and different points in time and, through the pressure which prices exert on production and consumption, in adapting stocks and demands to each other. If speculation began to exact higher prices at the beginning of the war, then it did indeed temporarily bring about a rise of prices beyond the level that would have been established in its absence. Indeed, since consumption would also thus be limited, the stock of goods available for use later in the war was bound to rise and thus would have led to a moderation of prices at that later time in relation to the level that was bound to have been established in the absence of speculation. If this indispensable economic function of speculation was to be excluded, something else should have immediately been put in its place, perhaps confiscation of all stocks and state management and rationing. In no way, however, was it suitable simply to be content with penal intervention.

When the war broke out, citizens expected a war lasting about three to six months. The merchant arranged his speculation accordingly. If the state had known better, it would have had the duty of intervening. If it thought that the war would already be ended in four weeks, then it could have intervened to keep price increases from being larger than seemed necessary for bringing stocks into harmony with demand. For that, too, fixing maximum prices would not have sufficed. If, however, the state thought that the war would last far longer than civilians thought, then it should have intervened, either by fixing minimum prices or by purchase of goods for the purpose of state stockpiling. For there was a danger that speculative traders, not familiar with the secret intentions and plans of the General Staff, would not immediately drive up prices to the extent necessary to assure the distribution of the small stocks on hand over the entire duration of the war. That would have been a case in which the intervention of the state in prices would have been thoroughly necessary and justified. That that did not happen is easy to explain. The military and political authorities were informed least of all about the prospective duration of the war. For that reason all their preparations failed, military as well as political and economic ones.

With regard to all those goods that even despite the war could be produced in territory of the Central Powers free of the enemy, the siege argument was already totally inapplicable. It was dilettantism of the worst sort to set maximum prices for these goods. Production could have been stimulated only by high prices; the limitation of price increases throttled it. It is hardly astonishing that state compulsion for cultivation and production failed.

It will be the task of economic history to describe in detail the stupidities of the economic policy of the Central Powers during the war. At one time, for example, the word was given to reduce the livestock by increased slaughtering because of a shortage of fodder; then prohibitions of slaughtering were issued and measures taken to promote the raising of livestock. Similar planlessness reigned in all sectors. Measures and countermeasures crossed each other until the whole structure of economic activity was in ruins.

The most harmful effect of the policy of siege socialism was the cutting off of districts with surpluses of agricultural production from territories in which consumption exceeded production. It is easy to understand why the Czech district leaders in the Sudetenland, whose hearts were on the side of the Entente, sought as much as possible to limit the export of foodstuffs out of the districts under their leadership to the German parts of Austria and, above all, to Vienna. It is less understandable that the Vienna government put up with this and that it also put up with its imitation by the German districts and also with the fact that Hungary shut itself off from Austria, so that famine was already prevailing in Vienna while abundant stocks were still on hand in the countryside and in Hungary. Quite incomprehensible, however, is the fact that the same policy of regional segmentation took hold in the German Reich also and that the agrarian districts there were permitted to cut themselves off from the industrial ones. That the population of the big cities did not rebel against this policy can be explained only by its being caught up in statist conceptions of economic life, by its blind belief in the omnipotence of official intervention, and by its decades-long ingrained mistrust of all freedom.

While statism sought to avoid the inevitable collapse, it only hastened it.

3   Autarky and Stockpiling

The clearer it had to become in the course of the war that the Central Powers were bound to be finally defeated in the war of starving out, the more energetically were references made from various sides to the necessity of preparing better for the next war. The economy would have to be reshaped in such a way that Germany would be capable of withstanding even a war of several years. It would have to be able to produce inside the country everything required for feeding its population and for equipping and arming its armies and fleets in order to be no longer dependent on foreign countries in this respect.

No long discussions are needed to show that this program cannot be carried out. It cannot be carried out because the German Reich is too densely populated for all foodstuffs needed by its population to be produced at home without use of foreign raw materials and because a number of raw materials needed for production of modern war material just do not exist in Germany. The theorists of the war economy commit a fallacy when they try to prove the possibility of an autarkic German economy by reference to the usability of substitute materials. One supposedly must not always use foreign products; there are domestic products scarcely inferior to foreign ones in quality and cheapness. For the German spirit, which has already famously distinguished itself in applied science, a great task arises here which it will solve splendidly. The efforts previously made in this field have led to favorable results. We are said already to be richer now than we were before, since we have learned how to exploit better than before materials that earlier were neglected or were used for less important purposes or not fully used.

The error in this line of thinking is obvious. It may well be true that applied science is far from yet having spoken the last word, that we may still count on improvements in technology that will be no less significant than the invention of the steam engine and of the electric motor. And it may happen that one or the other of these inventions will find the most favorable preconditions for its application precisely on German soil, that it will perhaps consist precisely in making useful a material that is abundantly available in Germany. But then the significance of this invention would lie precisely in shifting the locational circumstances of a branch of production, in making the productive conditions of a country that were previously to be regarded as less favorable more favorable under the given circumstances. Such shifts have often occurred in history and will occur again and again. We will hope that they occur in the future in such a way that Germany will become, to a higher degree than at present, a country of more favorable conditions of production. If that should happen, then many burdens will be lifted from the German people.

Yet these changes in the relative pattern of conditions of production must be sharply distinguished from introducing the use of substitute materials and producing goods under worse conditions of production. One can of course use linen instead of cotton and wooden soles instead of leather soles. However, in the former case one has replaced a cheaper by a dearer material, that is, by one in whose production more costs must be incurred, and in the latter case a better by a less usable material. That means, however, that the meeting of needs becomes worse. That we use paper sacks instead of jute sacks and iron tires on vehicles instead of rubber tires, that we drink "war" coffee instead of real coffee, shows that we become poorer, not richer. And if we now carefully put to use garbage that we had earlier thrown away, then this makes us richer just as little as if we obtained copper by melting works of art.[7] To be sure, living well is not the highest good; and there may be reasons for peoples as well as individuals to prefer a life of poverty to a life of luxury. But then let that be said openly without taking refuge in artificial theorems that try to make black out of white and white out of black; then let no one seek to obscure the clear case by allegedly economic arguments.[8]

It should not be disputed that war needs can beget and, in fact, have begotten many useful inventions. How much they represent a lasting enrichment of the German economy can be known only later.

Only those proponents of the idea of autarky who subordinate all other goals to the military one are thinking consistently. He who sees all values as realized only in the state and thinks of the state above all as a military organization always ready for war must demand of the economic policy of the future that it strive, pushing all other considerations aside, to organize the domestic economy for self-sufficiency in case of war. Regardless of the higher costs that thereby arise, production must be guided into the channels designated as most suitable by the economic general staff. If the standard of living of the population thereby suffers, well, in view of the high objective to be attained, that does not count at all. Not the standard of living is the greatest happiness of people, but fulfillment of duty.

But there is a grave error in this line of thinking also. Admittedly it is possible, if one disregards costs, to produce within the country everything necessary for waging war. But in war it is important not only that weapons and war material just be on hand but also that they be available

7. Cf. Dietzel, *Die Nationalisierung der Kriegsmilliarden* (Tübingen: 1919), pp. 31 ff.
8. Not only economists have been active in this direction; still more has been done by technicians, but most by physicians. Biologists who, before the war, declared the nutrition of the German industrial worker to be inadequate suddenly discovered during the war that food poor in protein is especially wholesome, that fat consumption in excess of the quantity permitted by the authorities is damaging to health, and that a limitation of the consumption of carbohydrates has little significance.

in sufficient quantity and in best quality. A people that must produce them under more unfavorable conditions of production, that is, with higher costs, will go into the field worse provisioned, equipped, and armed than its opponents. Of course, the inferiority of material supplies can to a certain extent be offset by the personal excellence of the combatants. But we have learned anew in this war that there is a limit beyond which all bravery and all sacrifice are of no use.

From recognition that efforts for autarky could not be carried through, there arose the plan for a future state stockpiling system. In preparation for the possible return of a war of starvation, the state must build up stockpiles of all important raw materials that cannot be produced at home. In that connection a large stock of grain was also thought of, and even stocks of fodder.[9]

From the economic standpoint, the realization of these proposals does not seem inconceivable. From the political standpoint, though, it is quite hopeless. It is scarcely to be assumed that other nations would calmly look on at the piling up of such war stocks in Germany and not, for their part, resort to countermeasures. To foil the whole plan, they indeed need only watch over the exports of the materials in question and each time permit the export only of such quantities as do not exceed the current demand.

What has quite incorrectly been called war economy is the economic preconditions for waging war. All waging of war is dependent on the state of the division of labor reached at the time. Autarkic economies can go to war against each other; the individual parts of a labor and trade community can do so, however, only insofar as they are in a position to go back to autarky. For that reason, with the progress of the division of labor we see the number of wars and battles diminishing ever more and more. The spirit of industrialism, which is indefatigably active in the development of trade relations, undermines the warlike spirit. The great steps forward that the world economy made in the age of liberalism considerably narrowed the scope remaining for military actions. When those strata of the German people who had the deepest insight into the world economic interdependence of the individual national economies doubted whether it was still at all possible that a war could develop and, if that should happen at all, expected at most a

9. Cf. Hermann Levy, *Vorratswirtschaft und Volkswirtschaft* (Berlin: Verlag von Julius Springer), 1915, pp. 9 ff.; Naumann, *Mitteleuropa*, pp. 149 f; Diehl, *Deutschland als geschlossener Handelsstaat im Weltkrieg* (Stuttgart: 1916), pp. 28 f.

war that would end quickly, they thereby showed better understanding of the realities of life than those who indulged in the delusion that even in the age of world trade one could practice the political and military principles of the Thirty Years' War.

When one examines the catchword about war economy for its content, it turns out that it contains nothing other than the demand to turn economic development back to a stage more favorable for waging war than the 1914 stage was. It is a question only of how far one should go in doing that. Should one go back only as far as to make warfare between great states possible, or should one try to make warfare possible between individual parts of a country and between city and countryside also? Should only Germany be put in a position to wage war against the entire remaining world, or should it also be made possible for Berlin to wage war against the rest of Germany?

Whoever on ethical grounds wants to maintain war permanently for its own sake as a feature of relations among peoples must clearly realize that this can happen only at the cost of the general welfare, since the economic development of the world would have to be turned back at least to the state of the year 1830 to realize this martial ideal even only to some extent.

4   The Economy's War Costs and the Inflation

The losses that the national economy suffers from war, apart from the disadvantages that exclusion from world trade entails, consist of the destruction of goods by military actions, the consumption of war materiel of all kinds, and the loss of productive labor that the persons drawn into military service would have rendered in their civilian activities. Further losses from loss of labor occur insofar as the number of workers is lastingly reduced by the number of the fallen and as the survivors become less fit in consequence of injuries suffered, hardships undergone, illnesses suffered, and worsened nutrition. These losses are only to the slightest degree offset by the fact that the war works as a dynamic factor and spurs the population to improve the technique of production. Even the increase in the number of workers that has taken place in the war by drawing on the otherwise unused labor of women and children and by extension of hours of work, as well as the saving achieved by limitation of consumption, still does not counterbalance them, so that the economy finally comes out of the war with a considerable loss of wealth. Economically considered, war and revolution are always bad business, unless such an improvement of the production process of the national economy results from them that the additional amount of goods produced after the war can compensate for the losses of the war. The socialist who is convinced that the socialist order of society will multiply the productivity of the economy may think little of the sacrifices that the social revolution will cost.

But even a war that is disadvantageous for the world economy can enrich individual nations or states. If the victorious state is able to lay such burdens on the vanquished that not only all of its war costs are thereby covered but a surplus is acquired also, then the war has been advantageous for it. The militaristic idea rests on the belief that such war gains are possible and can be lastingly held. A people who believes that it can gain its bread more easily by waging war than by work can hardly be convinced that it is more pleasing to God to suffer injustice than to commit injustice. The theory of militarism can be refuted; if, however, one cannot refute it, one cannot, by appeal to ethical factors, persuade the stronger party to forgo the use of its power.

The pacifistic line of argument goes too far if it simply denies that a people can gain by war. Criticism of militarism must begin by raising the question whether the victor can then definitely count on always remaining the stronger or whether he must not fear being displaced by still stronger parties. The militaristic argumentation can defend itself from objections raised against it from this point of view only if it starts with the assumption of unchangeable race characters. The members of the higher race, who behave according to pacifistic principles among themselves, hold firmly together against the lower races that they are striving to subjugate and thus assure themselves eternal predominance. But the possibility that differences will arise among the members of the higher races, leading part of their members to join with the lower races in battle against the remaining members of the higher ones, itself shows the danger of the militaristic state of affairs for all parties. If one entirely drops the assumption of the constancy of race characters and considers it conceivable that the race that had been stronger before will be surpassed by one that had been weaker, then it is evident that each party must consider that it could be faced with new battles in which it too could be defeated. Under these assumptions, the militaristic theory cannot be maintained. There no longer is any sure war gain, and the militaristic state of affairs appears as a situation of constant battles, at least, which shatter welfare so badly that finally even the victor obtains less than he would have harvested in the pacifistic situation.

In any case, not too much economic insight is needed to recognize that a war means at least direct destruction of goods, and misery. It was clear to everyone that the very outbreak of the war had to bring harmful interruptions in business life on the whole, and in Germany and Austria at the beginning of August 1914 people faced the future with fear. Astonishingly, however, things seemed to work otherwise. Instead of the expected crisis came a period of good business; instead of decline, boom. People found that war was prosperity; businessmen who, before the war, were thoroughly peace-minded and were always reproached by the friends of war for the anxiety that they were always showing at every flare-up of war rumors now began to reconcile themselves to the war. All at once there were no longer any unsalable products; enterprises that for years had run only at a loss yielded rich profits. Unemployment, which had assumed a menacing extent in the first days and weeks of the war, disappeared completely, and wages rose. The entire economy presented the picture of a gratifying boom. Soon writers appeared who sought to explain the causes of this boom.[10]

Every unprejudiced person can naturally have no doubt that war can really cause no economic boom, at least not directly, since an increase in wealth never does result from destruction of goods. It would scarcely have been too difficult to understand that war does bring good sales opportunities for all producers of weapons, munitions, and army equipment of every kind but that what these sellers gain is offset on the other hand by losses of other branches of production and that the real war losses of the economy are not affected thereby. War prosperity is like the prosperity that an earthquake or a plague brings. The earthquake means good business for construction workers, and cholera improves

---

10. The majority of authors, in conformity with the intellectual tendency of statism, did not occupy themselves with the explanation of the causes of the good course of business but rather discussed the question whether the war "should be allowed to bring prosperity." Among those who sought to give an explanation of the economic boom in war should be mentioned above all Neurath ("Die Kriegswirtschaft," reprint from the *Jahresbericht der Neuen Wiener Handelsakademie*, V [16], 1910, pp. 10 ff.), since he—following in the steps of Carey, List, and Henry George—had already before the war, in this as in other questions of "war economy," adopted the standpoint that gained broad diffusion in Germany during the war. The most naive representative of this view that war creates wealth is Steinmann-Bucher, *Deutschlands Volksvermögen im Krieg*, second edition (Stuttgart: 1916), pp. 40, 85 ff.

the business of physicians, pharmacists, and undertakers; but no one has for those reasons yet sought to celebrate earthquakes and cholera as stimulators of the productive forces in the general interest.

Starting with the observation that war furthers the business of the armament industry, many writers have sought to trace war to the machinations of those interested in war industry. This view appears to find superficial support in the behavior of the armament industry and of heavy industry in general. The most energetic advocates of the imperialistic policy were admittedly found in Germany not in the circles of industry but in those of the intellectual occupations, above all of officials and teachers. The financial means for war propaganda were provided before and during the war, however, by the armament industry. The armament industry created militarism and imperialism, however, just as little as, say, the distilleries created alcoholism or publishing houses trashy literature. The supply of weapons did not call forth the demand, but rather the other way around. The leaders of the armament industry are not themselves bloodthirsty; they would just as gladly earn money by producing other commodities. They produce cannons and guns because demand for them exists; they would just as gladly produce peacetime articles if they could do a better business with them.[11]

Recognition of this connection of things would have been bound to become widespread soon, and people would have quickly recognized that the war boom was to the advantage of only a small part of the population but that the economy as a whole was becoming poorer day by day, if inflation had not drawn a veil around all these facts, a veil impenetrable to a way of thinking that statism had made unaccustomed to every economic consideration.

To grasp the significance of inflation, it helps to imagine it and all of its consequences taken out of the picture of the war economy. Let us imagine that the state had forsworn that aid for its finances that it resorted

11. It is a mania of the statists to suspect the machinations of "special interests" in all that does not please them. Thus, Italy's entry into the war was traced to the work of propaganda paid for by England and France. Annunzio is said to have been bribed, and so on. Will one perhaps assert that Leopardi and Giusti, Silvio Pellico and Garibaldi, Mazzini and Cavour had also sold themselves? Yet their spirit influenced the position of Italy in this war more than the activity of any contemporary. The failures of German foreign policy are in large part to be traced to this way of thinking, which makes it impossible to grasp the realities of the world.

to by issuing paper money of every kind. It is clear that the issue of notes — if we disregard the relatively insignificant quantities of goods obtained from neutral foreign countries as a counterpart of gold withdrawn from circulation and exported — in no way increased the material and human means of waging war. By the issue of paper money not *one* cannon, not *one* grenade more was produced than could have been produced even without putting the printing press into operation. After all, war is waged not with "money" but with the goods that are acquired for money. For the production of war goods, it was a matter of indifference whether the quantity of money with which they were bought was greater or smaller.

The war considerably increased the demand for money. Many economic units were impelled to enlarge their cash balances, since the greater use of cash payments in place of the granting of long-term credit (which had been usual earlier), the worsening of trading arrangements, and growing insecurity had changed the entire structure of the payments system. The many military offices that were newly established during the war or whose range of activity was broadened, together with the extension of the monetary circulation of the Central Powers into the occupied territories, contributed to enlarging of the economy's demand for money. This rise in the demand for money created a tendency toward a rise in its value, that is to say, toward an increase in the purchasing power of the money unit, which worked against the opposite tendency unleashed by the increased issue of banknotes.

If the volume of note issue had not gone beyond what business could have absorbed in view of the war-induced increase in the demand for money, merely checking any increase in the value of money, then not many words would have to be spent on it. In fact, though, the banknote expansion was far greater. The longer war continued, the more actively was the printing press put into the service of the financial administration. The consequences occurred that the quantity theory describes. The prices of all goods and services, and with them the prices of foreign bills of exchange, went up.

The sinking of the value of money favored all debtors and harmed all creditors. That, however, does not exhaust the social symptoms of change in the value of money. The price rise caused by an increase in the quantity of money does not appear at one stroke in the entire economy and for all goods, for the additional quantity of money distributes itself only gradually. At first it flows to particular establishments and particular branches of production and therefore first increases only the demands for particular goods, not for all; only later do other goods also rise in price. "During the issue of notes," say Auspitz and Lieben, "the additional means of circulation will be concentrated in the hands of a small fraction of the population, e.g., of the suppliers and producers of war materials. Consequently, these persons' demands for various articles will increase; and thus the prices and also the sales of the latter will rise, notably, however, also those of luxury articles. The situation of the producers of all these articles thereby improves; their demands for other goods will also increase; the rise of prices and sales will therefore progress even further and spread to an ever larger number of articles, and finally to all." [12]

If the decline in the value of money were to pervade the entire economy at one stroke and be registered against all goods to the same extent, then it would cause no redistribution of income and wealth. For in this respect there can only be a question of redistribution. The national economy as such gains nothing from it, and what the individual gains others must lose. Those who bring to market the goods and services whose prices are caught up first in the upward price movement are in the favorable position of already being able to sell at higher prices while still able to buy the goods and services that they want to acquire at the older, lower prices. On the other hand, again, those who sell goods and services that rise in price only later must already buy at higher prices while they themselves, in selling, are able to obtain only the older, lower prices. As long as the process of change in the value of money is still under way, such gains of some and losses of others will keep occurring. When the process has finally come to an end, then these gains and losses do also cease, but the gains and losses of the interim are not made up for again. The war suppliers in the broadest sense of the word (also including workers in war industries and military personnel who received increased war incomes) have therefore gained not only from enjoying good business in the ordinary sense of the word but also from the fact that the additional quantity of money flowed first to them. The price rise of the goods and services that they brought to market was a double one: it was caused first by the increased demand for their labor, but then, too, by the increased supply of money.

12. Cf. Auspitz and Lieben, *Untersuchungen über die Theorie des Preises* (Leipzig: 1889), pp. 64 f.

That is the essence of so-called war prosperity; it enriches some by what it takes from others. It is not rising wealth but a shifting of wealth and income.[13]

The wealth of Germany and of German-Austria was above all an abundance of capital. One may estimate the riches of the soil and the natural resources of our country ever so high; yet one must still admit that there are other countries that are more richly endowed by nature, whose soil is more fruitful, whose mines are more productive, whose water power is stronger, and whose territories are more easily accessible because of location relative to the sea, mountain ranges, and river courses. The advantages of the German national economy rest not on the natural factor but on the human factor of production and on a historically given head start. These advantages showed themselves in the relatively great accumulation of capital, mainly in the improvement of lands used for agriculture and forestry and in the abundant stock of produced means of production of all kinds, of streets, railroads, and other means of transportation, of buildings and their equipment, of machines and tools, and, finally, of already produced raw materials and semifinished goods. This capital had been accumulated by the German people through long work; it was the tool that German industrial workers used for their work and from whose application they lived. From year to year this stock was increased by thrift.

The natural forces dormant in the soil are not destroyed by appropriate use in the process of production; in this sense they form an eternal factor of production. The amounts of raw materials amassed in the ground represent only a limited stock that man consumes bit by bit without being able to replace it in any way. Capital goods also have no eternal existence; as produced means of production, as semifinished goods, which they represent in a broader sense of the term, they are transformed little by little in the production process into consumption goods. With some, with so-called circulating capital, this takes place more quickly; with others, with so-called fixed capital, more slowly. But the latter also is consumed in production. Machines and tools also have

13. Cf. Mises, *Theorie des Geldes und der Umlaufsmittel* (Munich: 1912), pp. 222 ff.; second edition translated by H. E. Batson as *The Theory of Money and Credit* (Indianapolis: Liberty Fund, 1981), pp. 251 ff. A clear description of conditions in Austria during the Napoleonic Wars is found in Grünberg, *Studien zur österreichischen Agrargeschichte* (Leipzig: 1901), pp. 121 ff.; also Broda, "Zur Frage der Konjunktur im und nach dem Kriege," *Archiv für Sozialwissenschaft*, vol. 45, pp. 40 ff.; also Rosenberg, *Valutafragen* (Vienna: 1917), pp. 14 ff.

no eternal existence; sooner or later they become worn out and unusable. Not only the increase but even the mere maintenance of the capital stock therefore presupposes a continual renewal of capital goods. Raw materials and semifinished goods which, changed into goods ready for use, are conveyed to consumption must be replaced by others; and machines and tools of all kinds worn out in the production process must be replaced by others to the extent that they wear out. Performing this task presupposes making a clear assessment of the extent of the wearing out and using up of productive goods. With means of production that always are to be replaced only with others of the same kind, this is not difficult. The road system of a country can be maintained by trying to hold the condition of the individual sections technically the same by ceaseless maintenance work, and it can be extended by repeatedly adding new roads or enlarging the existing ones. In a static society in which no changes in the economy take place, this method would be applicable to all means of production. In an economy subject to change, this simple method does not suffice for most means of production, for the used-up and worn-out means of production are replaced not by ones of the same kind but by others. Worn-out tools are replaced not by ones of the same kind but by better ones, if indeed the whole orientation of production is not changed and the replacement of capital goods consumed in a shrinking branch of production does not take place by installation of new capital goods in other branches of production that are being expanded or newly established. Calculation in physical units, which suffices for the primitive conditions of a stationary economy, must therefore be replaced by calculation of value in money.

Individual capital goods disappear in the production process. Capital as such, however, is maintained and expanded. That is not a natural necessity independent of the will of economizing persons, however, but rather the result of deliberate activity that arranges production and consumption so as at least to maintain the sum of value of capital and that allots to consumption only surpluses earned in addition. The precondition for that is the calculation of value, whose auxiliary means is accounting. The economic task of accounting is to test the success of production. It has to determine whether capital was increased, maintained, or diminished. The economic plan and the distribution of goods between production and consumption is then based on the results that it achieves.

Accounting is not perfect. The exactness of its numbers, which strongly impresses the uninitiated, is only apparent. The evaluation of goods and claims that it must work with is always based on estimates resting on the interpretation of more or less uncertain elements. Insofar as this uncertainty stems from the side of goods, commercial practice, approved by the norms of commercial legislation, tries to avoid it by proceeding as cautiously as possible; that is, it requires a low evaluation of assets and a high evaluation of liabilities. But the deficiencies of accounting also stem from the fact that evaluations are uncertain from the side of money, since the value of money is also subject to change. So far as commodity money, so-called full-value metallic money, is concerned, real life pays no regard to these deficiencies. Commercial practice, as well as the law, has fully adopted the naive business view that money is stable in value, that is, that the existing exchange relation between money and goods is subject to no change from the side of money.[14] Accounting assumes money to be stable in value. Only the fluctuations of credit and token-money currencies, so-called paper currencies, against commodity money were taken account of by commercial practice by setting up corresponding reserves and by write-offs. Unfortunately, German statist economics has paved the way for a change of perception on this point also. In nominalistic money theory, by extending the idea of the stability of value of metal money to all money as such, it created the preconditions for the calamitous effects of decline in the value of money that we now have to describe.

Entrepreneurs did not pay attention to the fact that the decline in the value of money now made all items in balance sheets become inaccurate. In drawing up balance sheets, they neglected to take account of the change in the value of money that had occurred since the last balance sheet. Thus it could happen that they regularly added a part of the original capital to the net revenue of the year, regarded it as profit, paid it out, and consumed it. The error which (in the balance sheet of a corporation) was made by not taking account of the depreciation of money on the liability side was only partly made up for by the fact that on the asset side also the components of wealth were not reported at a higher value. For this disregard of the rise in nominal value did not

14. On this, cf. Mises, *Theorie des Geldes und der Umlaufsmittel*, pp. 237 ff. (English translation, pp. 268 ff.).

apply to circulating capital also, since for inventories that were sold, the higher valuation did appear; it was precisely this that constituted the inflationary extra profit of enterprises. The disregard of the depreciation of money on the asset side remained limited to fixed investment capital and had as a consequence that in calculating depreciation, people used the smaller original amounts that corresponded to the old value of money. That enterprises often set up special reserves to prepare for reconversion to the peacetime economy could not, as a rule, make up for this.

The German economy entered the war with an abundant stock of raw materials and semifinished goods of all kinds. In peacetime, whatever of these stocks was devoted to use or consumption was regularly replaced. During the war the stocks were consumed without being able to be replaced. They disappeared out of the economy; the national wealth was reduced by their value. This could be obscured by the fact that in the wealth of the trader or producer, money claims appeared in their place — as a rule, war-loan claims. The businessman thought that he was as rich as before; generally he had sold the goods at better prices than he had hoped for in peacetime and now believed that he had become richer. At first he did not notice that his claims were being ever more devalued through the sinking of the value of money. The foreign securities that he possessed rose in price as expressed in marks or crowns. This too he counted as a gain.[15] If he wholly or partially consumed these apparent profits, then he diminished his capital without noticing it.[16]

The inflation thus drew a veil over capital consumption. The individual believed that he had become richer or had at least not lost, while in truth his wealth was dwindling. The state taxed these losses of individual economic units as "war profits" and spent the amounts collected for unproductive purposes. The public did not become tired, however, of concerning itself about the large war profits, which, in good part, were no profits at all.

15. The nominalists and chartalists among monetary theorists naturally agreed with this layman's view: that upon the sale of foreign securities, the increased nominal value received because of the decline of the currency represented a profit; cf. Bendixen, *Währungspolitik und Geldtheorie im Lichte des Weltkrieges* (Munich: 1916), p. 37. That is probably the lowest level to which monetary theory could sink.

16. It naturally would not have been possible to take account of these changes in accounting serving official purposes; this accounting had to be carried out in the legal currency. It would indeed have been possible, though, to base economic calculation on the recalculation of balance sheets and of profit-and-loss calculation in gold money.

All fell into ecstasy. Whoever took in more money than earlier — and that was true of most entrepreneurs and wage earners and, finally, with the further progress of the depreciation of money, of all persons except capitalists receiving fixed incomes — was happy about his apparent profits. While the entire economy was consuming its capital and while even stocks of goods ready for consumption held in individual households were dwindling, all were happy about prosperity. And to cap it all, economists began to undertake profound investigations into its causes.

Rational economy first became possible when mankind became accustomed to the use of money, for economic calculation cannot dispense with reducing all values to one common denominator. In all great wars monetary calculation was disrupted by inflation. Earlier it was the debasement of coin; today it is paper-money inflation. The economic behavior of the belligerents was thereby led astray; the true consequences of the war were removed from their view. One can say without exaggeration that inflation is an indispensable intellectual means of militarism. Without it, the repercussions of war on welfare would become obvious much more quickly and penetratingly; war-weariness would set in much earlier.

Today is too soon to survey the entire extent of the material damage that the war has brought to the German people. Such an attempt is bound in advance to start from the conditions of the economy before the war. Even for that reason alone it must remain incomplete. For the dynamic effects of the World War on the economic life of the world cannot thus be considered at all, since we lack all possibility of surveying the entire magnitude of the loss that the disorganization of the liberal economic order, the so-called capitalistic system of national economy, entails. Nowhere do opinions diverge so much as on this point. While some express the view that the destruction of the capitalistic apparatus of production opens the way for an undreamed-of development of civilization, others fear from it a relapse into barbarism.

But even if we disregard all that, we should, in judging the economic consequences of the World War for the German people, in no way limit ourselves to taking account only of war damages and war losses that have already actually appeared. These losses of wealth, which in and for themselves are immense, are outweighed by disadvantages of a dynamic nature. The German people will remain economically confined to their inadequate territory of settlement in Europe. Millions of Germans who previously earned their bread abroad are being compulsorily repatriated. Moreover, the German people have lost their considerable capital investment abroad. Beyond that, the basis of the German economy, the processing of foreign raw materials for foreign consumption, has been shattered. The German people are thereby being made into a poor people for a long time.

The position of the German-Austrians is turning out still more unfavorable in general than the position of the German people. The war costs of the Habsburg Empire have been borne almost completely by the German-Austrians. The Austrian half of the Empire has contributed in a far greater degree than the Hungarian half of the Empire to the outlays of the Monarchy. The contributions that were incumbent on the Austrian half of the Empire were made, furthermore, almost exclusively by the Germans. The Austrian tax system laid the direct taxes almost exclusively on the industrial and commercial entrepreneurs and left agriculture almost free. This mode of taxation in reality meant nothing other than the overburdening of the Germans with taxes and the exemption of the non-Germans. Still more to be considered is that the war loans were subscribed to almost entirely by the German population of Austria and that now, after the dissolution of the state, the non-Germans are refusing any contribution toward interest payments and amortization of the war loans. Moreover, the large German holding of money claims on the non-Germans has been greatly reduced by the depreciation of money. The very considerable ownership by German-Austrians of industrial and trade enterprises and also of agricultural properties in non-German territories, however, is being expropriated partly by nationalization and socialization measures, partly by the provisions of the peace treaty.

5 Covering the State's War Costs

There were three ways available to cover the costs that the State Treasury incurred in the war.

The first way was confiscating the material goods needed for waging war and drafting the personal services needed for waging war without compensation or for inadequate compensation. This method seemed the simplest, and the most consistent representatives of militarism and socialism resolutely advocated employing it. It was used extensively in drafting persons into actually waging war. The universal military-service obligation was newly introduced in many states during the war and in others was substantially extended. That the soldier received only a trifling compensation for his services in relation to the wages of free labor, while the worker in the munitions industry was highly paid and while the possessors of expropriated or confiscated material means of war received an at least partially corresponding compensation, has rightly been called a striking fact. The explanation for this anomaly may be found in the fact that only a few people enlist today even for the highest wages and that in any case prospects of putting together any army of millions on the basis of enlistments would not be very good. In relation to the immense sacrifices that the state demands of the individual through the blood tax, it seems rather incidental whether it compensates the soldier more or less abundantly for the loss of time that he suffers from his military-service obligation. In the industrial society there is no appropriate compensation for war services. In such a society they have no price at all; they can be demanded only compulsorily, and then it is surely of slight significance whether they are paid for more generously or at the laughably low rates at which a man was compensated in Germany. In Austria the soldier at the front received a wage of 16 heller and a field supplement of 20 heller, 36 heller a day in all![17] That reserve officers, even in the continental states, and that the English and American troops received a higher compensation is explained by the fact that a peacetime wage rate had been established for officer service in the continental states and for all military service in England and America which had to be taken as a point of departure in the war. But however high or however low the compensation of the warrior may be, it is never to be regarded as a full compensation for the compulsorily recruited man. The sacrifice that is demanded of the soldier serving by compulsion can be compensated only with intangible values, never with material ones.[18]

In other respects the uncompensated expropriation of war material was scarcely considered. By its very nature alone it could occur only

17. And, moreover, the troops that had to fight through the fearful battles in the Carpathians and in the swamps of the Sarmatian plain, in the high mountains of the Alps, and in the Karst were poorly supported and inadequately clothed and armed! [In 1914, the Austrian monetary unit mentioned here, the heller, was a small coin then worth about 1/20th of one U.S. cent (A Satchel Guide to Europe, Boston: Houghton Mifflin, 1914, 191).]

18. From the political point of view it was a grave mistake to follow completely different principles in the compensation of the officer and the enlisted man and to pay the soldier at the front worse than the worker behind the lines. That contributed much to demoralizing the army!

with regard to goods on hand in individual economic units in sufficient quantity at the beginning of the war, but not also where producing new goods was concerned.

The second way available to the state for acquiring resources was introducing new taxes and raising already existing taxes. This method too was used everywhere as much as possible during the war. The demand was made from many sides that the state should try, even during the war, to cover the total war costs by taxes; in that connection reference was made to England, which was said to have followed this policy in earlier wars. It is true that England covered the costs of smaller wars that were only insignificant in relation to its national wealth in greatest part by taxes during the war itself. In the great wars that England waged, however, this was not true, neither in the Napoleonic Wars nor in the World War. If one had wanted immediately to raise such immense sums as this war required entirely by taxation without incurring debt, then, in assessing and collecting taxes, one would have had to put aside regard for justice and uniformity in the distribution of tax burdens and take from where it was possible to take at the moment. One would have had to take everything from the owners of movable capital (not only from large owners but also from small ones, e.g., savings-bank depositors) and on the other hand leave the owners of real property more or less free.

If, however, the high war taxes were assessed uniformly (for they would have had to be very high if they were fully to cover each year the war costs incurred in the same year), then those who had no cash for paying taxes would have had to acquire the means for paying by going into debt. Landowners and owners of industrial enterprises would then have been compelled to incur debt or even to sell part of their possessions. In the first case, therefore, not the state itself but rather many private parties would have had to incur debts and thereby obligate themselves to interest payments to the owners of capital. However, private credit is in general dearer than public credit. Those land and house owners would therefore have had to pay more interest on their private debts than they had to pay indirectly in interest on the state debt. If, however, they had found themselves forced to sell a smaller or larger part of their property in order to pay taxes, then this sudden offer of a large part of real property for sale would have severely depressed prices, so that the earlier owners would have suffered a loss; and the capitalists who at this moment had had cash at their disposal would have gained a profit by buying cheaply. That the state did not fully cover the costs of the war by taxes but rather in largest part by incurring state debt, whose interest was paid from the proceeds of taxes, therefore does not signify, as is often assumed, a favoring of the capitalists.[19]

One now and then hears the interpretation expressed that financing war by state loans signifies shifting the war costs from the present onto following generations. Many add that this shifting is also just, since, after all, the war was being waged not only in the interest of the present generation but also in the interest of our children and grandchildren. This interpretation is completely wrong. War can be waged only with present goods. One can fight only with weapons that are already on hand; one can take everything needed for war only from wealth already on hand. From the economic point of view, the present generation wages war, and it must also bear all material costs of war. Future generations are also affected only insofar as they are our heirs and we leave less to them than we would have been able to leave without the war's intervening. Whether the state now finances the war by debts or otherwise can change nothing about this fact. That the greatest part of the war costs was financed by state loans in no way signifies a shifting of war burdens onto the future but only a particular principle of distributing the war costs. If, for example, the state had to take half of his wealth from each citizen to be able to pay for the war financially, then it is fundamentally a matter of indifference whether it does so in such a way that it imposes a *one-time* tax on him of half of his wealth or takes from him every year as a tax the amount that corresponds to interest payments on half of his wealth. It is fundamentally a matter of indifference to the citizen whether he has to pay 50,000 crowns as tax one time or pay the interest on 50,000 crowns year in, year out. This becomes of greater significance, however, for all those citizens who would not be able to pay the 50,000 crowns without incurring debt, those who would first have to borrow the share of tax falling on them. For they would have to pay more interest on these loans that they take out as private parties than the state, which enjoys the cheapest credit, pays to its creditors. If we set this difference between the dearer private credit and the cheaper state credit at only one percentage point, this means, in our example, a yearly saving of 500 crowns for the taxpayer. If year after year he has to pay his contribution to interest on his share of the state debt,

19. Cf. Dietzel, *Kriegssteuer oder Kriegsanleihe?* (Tübingen: 1912), pp. 13 ff.

he saves 500 crowns in comparison with the amount that he would have had to pay every year as interest on a private loan that would have enabled him to pay the temporary high war taxes.

The more socialist thinking gained strength in the course of the war, the more were people bent on covering the war costs by special taxes on property.

The idea of subjecting additional income and the growth of property obtained during the war to special progressive taxation need not, fundamentally, be socialistic. In and of itself the principle of taxation according to ability to pay is not socialistic. It cannot be denied that those who achieved a higher income in the war than in peacetime or had increased their property were *ceteris paribus* more able to pay than those who did not succeed in increasing their income or their property. Moreover, one can quite rule out the question of how far these nominal increases in wealth and income were to be regarded as real increases in income and wealth and whether it was not a question here merely of nominal increases in amounts expressed in money in consequence of the decline in the value of money. Someone who had an income of 10,000 crowns before the war and increased it during the war to 20,000 crowns doubtless found himself in a more favorable position than someone who had remained with his prewar income of 10,000 crowns. In this disregard of the value of money, which only goes without saying in view of the general tenor of German and Austrian legislation, there did lie, to be sure, a deliberate disadvantaging of movable capital and a deliberate preference for landowners, especially farmers.

The socialistic tendencies of war-profit taxation came to light above all in their motives. War-profit taxes are supported by the view that all entrepreneurial profit represents robbery from the community as a whole and that by rights it should be entirely taken away. This tendency comes to light in the scale of the rates, which more and more approach complete confiscation of the entire increase in property or income and doubtless finally will reach even this goal set for them. For one should indeed suffer no illusion about the fact that the unfavorable opinion of entrepreneurial income manifested in these war taxes is not attributable to wartime conditions alone and that the line of argument used for the war taxes — that in this time of national distress every increase in wealth and every increase in income is indeed unethical — can also be maintained in the period after the war with the same justification, even if with differences in detail.

Socialistic tendencies are also quite clear in the idea of a one-time capital levy. The popularity that the slogan about a one-time capital levy enjoys, a popularity so great that it makes any serious discussion of its appropriateness quite impossible, can be explained only by the entire population's aversion to private property. Socialists and liberals will answer quite differently the question whether a one-time property tax is preferable to an adjustable one. One can refer to the fact that the adjustable, yearly recurring property tax offers the advantage in comparison with the one-time property tax that it does not remove capital goods from the disposal of the individual (quite apart from the fact that it is fairer and more uniform, since it permits errors made in one year's assessment to be corrected the next year and that it is independent of the accident of possession and evaluation of property at a particular moment because it deals with property year in and year out according to the current amount of wealth that it constitutes). When someone operates an enterprise with a capital of his own of 100,000 marks, then it is not at all a matter of indifference to him whether he has to pay an amount of 50,000 marks at one time as a property tax or pay each year only the amount corresponding to the interest that the state has to pay on a debt of 50,000 marks. For it is to be expected that with this capital beyond the amount that the state would have to demand from him for paying interest on the 50,000 marks, he could earn a profit that he could then keep. This is not what is decisive for the liberal's position, however, but rather the social consideration that by the one-time capital levy the state would transfer capital out of the hands of entrepreneurs into the hands of capitalists and lenders. If the entrepreneur is to carry on his business after the capital levy on the same scale as before it, then he must acquire the missing amount by obtaining credit, and as a private party he will have to pay more interest than the state would have had to pay. The consequence of the capital levy will therefore be a greater indebtedness of the enterprising strata of the population to the nonenterprising capitalists, who, as a result of the reduction of the war debt, will have exchanged part of their claims on the state for claims on private parties.

The socialists, of course, go still further. They want to use the capital levy not only for lightening the burden of war debts — many of them want to get rid of war debts in a simple manner by state bankruptcy — but they demand the capital levy in order to give the state shares of ownership in economic enterprises of all kinds, in industrial corporations, in mining, and in agricultural estates. They campaign for it with the slogan about the state's and society's sharing in the profit of private enterprises,[20] as if the state were not sharing in the profits of all enterprises through tax legislation anyway, so that it does not first need a civil-law title to draw profit from the enterprises. Today the state shares in the profits of enterprises without being obliged to cooperate at all in the management of the production process and without being exposed to harm in any way by possible losses of the enterprise. If, however, the state owns shares in all enterprises, it will also share in losses; moreover, it will even be forced to concern itself with the administration of individual businesses. Just that, however, is what the socialists want.

6   War Socialism and True Socialism

The question whether so-called war socialism is true socialism has been discussed repeatedly and with great passion. Some have answered yes just as firmly as others have answered no. In that connection the striking phenomenon could be observed that as the war continued and as it became even more obvious that it would end with failure of the German cause, the tendency to characterize war socialism as true socialism diminished also.

To be able to handle the problem correctly, one must first of all keep in mind that socialism means the transfer of the means of production out of the private ownership of individuals into the ownership of society. That alone and nothing else is socialism. All the rest is unimportant. It is a matter of complete indifference for deciding our question, for example, who holds power in a socialized community, whether a hereditary emperor, a Caesar, or the democratically organized whole of the people. It does not belong to the essence of a socialized community that it is under the leadership of soviets of workers and soldiers. Other authorities also can implement socialism, perhaps the church or the military state. It is to be noted, furthermore, that an election of the general directorship of the socialist economy in Germany, carried out on the basis of full universality and equality of the right to vote, would have produced a far stronger majority for Hindenburg and Ludendorff

20. Cf. above all Goldscheid, *Staatssozialismus oder Staatskapitalismus*, fifth edition (Vienna: 1917); idem., *Sozialisierung der Wirtschaft oder Staatsbankerott* (Vienna: 1919).

in the first years of the war than Lenin and Trotsky could ever have achieved in Russia.

Also nonessential is how the outputs of the socialized economy are used. It is of no consequence for our problem whether this output primarily serves cultural purposes or the waging of war. In the minds of the German people or at least of its preponderant majority, victory in the war was seen beyond doubt as the most urgent goal of the moment. Whether one approves of that or not is of no consequence.[21]

It is equally of no consequence that war socialism was carried out without formal reorganization of ownership relations. What counts is not the letter of the law but the substantive content of the legal norm.

If we keep all this in mind, then it is not hard to recognize that the measures of war socialism amounted to putting the economy on a socialistic basis. The right of ownership remained formally unimpaired. By the letter of the law the owner still continued to be the owner of the means of production. Yet the power of disposal over the enterprise was taken away from him. It was no longer up to him to determine what should be produced, to acquire raw materials, to recruit workers, and finally to sell the product. The goal of production was prescribed to him, the raw materials were delivered to him at definite prices, the workers were assigned to him and had to be paid by him at rates on whose determination he had no direct influence. The product, furthermore, was taken from him at a definite price, if he was not actually carrying out all the production as a mere manager. This organization was not uniformly and simultaneously implemented in all branches of industry — in many not at all. Also, its net had big enough meshes to let much get through. Such an extreme reform, which completely turns the conditions of production around, just cannot be carried out at one blow. But the goal being aimed at and being approached ever more closely with every new decree was this and

21. Max Adler (*Zwei Jahre . . . ! Weltkriegsbetrachtungen eines Sozialisten* [Nürnberg: 1916], p. 64) disputes the idea that war socialism is true socialism: "Socialism strives for the organization of the national economy for the sufficient and uniform satisfaction of the needs of all; it is the organization of sufficiency, even of superfluity; 'war socialism,' on the other hand, is the *organization of scarcity* and of need." Here the means is confused with the end. In the view of socialist theoreticians, socialism should be the means for achieving the highest productivity of the economy attainable under the given conditions. Whether superfluity or shortage reigns then is not essential. The criterion of socialism is, after all, not that it strives for the general welfare but rather that it strives for welfare by way of production based on the socialization of the means of production. Socialism distinguishes itself from liberalism only in the method that it chooses; the goal that they strive for is common to both. Cf. below, pp. 150 ff.

nothing else. War socialism was by no means complete socialism, but it was full and true socialization without exception if one had kept on the path that had been taken.

Nothing about that is changed by the fact that the proceeds of production went first to the entrepreneur. The measures characterized as war-socialist in the narrow sense did not abolish entrepreneurial profit and interest on capital in principle, although the fixing of prices by the authorities took many steps in this direction. But precisely all the economic-policy decrees of the war period do belong to the full picture of war socialism; it would be mistaken to keep only particular measures in view and disregard others. Whatever the economic dictatorship of the various agencies of the war economy left free was gotten at by tax policy. War tax policy established the principle that all additional profit achieved beyond the profits of the prewar period was to be taxed away. From the beginning this was the goal that the policy aimed at and that it came closer to with each later decree. No doubt it would have completely reached this goal also if only it had had a little more time. It was carried out without regard to the change in the value of money that had occurred in the meanwhile, so that this meant a limitation of entrepreneural profit not just to the amount obtained before the war but to a fraction of this amount. While entrepreneurial profit was thus limited on the top side, on the other side the entrepreneur was guaranteed no definite profit. As before, he still had to bear losses alone, while keeping no more chance of gain.

Many socialists declared that they were not thinking of an uncompensated expropriation of entrepreneurs, capitalists, and landowners. Many of them had the notion that a socialist community could allow the possessing classes to continue receiving their most recently received incomes, since socialization would bring such a great rise in productivity that it would be easy to pay this compensation. Under that kind of transition to socialism, entrepreneurs would have been compensated with larger amounts than under the one introduced by war socialism. They would have continued to receive as guaranteed income the profits that they had last received. It is incidental whether these incomes of the possessing classes would have had to continue only for a definite time or forever. War socialism also did not settle the question finally for all time. The development of wealth, income, and inheritance taxes would have been able, especially through extension of the progressivity of the tax rates, to achieve a complete confiscation soon.

The continued receipt of interest remained temporarily permitted to the owners of loan capital. Since they were suffering persistent losses of property and income from inflation, they offered no propitious object for greater intervention by the tax office. With regard to them, inflation was already performing the task of confiscation.

Public opinion in Germany and Austria, entirely dominated by the socialistic spirit, complained again and again that the taxation of war profits had been delayed too long and that even later it had not been applied with appropriate severity. One supposedly should have acted at once to collect all war profits, that is to say, all increases in wealth and income obtained during the war. Even on the first day of the war, therefore, complete socialization should have been introduced — leaving alone property incomes received before the war. It has already been explained why this was not done and what consequences for the conversion of industry onto a war footing would have resulted if this advice had been followed.

The more fully war socialism was developed, the more palpable did individual consequences of a socialistic order of society already become. In technical respects enterprises did operate no more irrationally than before, since the entrepreneurs, who remained at the head of the enterprises and formally filled their old positions, still harbored the hope of being able to keep for themselves — even if only by illegal means — a larger or smaller part of the surpluses earned and at least hoped for future removal of all measures of war socialism, which, after all, were still always officially declared exceptional wartime orders. Yet a tendency toward increasing expenses became noticeable, especially in trade, because of the price policy of the authorities and the practice of the courts in handling the provisions of penal law regarding exceeding the maximum prices: permitted prices were ascertained on the basis of the entrepreneur's outlays plus a margin of "simple profit," so that the entrepreneur's profit became all the greater the more dearly he had made purchases and the more expenses he had incurred.

Of greatest significance was impairment of the initiative of entrepreneurs. Since they shared more heavily in losses than in profits, the incentive to undertake risky ventures was only slight. Many production possibilities remained unused in the second half of the war because entrepreneurs shied away from the risk bound up with new investments and with introducing new production methods. Thus the policy of the state's taking over responsibility for possible losses, adopted especially in Austria right at the beginning of the war, was better suited for stimulating production. Toward the end of the war, views on this point had changed. With regard to importing particular raw materials into Austria from abroad, the question arose of who should bear the "peace risk," the danger of a loss from the price crash that was expected in the event of peace. The entrepreneurs associated with the Central Powers, whose chances of profit were limited, wanted to undertake the business only if the state were ready to bear the possible loss. Since this could not be arranged, the importation did not take place.

War socialism was only the continuation at an accelerated tempo of the state-socialist policy that had already been introduced long before the war. From the beginning the intention prevailed in all socialist groups of dropping none of the measures adopted during the war after the war but rather of advancing on the way toward the completion of socialism. If one heard differently in public, and if government offices, above all, always spoke only of exceptional provisions for the duration of the war, this had only the purpose of dissipating possible doubts about the rapid tempo of socialization and about individual measures and of stifling opposition to them. The slogan had already been found, however, under which further socializing measures should sail; it was called *transitional economy.*

The militarism of General Staff officers fell apart; other powers took the transitional economy in hand.

Socialism and Imperialism

1   Socialism and Its Opponents

The authoritarian-militaristic spirit of the Prussian authoritarian state finds its counterpart and completion in the ideas of German Social Democracy and of German socialism in general. To hasty observation the authoritarian state and Social Democracy appear as irreconcilable opposites between which there is no mediation. It is true that they confronted each other for more than fifty years in blunt hostility. Their relation was not that of political opposition, as occurs between different parties in other nations also; it was complete estrangement and mortal enmity. Between Junkers and bureaucrats on the one hand and Social Democrats on the other hand, even every personal, purely human contact was ruled out; scarcely ever did one side or the other make an attempt to understand its opponent or have a discussion with him.

The irreconcilable hatred of the monarchy and of the Junker class did not concern, however, the social-economic program of the Social Democratic Party. The program of the German Social Democratic Party contains two elements of different origins tied together only loosely. It includes on the one hand all those political demands that liberalism, especially its left wing, represents and also has partly implemented already in most civilized states. This part of the Social Democratic Party program is built on the great political idea of a republic, which wants to dissolve the princely and authoritarian state and turn the subject into a citizen of the state. That the Social Democratic Party has pursued this goal, that it took the banner of democracy from the enfeebled hands of dying German liberalism and alone held it high in the darkest decades of German politics despite all persecutions — that is its great pride and fame, to which it owes the sympathy that the world accords it and that first brought it many of its best men and the masses of the oppressed and

of "bourgeois fellow-travelers." The very fact, however, that it was republican and democratic drew onto it the inextinguishable hatred of
the Junkers and bureaucrats; that alone brought it into conflict with authorities and courts and made it into an outlawed sect of enemies of the
state, despised by all "right-thinking people."

The other component of the program of German Social Democracy
was Marxian socialism. The attraction that the slogan about the capitalistic exploitation of the workers and that the promising utopia of a future state exerted on the great majority was the basis of an imposing
party and labor union organization. Many, however, were won over to
socialism only through democracy. As the German bourgeoisie submit-
ted unconditionally to the authoritarian state of Bismarck, after the
annihilating defeats that German liberalism had suffered, and as the
German protective-tariff policy permitted the German entrepreneurial
class to identify itself with the Prussian state, militarism and industrialism became politically related concepts for Germany, and the socialist
side of the party program absorbed new strength from democratic aspirations. Many refrained from criticizing socialism in order not to harm
the cause of democracy. Many became socialists because they were
democrats and believed that democracy and socialism were inseparably
connected.

Still, close relations corresponding to the essence of both socialism[1]
and the autocratic-authoritarian form of state really exist.[2] For that reason also the authoritarian state did not fight socialist efforts at all as
harshly as it confronted all democratic impulses. On the contrary, the
Prussian-German authoritarian state evolved strongly toward the side

---

1. In regard to economic policy, socialism and communism are identical—both strive for socialization of the means of production, in contrast with liberalism, which wants on principle to let
private ownership even of the means of production continue. The distinction that has recently
come into use between socialism and communism is irrelevant with regard to economic policy
unless one also foists on the communists the plan of wanting to discontinue private ownership of
consumption goods. On centralist and syndicalist socialism (actually, only centralist socialism is
true socialism), see below, pp. 162 ff.

2. On the intimate relation between militarism and socialism, cf. Herbert Spencer, loc. cit., vol. 3,
p. 712. The imperialistic tendencies of socialism are treated by Seillière, Die Philosophie des Imperialismus, second edition of the German version (Berlin: 1911), vol. 2, pp. 171 ff., vol. 3, pp. 59 ff.
Sometimes socialism does not even outwardly deny its intimate relation with militarism. That
comes to light especially clearly in those socialistic programs that want to arrange the future state
on the model of an army. Examples: wanting to solve the social question by setting up a "food army"
or a "worker army" (cf. Popper-Lynkeus, Die allgemeine Nährpflicht [Dresden: 1912], pp. 373 ff.; further, Ballod, Der Zukunftsstaat, second edition [Stuttgart: 1919], pp. 32 ff.). The Communist

of "social kingship" and would have turned still more toward socialism if the great workers' party of Germany had been ready before August 1914 to give up its democratic program in exchange for the gradual realization of its socialistic goals. The sociopolitical doctrine of Prussian militarism can best be recognized in the literary products of the Prussian school of economic policy. Here we find complete harmony established between the ideal of the authoritarian state and that of a far-reaching socialization of large industrial enterprise. Many German social thinkers reject Marxism — not, however, because they reject its goals but because they cannot share its theoretical interpretation of social and economic developments. Marxism, whatever one may say against it, nevertheless has one thing in common with all scientific economics: it recognizes a conformity to law in the historical process and presupposes the causal interconnection of all that happens. German statism could not follow it in this respect because it sees everywhere only marks of the activity of great kings and powerful states. The heroic and teleological interpretation of history seems more obvious to statism than the causal; it knows no economic law; it denies the possibility of economic theory.[3] In that respect Marxism is superior to German social-policy doctrine, which has no theoretical basis at all and never has sought to create one. All social problems appear to this school as tasks of state administration and politics, and there is no problem on whose solution it does not venture with a light heart. Always, however, it is the same prescription that it issues: commands and prohibitions as lesser means, state ownership as the great, never-failing means.

Under such circumstances Social Democracy had an easy position. Marxian economic theory, which in Western Europe and America was able to win only a small following and was not able to assert itself alongside the accomplishments of modern economic theory, did not have to

---

Manifesto already demands the "establishment of industrial armies." It should be noted that imperialism and socialism go hand in hand in literature and politics. Reference was already made earlier (pp. 78 ff.) to Engels and Rodbertus; one could name many others, e.g., Carlyle (cf. Kemper, "Carlyle als Imperialist," *Zeitschrift für Politik*, XI, 115 ff.). Australia, which, as the only one among the Anglo-Saxon states, has turned away from liberalism and come closer to socialism than any other country, is the imperialistic state par excellence in its immigration legislation.

3. This spirit of hostility to theoretical investigation has also infected the German Social Democrats. It is characteristic that just as theoretical economics could flourish on German-speaking territory only in Austria, so also the best representatives of German Marxism, Kautsky, Otto Bauer, Hilferding, and Max Adler, come from Austria.

suffer much under the criticism of the empirical-realistic and historical school of German economics. The critical work to be done against Marxian economic theory was carried out by the Austrian school, ostracized in Germany, and above all by Böhm-Bawerk.[4] Marxism could easily dispose of the Prussian school; it was dangerous to it not as an opponent but as a friend. Social Democracy had to take care to show that social reform, such as German social policy strove for, could not replace the social revolution and that state ownership in the Prussian sense was not identical with socialization. This demonstration could not succeed, but its failure did not damage Social Democracy. For it was, after all, the party eternally condemned to fruitless opposition, which was always able to make capital for its party position precisely out of the defects of the social-reform and socialization measures.

That Social Democracy became the most powerful party in the German Reich it owes primarily to the democratic part of its program, taken over as the heir of liberalism. That, however, socialism as such also enjoys the greatest sympathy among the German people, so that only isolated voices speak out seriously and in principle against socialization and that even so-called bourgeois parties want to socialize the branches of production that are "ripe" for socialization — that is the result of the propaganda work that statism has performed. Socialist ideas constitute no victory over the Prussian authoritarian state but are its consistent development; their popularity in Germany has been furthered no less by the academic socialism of privy councilors than by the propaganda work of Social Democratic agitators.

Among the German people today, thanks to the views advocated for fifty years by the Prussian school of economic policy, there is no longer even any understanding of what the contrast between liberalism in economic policy and socialism really consists of. That the distinction between the two orientations lies not in the goal but in the means is not clear to many. Even to the antisocialist German, socialism appears as the sole just form of economic organization, assuring the people the most abundant satisfaction of their needs; and if he himself opposes it, he does so in the consciousness of resisting what is best for the common interest, doing so for his own benefit because he feels himself threatened in his

---

4. It is naturally not intended here to undertake a critical assessment of Marxism. The discussion in this section is intended only to explain the imperialistic tendencies of socialism. Also, enough writings are available anyway to whoever is interested in these problems (e.g., Simkhowitsch, *Marxismus versus Sozialismus*, translated by Jappe [Jena: 1913]).

rights or privileges. The bureaucrats mostly take this position, which is often enough found, however, among entrepreneurs also. It has long been forgotten in Germany that liberalism, like socialism, also recommends its economic system out of concern, not for the interests of individuals, but for those of all, of the masses. That "the greatest happiness of the greatest number" should be the goal of policy was first maintained by a radical free-trader, Jeremy Bentham. Bentham also carried on his famous struggle against usury laws, for example, not out of concern for the interests of the moneylenders but out of concern for the interests of all.[5] The point of departure of all liberalism lies in the thesis of the harmony of rightly understood interests of individuals, of classes, and of peoples. It rejects the basic idea of mercantilism that the advantage of the one is the disadvantage of the other. That is a principle that may hold true for war and plunder; for economics and trade it does not hold. Therefore liberalism sees no basis for opposition between classes; therefore it is pacifist in relations between peoples. Not because it considers itself called upon to represent the special interests of the possessing classes does it advocate maintenance of private ownership of the means of production, but rather because it sees the economic order resting on private ownership as the system of production and distribution that assures the best and highest material satisfaction for all sections of the people. And just as it calls for free trade at home not out of regard for particular classes but out of regard for the welfare of all, so it demands free trade in international relations, not for the sake of foreigners, but for the sake of its own people.

Interventionist economic policy takes another standpoint. It sees irreconcilable antagonisms in relations among states. Marxism, however, has proclaimed the doctrine of class struggle; on the irreconcilable opposition of classes it erects its doctrine and its tactics.

In Germany liberalism was never understood; it never took root. Only thus can it be explained that even the opponents of socialism more or less accepted socialist doctrines. That appears most clearly in the position of the opponents of socialism on the problem of the class struggle. Marxian socialism preaches the struggle of the proletariat against the bourgeoisie. Elsewhere this battle cry is opposed by that of the solidarity of interests. Not so in Germany. Here the proletarians are confronted by the bourgeoisie as a class. The united bourgeois parties confront the

---

5. Cf. Bentham, *Defence of Usury*, second edition (London: 1790), pp. 108 f.

proletarian party. They do not see that in this way they recognize the argumentation of the Marxists as correct and thereby make their struggle hopeless. He who can advance in favor of private ownership of the means of production nothing other than that its abolition would harm the rights of owners limits the supporters of the antisocialist parties to the nonproletarians. In an industrial state the "proletarians" naturally have numerical superiority over the other classes. If party formation is determined by class membership, then it is clear that the proletarian party must gain victory over the others.

2   Socialism and Utopia

Marxism sees the coming of socialism as an inescapable necessity. Even if one were willing to grant the correctness of this opinion, one still would by no means be bound to embrace socialism. It may be that despite everything we cannot escape socialism, yet whoever considers it an evil must not wish it onward for that reason and seek to hasten its arrival; on the contrary, he would have the moral duty to do everything to postpone it as long as possible. No person can escape death; yet the recognition of this necessity certainly does not force us to bring about death as quickly as possible. If Marxists were convinced that socialism was bound to bring about no improvement but rather a worsening of our social conditions they would have no more reason to become socialists than we would to commit suicide.[6]

Socialists and liberals agree in seeing the ultimate goal of economic policy as attainment of a state of society assuring the greatest happiness for the greatest number. Welfare for all, the greatest possible welfare for the greatest possible number — that is the goal of both liberalism and of socialism, even though this may now and then be not only misunderstood but even disputed. Both reject all ascetic ideals that want to restrain people to frugality and preach renunciation and flight from life; both strive for social wealth. Only over the way of reaching this ultimate goal of economic policy do their views disagree. An economic order resting on private ownership of the means of production and according the greatest possible scope to the activity and free initiative of the individual assures to the liberal the attainment of the goal aspired

---

6. Cf. Hilferding, *Das Finanzkapital* (Vienna: 1910), p. X.

to. The socialist, on the other hand, seeks to attain it by socialization of the means of production.

The older socialism and communism strove for equality of property and of income distribution. Inequality was said to be unjust; it contradicted divine laws and had to be abolished. To that liberals reply that fettering the free activity of the individual would harm the general interest. In the socialist society the distinction between rich and poor would fall away; no one would any longer possess more than another, but every individual would be poorer than even the poorest today, since the communistic system would work to impede production and progress. It may indeed be true that the liberal economic order permits great differences in income, but that in no way involves exploitation of the poor by richer people; what the rich have they have not taken away from the poor. In the socialist society, their surplus could not be distributed to the poor, since in that society it would not be produced at all. The surplus produced in the liberal economic order beyond what could also be produced by a communistic economic order is not even entirely distributed to the possessors; a part of it even accrues to the propertyless so that everyone, even the poorest, has an interest in the establishment and maintenance of a liberal economic order. Fighting erroneous socialist doctrines is therefore not a special interest of a single class but the concern of everyone; everyone would suffer under the limitation of production and of progress entailed by socialism. That one has more to lose, another less, is incidental in relation to the fact that all would be harmed and that the misery awaiting them is equally great.

That is the argument in favor of private ownership of the means of production that every socialism that does not set up ascetic ideals would have to refute. Marx did indeed perceive the necessity of this refutation. When he sees the driving factor of the social revolution in the fact that the relations of ownership change from forms of development of the productive forces into fetters on them,[7] when he once in passing tries to offer a proof—which failed—that the capitalist manner of production impedes the development of productivity in a particular case,[8] he does incidentally recognize the importance of this problem. But neither he nor his followers could attribute to it the significance it deserves for deciding the question of socialism or liberalism. They are hampered

7. Cf. Marx, *Zur Kritik der politischen Ökonomie*, edited by Kautsky (Stuttgart: 1897), p. xi.
8. Cf. Marx, *Das Kapital*, vol. 3, first part, third edition (Hamburg: 1911), pp. 242 ff.

in doing so even by the entire orientation of their thinking around the materialist interpretation of history. Their determinism just cannot understand how one can be for or against socialism, since the communist society is molding the inescapable future. It is moreover settled for Marx, as a Hegelian, that this development toward socialism is also rational in the Hegelian sense and represents progress toward a higher stage. The idea that socialism could mean a catastrophe for civilization would necessarily have seemed completely incomprehensible to him.

Marxian socialism therefore had no incentive to consider the question whether or not socialism as an economic form was superior to liberalism. To it, it seemed settled that socialism alone signified welfare for all, while liberalism enriched a few but abandoned the great masses to misery. With the appearance of Marxism, therefore, controversy over the advantages of the two economic orders died away. Marxists do not enter into such discussions. *Ex professo* [avowedly] they have not even tried to refute the liberal arguments in favor of private ownership of the means of production, not to mention actually refuting them.

In the view of individualists, private ownership of the means of production fulfills its social function by conveying the means of production into the hands of those who best understand how to use them. Every owner must use his means of production in such a way that they yield the greatest output, that is, the highest utility for society. If he does not do this, then this must lead to his economic failure, and the means of production shift over to the disposal of those who better understand how to use them. In that way the inappropriate or negligent application of means of production is avoided and their most effective utilization assured. For means of production that are not under the private ownership of individuals but rather are under social ownership, this is not true in the same way. What is missing here is the incentive of the owner's self-interest. The utilization of equipment is therefore not as complete as in the private sector; with the same input the same output cannot therefore be achieved. The result of social production must therefore remain behind that of private production. Evidence of that has been supplied by public enterprises of the state and municipalities (so individualists further argue). It is demonstrated and well known that less is accomplished in these than in the private sector. The output of enterprises that had been quite profitable under private ownership sank at once after coming under state or municipal ownership. The public firm can nowhere maintain itself in free competition with the private firm; it is possible today only where it has a monopoly that excludes competition. Even that alone is evidence of its lesser economic productivity.

Only a few socialists of Marxist orientation have recognized the significance of this counterargument; otherwise they would have had to admit that this is a point on which everything depends. If the socialist mode of production will be able to achieve no additional output in comparison with private enterprise, if, on the contrary, it will produce less than the latter, then no improvement but rather a worsening of the lot of the worker is to be expected from it. All argumentation of the socialists would therefore have to concentrate on showing that socialism will succeed in raising production beyond the amount possible in the individualistic economic order.

Most Social Democratic writers are quite silent on this point; others touch on it only incidentally. Thus, Kautsky names two methods that the future state will use for raising production. The first is the concentration of all production in the most efficient firms and the shutting down of all other, less high-ranking, firms.[9] That this is a means of raising production cannot be disputed. But this method is in best operation precisely under the rule of free competition. Free competition pitilessly culls out all less-productive enterprises and firms. Precisely that it does so is again and again used as a reproach against it by the affected parties; precisely for that reason do the weaker enterprises demand state subsidies and special consideration in sales to public agencies, in short, limitation of free competition in every possible way. That the trusts organized on a private-enterprise basis work in the highest degree with these methods for achieving higher productivity must be admitted even by Kautsky, since he actually cites them as models for the social revolution. It is more than doubtful whether the socialist state will also feel the same urgency to carry out such improvements in production. Will it not continue a firm that is less profitable in order to avoid local disadvantages from its abandonment? The private entrepreneur ruthlessly abandons enterprises that no longer pay; he thereby makes it necessary for the workers to move, perhaps also to change their occupations. That is doubtless harmful above all for the persons affected, but an advantage for the whole, since it makes possible cheaper and better supply of the markets. Will the socialist state also do that? Will it not, precisely on the contrary,

9. Cf. Kautsky, *Die Soziale Revolution*, third edition (Berlin: 1911), II, pp. 21 ff.

out of political considerations, try to avoid local discontent? In the Austrian state railroads, all reforms of this kind were wrecked because people sought to avoid the damage to particular localities that would have resulted from abandonment of superfluous administrative offices, workshops, and heating plants. Even the Army administration ran into parliamentary difficulties when, for military reasons, it wanted to withdraw the garrison from a locality.

The second method of raising production that Kautsky mentions, "savings of very many kinds," he also, by his own admission, finds already realized by the trusts of today. He names, above all, savings in materials and equipment, transport costs, and advertising and publicity expenses.[10] Now, as far as savings of material and transport are concerned, experience shows that nowhere are operations carried on with so little thrift in this respect and nowhere with such waste of labor and materials of all kinds as in public service and public enterprises. Private enterprise, on the contrary, seeks, even in the owner's own interest alone, to work as thriftily as possible.

The socialist state will, of course, save all advertising expenses and all costs for traveling salesmen and for agents. Yet it is more than doubtful whether it will not employ many more persons in the service of the social apparatus of distribution. We have already had the experience in the war that the socialist apparatus of distribution can be quite ponderous and costly. Or are the costs of the bread, flour, meat, sugar, and other items really smaller than the costs of advertisements? Is the large staff that is necessary for the issue and administration of these rationing devices cheaper than the expenditure on traveling salesmen and agents?

Socialism will abolish small retail shops. But it will have to replace them with goods-delivery stations, which will not be cheaper. Even consumer cooperatives, after all, have no fewer employees than retail trade organized in a modern way employs; and precisely because of their higher expenses, they often could not stand the competition with merchants if they were not given tax advantages.

We see on what weak ground Kautsky's argumentation stands here. When he now asserts that "by application of these two methods a proletarian regime can raise production at once to so high a level that

10. Ibid., p. 26.

it becomes possible to raise wages considerably and at the same time reduce hours of work," well, this is an assertion for which no proof has so far been provided.[11]

The social functions of private ownership of the means of production are not yet exhausted in assuring the highest attainable productivity of labor. Economic progress rests on the continuing accumulation of capital. That was never disputed either by liberals or by socialists. The socialists who have concerned themselves somewhat more closely with the problem of the organization of the socialist society also do not neglect, then, always to mention that in the socialist state the accumulation of capital, which today is undertaken by private parties, will be society's responsibility.

In the individualistic society the individual, not society, accumulates. Capital accumulation takes place by saving; the saver has the incentive of receiving income from the saved capital as the reward of saving. In the communist society, society as such will receive the income that today flows to the capitalists alone; it will then distribute this income equally to all members or otherwise use it for the good of the whole. Will that alone be a sufficient incentive for saving? To be able to answer this question, one must imagine that the society of the socialist state will be faced every day with the choice whether it should devote itself more to the production of consumer goods or more to that of capital goods, whether it should choose productive processes that do indeed take a shorter time but correspondingly yield less output or choose ones that take more time but then also bring greater output. The liberal thinks that the socialist society will always decide for the shorter production period, that it will prefer to produce consumer goods instead of capital goods, that it will consume the means of production it will have taken over as heir of the liberal society or at best maintain them but in no case increase them. That, however, would mean that socialism will bring stagnation, if not the decline of our whole economic civilization, and misery and need

11. One has heard often enough in recent years of frozen potatoes, rotten fruit, and spoiled vegetables. Did not things like that happen earlier? Of course, but to a much smaller extent. The dealer whose fruit spoiled suffered losses of wealth that made him more careful in the future; if he did not pay better attention, then this was finally bound to lead to his economic disappearance. He left the management of production and was shifted to a position in economic life where he was no longer able to do harm. It is otherwise in dealings with state-traded articles. Here no self-interest stands behind the goods; here officials manage whose responsibility is so divided that no one particularly concerns himself about a small misfortune.

for all. That the state and the cities have already pursued investment policy on a large scale is no disproof of this assertion, since they pursued this activity entirely with the means of the liberal system. The means were raised by loans, that is, they were provided by private parties who expected from them an increase in their capital incomes. If in the future, however, the socialist society should face the question whether it will feed, clothe, and house its members better or whether it will save on all these things in order to build railroads and canals, to open mines, to undertake agricultural improvements for the coming generations, then it will decide for the former, even on psychological and political grounds alone.

A third objection to socialism is the famous argument of Malthus. Population is said to have a tendency to grow faster than the means of subsistence. In the social order resting on private ownership, a limitation of the increase in population is posed by the fact that each person is able to raise only a limited number of children. In the socialist society this impediment to population increase will fall away, since no longer the individual but rather the society will have to take care of raising the new generation. Then, however, such a growth of population would soon occur that need and misery for all would be bound to appear.[12]

Those are the objections to the socialist society with which everyone would have to come to grips before he took the side of socialism.

It is no refutation at all of the objections raised against socialism that the socialists seek to stigmatize everyone who is not of their opinion with the label "bourgeois economist" as representative of a class whose special interests run counter to the general interest. That the interests of the property owners run counter to those of the whole would indeed first have to be proved; that is precisely what the entire controversy revolves around.

The liberal doctrine starts with the fact that the economic order resting on private ownership of the means of production removes the opposition between private and social interest because each individual's pursuit of his rightly understood self-interest assures the highest attainable degree of general welfare. Socialism wants to establish a social order in which the self-interest of the individual, selfishness, is excluded,

12. While the socialists have scarcely deigned to reply to the two first arguments mentioned, they have concerned themselves more exhaustively with the Malthusian law, without, to be sure, in the view of the liberals, refuting the conclusions that follow from it.

a society in which everyone has to serve the common good directly. It would now be the task of the socialists to show in what manner this goal could be reached. Even the socialist cannot call into question the existence of a primary and direct opposition between the special interests of the individual and those of the whole, and he must also admit that a labor order can be based just as little on the categorical imperative alone as on the compulsory force of penal law. Up to now, however, no socialist has ever made even the mere attempt to show how this gap between special interest and general welfare could be bridged over. The opponents of socialism, however, along with Schäffle, consider precisely that question to be "the decisive but up to now entirely undecided point on which in the long run everything would depend, on which victory or defeat of socialism, reform or destruction of civilization by it, would be dependent from the economic side."[13]

Marxian socialism calls the older socialism utopian because it tries to construct the elements of a new society out of one's head and because it seeks ways and means of implementing the contrived social plan. In contrast, Marxism is supposed to be scientific communism. It discovers the elements of the new society in the laws of development of capitalist society, but it constructs no future state. It recognizes that the proletariat, because of its conditions of life, can do nothing else than finally overcome every class opposition and thereby realize socialism; however, it does not seek philanthropists, as the utopians do, who would be ready to make the world happy by the introduction of socialism. If one wants to see the distinction between science and utopia in that, then Marxian socialism rightly claims its name. One could, however, make the distinction in another sense also. If one calls utopian all those social theories which, in outlining the future social system, start with the view that after introduction of the new social order people will be guided by essentially different motives than in our present conditions,[14] then the socialist ideal of Marxism is also a utopia.[15] Its

13. Cf. Schäffle, *Die Quintessenz des Sozialismus*, 18th edition (Gotha: 1919), p. 30.
14. Cf. Anton Menger, *Das Recht auf den vollen Arbeitsertrag*, fourth edition (Stuttgart: 1910), pp. 105 ff.
15. In another sense than is usual, of course, one can distinguish between scientific and philanthropic socialism. Those socialists who are concerned in their programs to start with economic lines of thinking and take the necessity of production into account can be called scientific socialists, in contrast with those who know how to bring forth only ethical and moral discussions and set up only a program for distribution but not for production also. Marx clearly noted the defects of merely philanthropic socialism when, after moving to London, he proceeded to study the

continued existence presupposes men who are in no position to pursue any special interest against the general interest.[16] Again and again, when this objection is made to him, the socialist refers to the fact that both today and in every earlier stage of society very much work, and often precisely the most highly qualified work, was indeed performed for its own sake and for the community and not for the direct advantage of the worker. He points to the indefatigable effort of the researcher, to the sacrifice of the physician, to the conduct of the warrior in the field. In recent years one could hear again and again that the great deeds performed by soldiers in the field were to be explained only by pure devotion to the cause and by a high sense of sacrifice, or at worst, perhaps, by striving for distinction, but never by striving for private gain. This argumentation overlooks the fundamental distinction that exists, however, between economic work of the usual kind and those special performances. The artist and the researcher find their satisfaction in the pleasure that the work in itself affords them and in the recognition that they hope to reap at some time, even if perhaps only from posterity when material success would be lacking. The physician in the area of pestilence and the soldier in the field repress not only their economic interests but also their drive for self-preservation; even that alone shows that there can be no question of a regular state of affairs but only of a transitory, exceptional state from which no far-reaching conclusions can be drawn.

The treatment that socialism allots to the problem of self-interest points clearly to its origin. Socialism comes from the circles of intellectuals; at its cradle stand poets and thinkers, writers and men of letters. It does not deny its derivation from those strata that even on professional grounds alone have to concern themselves with ideals. It is an ideal of noneconomic people. Therefore, it is not much more striking

---

economic theorists. The result of this study was the doctrine presented in *Das Kapital*. Later Marxists, however, have badly neglected this side of Marxism. They are much more politicians and philosophers than economists. One of the chief defects of the economic side of the Marxian system is its connection with classical economics, which corresponded to the state of economic science at that time. Today socialism would have to seek a scientific support in modern economics in the theory of marginal utility. Cf. Joseph Schumpeter, "Das Grundprinzip der Verteilungslehre," *Archiv für Sozialwissenschaft und Sozialpolitik*, vol. 42, 1916/1917, p. 88.

16. How easily the Marxists disregard this argument can be seen in Kautsky: "If socialism is a social necessity, then if it came into conflict with human nature, it would be the latter that would get the worse of the matter and not socialism." Preface to Atlanticus [Ballod], *Produktion und Konsum im Sozialstatt* (Stuttgart: 1898), p. xiv.

that writers and men of letters of every kind were always represented among its adherents in large numbers and that it could always count on fundamental agreement among officials.

The view characteristic of officials comes clearly to light in the treatment of the problem of socialization. From the bureaucratic point of view, it involves only questions of management and administrative technique that can easily be solved if only one allows the officials more freedom of action. Then socialization could be carried out without danger of "eliminating free initiative and individual readiness to bear responsibility on which the successes of private business management rest."[17] Actually, free initiative of individuals cannot exist in the socialized economy. It is a fateful error to believe it possible, by some sort of organizational measures, to leave scope for free initiative in the socialized enterprise. Its absence does not hinge on defects of organization; it is grounded in the essence of the socialized enterprise. Free initiative means taking risks in order to win; it means putting up stakes in a game that can bring gain or loss. All economic activity is composed of such risky undertakings. Every act of production, every purchase by the trader and by the producer, every delay in selling, is such a risky undertaking. Still more so is undertaking every sizable investment or change in the enterprise, not to mention the investment of new capital. Capitalists and entrepreneurs must take chances; they cannot do otherwise, since they have no possibility of maintaining their property without undertaking such ventures.

Anyone who has means of production at his disposal without being their owner has neither the risk of loss nor the chance of gain, as an owner does. The official or functionary need not fear loss, and for that reason he cannot be allowed to act freely and unrestrictedly like the owner. He must be restricted in some manner. If he could manage without restrictions, then he simply would be the owner. It is playing with words to say one wants to impose on the nonowner *readiness* to bear responsibility. The owner does not simply have a *readiness* to bear responsibility; he actually *does* bear responsibility because he feels the consequences of his actions. The functionary may have ever so much readiness to bear responsibility, yet he never can bear responsibility other than morally. Yet the more moral responsibility one imposes on him, the

17. Cf. Bericht der Sozialisierungskommission über die Sozialisierung der Kohle [Report of the Socialization Commission on the Socialization of Coal], *Frankfurter Zeitung*, 12 March 1919.

more one cramps his initiative. The problem of socialization cannot be solved by civil-service instructions and reforms of organization.

3 Centralist and Syndicalist Socialism

The question whether or not our economic development is already "ripe" for socialism originates in the Marxian idea of the development of the productive forces. Socialism can be realized only when its time has come. A form of society cannot perish before it has developed all the productive forces that it is capable of developing; only then is it replaced by another, higher, form. Before capitalism has lived out its course, socialism cannot take over its inheritance.

Marxism likes to compare the social revolution with birth. Premature births are failures; they lead to the death of the new creature.[18] From this point of view Marxists inquire whether the attempts of the Bolsheviks in Russia to establish a socialist commonwealth are not premature. It must be difficult indeed for the Marxist, who regards a definite degree of development of the capitalistic mode of production and of heavy industry as a necessary condition for the appearance of socialism, to understand why socialism has achieved victory precisely in the Russia of small peasants and not in highly industrialized Western Europe or in the United States.

It is different when the question is raised whether or not this or that branch of production is ripe for socialization. This question is as a rule posed in such a way that the very posing of the question basically admits that socialized enterprises in general yield smaller outputs than those operating under private ownership and that, therefore, only particular branches of production should be socialized in which no excessive disadvantages are to be expected from this lesser productivity. Thus it is explained that mines, above all coal mines, are already ripe for socialization. Obviously people thus proceed from the view that it is easier to operate a mine than, say, a factory producing for the fashion market; people evidently believe that mining only involves exploiting the gifts of nature, which even the ponderous socialist enterprise can manage. And, again, when others regard the large industrial enterprise as above all ripe for socialization, they are proceeding from the idea that in the

18. Cf. Kautsky, *Die Soziale Revolution*, loc. cit., I, pp. 13 ff.

large enterprise, which already is working with a certain bureaucratic apparatus anyway, the organizational preconditions for socialization are given. Such ideas involve a serious fallacy. To prove the necessity of the socialization of particular enterprises, it is not enough to show that socialization does little harm in them because they still would not fail then even if they did work more poorly than would be the case under the administration of private enterprise. Whoever does not believe that socialization brings a rise of productivity would, to be consistent, have to consider any socialization as mistaken.

We can also find a hidden admission of the lesser productivity of the economy in a socialist social order in the idea on which many writers base the proposition that the war has set us back in development and has, therefore, further postponed the time of ripeness for socialism. Thus, Kautsky says: "Socialism, that is, general welfare within modern civilization, becomes possible only through the great development of productive forces that capitalism brings, through the enormous riches that it creates and that are concentrated in the hands of the capitalist class. A state that has squandered these riches through a senseless policy, perhaps an unsuccessful war, offers from the outset no favorable point of departure for the quickest diffusion of welfare in all classes." [19] Whoever — like Kautsky — expects a multiplication of productivity from socialistic production would, however, really have to see one more reason for hastening socialization precisely in the fact that we have become poorer because of the war.

The liberals are much more consistent in this. They are not waiting for another mode of production, perhaps the socialist one, to make the world ripe for liberalism; they see the time for liberalism as always and everywhere given, since, in general and without exception, they assert the superiority of the mode of production resting on private ownership of the means of production and on the free competition of producers.

The way that the socialization of enterprises would have to take place is clearly and distinctly indicated by the public ownership measures of the states and municipalities. One could even say that the administration of German states and cities is no more skillful than this procedure, which has been followed for many years. With regard to administrative technique, socialization is nothing new, and the socialist governments that are now at work everywhere would have to do nothing beyond

19. Cf. Kautsky, *Die Diktatur des Proletariats*, second edition (Vienna: 1918), p. 40.

continuing what their predecessors in state and communal socialism have already done before.

Of course, neither the new power-holders nor their constituents want to hear anything about that. The masses, which today stormily demand the most rapid accomplishment of socialism, imagine it as something quite different from the extension of state and municipal enterprise. Indeed, they have heard from their leaders again and again that these public enterprises have nothing in common with socialism. What socialization should be, however, if not state and municipal ownership, no one can say.[20] What Social Democracy previously cultivated is now bitterly taking revenge on it, namely, its always engaging for decades only in demagogic everyday politics and not in principled politics for the final triumph. In fact, Social Democracy has long since given up centralist socialism; in daily politics it has ever more and more become union-oriented, syndicalistic, and, in the Marxian sense, "petty bourgeois." Now syndicalism raises its demands, which stand in irreconcilable contradiction to the program of centralist socialism.

Both orientations have one point in common: they want to make the worker the owner of the means of production again. Centralist socialism wants to achieve this by making the whole working class of the entire world or at least of an entire country the owner of the means of production; syndicalism wants to make the workforces of individual enterprises or individual branches of production the owners of the means of production that they use. The ideal of centralist socialism is at least discussible; that of syndicalism is so absurd that one need waste few words on it.

One of the great ideas of liberalism is that it lets the consumer interest alone count and disregards the producer interest. No production is worth maintaining if it is not suited to bring about the cheapest and best supply. No producer is recognized as having a right to oppose any change in the conditions of production because it runs counter to his

20. According to Engels (*Herrn Eugen Dührings Umwälzung der Wissenschaft*, seventh edition [Stuttgart: 1910], p. 299 n.) [*Anti-Dühring: Herr Eugen Dühring's Revolution in Science* (New York: International Publishers, 1936) p. 305 n], referring to "the case in which the means of production or of transport and communications have really outgrown the control by corporations and in which state ownership has thus become *economically* imperative," state ownership means economic progress and "the attainment of a new stage in the taking possession of all productive forces by society itself, even when the state of today carries it out." [Wording in 1936 English translation differs slightly.]

interest as a producer. The highest goal of all economic activity is the achievement of the best and most abundant satisfaction of wants at the smallest cost.

This position follows with compelling logic from the consideration that all production is carried on only for the sake of consumption, that it is never a goal but always only a means. The reproach made against liberalism that it thereby takes account only of the consumer viewpoint and disdains labor is so stupid that it scarcely needs refutation. Preferring the producer interest over the consumer interest, which is characteristic of antiliberalism, means nothing other than striving artificially to maintain conditions of production that have been rendered inefficient by continuing progress. Such a system may seem discussible when the special interests of small groups are protected against the great mass of others, since the privileged party then gains more from his privilege as a producer than he loses on the other hand as a consumer; it becomes absurd when it is raised to a general principle, since then every individual loses infinitely more as a consumer than he may be able to gain as a producer. The victory of the producer interest over the consumer interest means turning away from rational economic organization and impeding all economic progress.

Centralist socialism knows this very well. It joins liberalism in fighting all traditional producer privileges. It proceeds from the view that there would be no producer interest at all in the socialist commonwealth, since each one would recognize there that the consumer interest alone is worth considering. Whether or not this assumption is justified will not be discussed here; it is immediately evident that if it should not hold true, socialism could not be what it pretends to be.

Syndicalism deliberately places the producer interest of the workers in the foreground. In making worker groups owners of the means of production (not in so many words but in substance), it does not abolish private property. It also does not assure equality. It does remove the existing inequality of distribution but introduces a new one, for the value of the capital invested in individual enterprises or sectors of production does not correspond at all to the number of workers employed in them. The income of each single worker will be all the greater, the smaller the number of fellow workers employed in his enterprise or sector of production and the greater the value of the material means of production employed in it. The syndicalistically organized state would be no socialist state but a state of worker capitalism, since the individual worker groups would be owners of the capital. Syndicalism would make all repatterning of production impossible; it leaves no room free for economic progress. In its entire intellectual character it suits the age of peasants and craftsmen, in which economic relations are rather stationary.

The centralist socialism of Karl Marx, which once had triumphed over Proudhon and Lassalle, has, in the course of development of recent decades, been pushed back step by step by syndicalism. The struggle between the two views, which outwardly occurred in the form of a struggle between the political party organization and the labor union organization and behind the scenes took on the shape of a struggle of leaders risen from the working class against intellectual leaders, has ended with a complete victory of syndicalism. The theories and writings of the party chiefs still outwardly wear the garment of centralist socialism, but the practice of the party has gradually become syndicalist, and in the consciousness of the masses the syndicalist ideology lives exclusively. The theoreticians of centralist socialism have not had the courage — out of tactical concerns, because they wanted to avoid an open breach between the two positions, as in France — to take a decisive stand against the syndicalist policy; if they had mustered the courage for that, they would doubtless have been defeated in this struggle. In many respects they have directly furthered the development of the syndicalist line of thinking, since they fought the development toward centralist socialism that was taking place under the leadership of statist socialism. They had to do this, on the one hand to mark a sharp distinction between their position and that of the authoritarian state, and on the other hand because the economic failures being caused by state and municipal ownership were, after all, becoming so broadly and generally visible that they could become dangerous to the ardent enthusiasm with which the masses were following the obscure ideal of socialism. If one kept pointing out again and again that state railroads and city lighting works were in no way a first step toward realizing the state of the future, one could not educate the population in favor of centralist socialism.

As workers had become unemployed through introduction of improved methods of work, it was syndicalism that sought to destroy the new machines. Sabotage is syndicalistic; in the final analysis, however, every strike is also syndicalistic; the demand for introduction of the social protective tariff is syndicalistic. In a word, all those means of the class struggle that the Social Democratic Party did not want to give up because it feared losing influence on the working masses only stimulated the syndicalistic — Marx would have said "petty-bourgeois" — instincts of the masses. If centralist socialism has any adherents at all today, this is not the accomplishment of Social Democratic agitation but of statism. State and municipal socialism provided publicity for centralist socialism by putting socialism into practice; academic socialism provided literary propaganda for it.

What is going on before our eyes today is of course neither centralist socialism nor syndicalism; it is not organization of production at all and also not organization of distribution, but rather distribution and consumption of consumer goods already on hand and annihilation and destruction of means of production already on hand. Whatever is still being produced is being produced by the remnants of the free economy that are still allowed to exist; wherever this socialism of today has already penetrated, there is no longer any question of production. The forms in which this process is occurring are manifold. Strikes shut enterprises down, and where work is still being done, the ca' canny system[21] itself sees to it that the output is only slight. By high taxes and by compulsion to pay high wages to the workers even when there is no work for them, the entrepreneur is forced to consume his capital. Working in the same direction is inflationism, which, as has been shown, conceals and thereby fosters capital consumption. Acts of sabotage by the workers and inept interventions by the authorities destroy the material apparatus of production and complete the work that war and revolutionary struggles began.

In the midst of all this destruction only agriculture remains, above all small farms. It too has suffered severely under the circumstances, and here, too, much of the working capital has already been consumed, and ever more of it is being consumed. The large units will probably be socialized or even broken up into small farms. In any case, their productive power will thereby suffer, even apart from the impairment of their capital. Still, the devastation of agriculture remains relatively slight in comparison with the ever-worsening dissolution of the apparatus of industrial production.

The dying out of the spirit of social cooperation, which constitutes the essence of the social revolutionary process that is occurring before our eyes, must entail different consequences in industry, in transport, and in trade — in short, in the city — than in agriculture. A railroad, a factory,

21. A deliberate slowdown of workers.

a mine simply cannot be operated without that spirit, on which the division of labor and the coordination of labor rest. It is otherwise in agriculture. If the peasant withdraws from exchange and shifts his production back to the autarky of the self-sufficient household economy, he does live worse than he once lived, but he can keep on living anyway. Thus we see the peasantry becoming ever more and more self-sufficient. The peasant is again beginning to produce everything that he wishes to consume in his household and, on the other hand, to cut back his production for the needs of the city-dweller.[22]

What that means for the future of the city population is clear. The industry of Germany and German-Austria has largely lost its foreign market; now it is losing the domestic market also. When work in the workshops is again resumed, the peasants will face the question whether it is not more advantageous for them to obtain industrial products cheaper and better from abroad. The German peasant will again be a free-trader, as he had been up to forty years ago.

It is scarcely thinkable that this process should go on in Germany without the greatest disruptions. For it does signify no less than the decay of German urban civilization, the slow starvation of millions of German city-dwellers.

If revolutionary syndicalism and destructionism should not remain limited to Germany but instead should spread over all Europe and even to America also, then we would face a catastrophe comparable only with the collapse of the ancient world. Ancient civilization also was built on a far-reaching division of labor and coordination of labor; in it too the — even if limited[23] — operation of the liberal principle had brought about a great flourishing of material and intellectual culture. All that disappeared as the immaterial bond that held this whole system together, the spirit of social cooperation, disappeared. In the dying Roman Empire also the cities were depopulated; the man who owned no land sank into misery; whoever could somehow do so moved to the countryside to escape starvation.[24] Then, too, there occurred, accompanied outwardly by the most severe disturbances of the monetary system, the process of reversion of the monetary economy to a barter economy, the exchange

---

22. That holds true of German-Austria especially. In the Reich the conditions are still different for the time being.

23. We too have never really had "free competition."

24. Numerous documents in late Roman legal sources. Cf., e.g., 1. un. C. Si curialis relicta civitate rus habitare maluerit, X, 37.

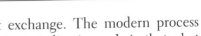

economy to the economy without exchange. The modern process would differ from the decline of ancient civilization only in that what once occurred over centuries would now complete itself in an incomparably more rapid tempo.

4 Socialist Imperialism

The older socialists were opponents of democracy. They want to make the whole world happy with their plans and are impatient with anyone who is of another opinion. Their favorite form of state would be enlightened absolutism in which they always secretly dream of themselves occupying the position of enlightened despot. Recognizing that they neither occupy this position nor can attain it, they seek the despot who would be ready to adopt their plans and become their tool. Other socialists, again, are oligarchically minded and want to have the world ruled by an aristocracy that includes the — in their opinion — really best people. In that regard it is a matter of indifference whether these aristocrats should be the philosophers of Plato, the priests of the Church, or the Newtonian Council of Saint-Simon.

With Marx there occurs in this respect, also, a complete change of interpretation. The proletarians form the immense majority of the population. They all necessarily have to become socialists, though, since consciousness is determined by social reality. Thus socialism, in contrast with all earlier class struggles, which had been movements of minorities or in the interests of minorities, is said to be the movement of the vast majority in the interest of the vast majority for the first time in history. It follows that democracy is the best means for realizing socialism. The real bedrock on which democratic socialism was built was that it found its base primarily in Germany, Austria, and Russia, thus in countries in which democracy had not been realized. There the democratic program was the obvious program of every opposition party and so necessarily of socialism also.

When the possibility offered itself in Russia to a very small number of socialists in relation to the millions of the people to grasp rule for themselves by capturing the means of power of broken-down Czarism, the principles of democracy were quickly thrown overboard. In Russia socialism certainly is not a movement of the immense majority. That it claims to be a movement in the interest of the immense majority is nothing special; all movements have claimed that. It is certain that the rule of the Bolsheviks in Russia rests just as much on possession of the government apparatus as the rule of the Romanovs once did. A democratic Russia would not be Bolshevik.

In Germany under the dictatorship of the proletariat there can be no problem, as its proponents assert, of defeating the resistance of the bourgeoisie to the socialization of the means of production. If the socialization of small peasant farms is renounced in advance and the continued receipt of small rentier (fixed) incomes allowed also, as present-day socialism intends, then scarcely any resistance to socialization is to be expected in Germany. Liberal ideas, with which alone resistance against socialism could be mounted, have never won much ground in Germany; today they are shared by scarcely a dozen persons in Germany. Resistance to socialization based on the standpoint of private interests never has, however — rightly — any prospect of success, least of all in a country in which all industrial and mercantile wealth has always seemed to the great masses to be a crime. The expropriation of industry, of mining, and of big landholdings and the elimination of trade are the impetuous demand in Germany today of the overwhelming majority of the German people. To carry it out, dictatorship is needed least of all. Socialism can rely on the great masses at the moment; it does not yet have to fear democracy.

The German economy is today in the most difficult position imaginable. On the one hand the war has destroyed immense property values and laid upon the German people the obligation to pay huge reparations to the opponents; on the other hand it has brought clearly to consciousness the fact of the relative overpopulation of the German land. Everyone must recognize today that it will be extraordinarily difficult, if not impossible, for German industry after the war to compete with foreign industry without a sharp reduction of the wage level. Hundreds of thousands, even millions, of Germans are today seeing their small possessions melting away day by day. People who still considered themselves rich a few months ago, who were envied by thousands and, as "war winners," did not exactly enjoy affectionate attention in public, can today calculate exactly when they will have consumed the modest remains of their apparent wealth and will be left beggars. Members of the independent professions see how their standard of living is sinking day by day without hope of improvement.

That a people in such a position can be gripped by despair is not astonishing. It is easy to say that there is only one single remedy for the danger of the increasing misery of the entire German people, namely, to resume work as fast as possible and try, through improvements in the productive process, to make up for the damages inflicted on the German economy. But it is understandable that a people to whom the idea of power was preached for decades, whose instinct for force was awakened by the horrors of the long war, also seeks first of all in this crisis to resort again to power politics. The terrorism of the Spartacists continues the policy of the Junkers, as the terrorism of the Bolsheviks continues the policy of Czarism.

The dictatorship of the proletariat would facilitate getting over economic difficulties for the moment by expropriating the consumption goods held by the propertied classes. It is clear that that is not socialism and that no socialist theorist has ever advocated it. In this way one can only badly and only for a short time disguise the difficulties that confront production on a socialist basis. Imports of foodstuffs from abroad can be financed for a certain time by selling foreign securities and by exporting works of art and jewels. Sooner or later, however, this means must fail.

The dictatorship of the proletariat wants to use terror to nip any stirring up of opposition in the bud. Socialism is believed established for all eternity once its property has been taken away from the bourgeoisie and all possibility of public criticism has been abolished. It cannot be denied, of course, that much can be done in this way, that, above all, all European civilization can thus be destroyed; but one does not thereby build a socialist order of society. If the communist social order is less suited than one resting on private ownership of the means of production to bring about "the greatest happiness of the greatest number," then the ideas of liberalism cannot be killed off even by terrorist measures.

Marxian socialism, as a fundamentally revolutionary movement, is inwardly inclined toward imperialism. No one will dispute that, least of all the Marxists themselves, who straightforwardly proclaim the cult of revolution. It is less noted, however, that modern socialism of necessity must be imperialistic outwardly also.

Modern socialism does not come forth in propaganda as a rationalist demand; it is an economic-policy position that presents itself as a doctrine of salvation in the manner of religions. As an economic-policy idea it would have had to compete intellectually with liberalism; it would have had to try to invalidate the arguments of its opponents logically and to turn aside their objections against its own doctrines. Individual socialists have done that too. By and large, though, socialists have scarcely bothered themselves with scientific discussion of the advantages and disadvantages of the two conceivable systems of social production. They have proclaimed the socialist program as a doctrine of salvation. They have represented all earthly suffering as an emanation of the capitalist social order and have promised, with the implementation of socialism, the removal of everything painful. They held the capitalist economy responsible for all shortcomings of the past and present. In the state of the future all longing and hoping will be fulfilled; there the restless will find rest; the unhappy, happiness; the inadequate, strength; the sick, cure; the poor, wealth; the abstinent, enjoyment. In the state of the future, work will be a pleasure and no longer a torment. In the state of the future, an art will flourish of whose magnificence "bourgeois" art gives no idea, and a science that will solve all riddles of the universe without remnant. All sexual need will disappear; man and wife will give each other happiness in love that earlier generations never dreamed of. Human character will undergo a thoroughgoing change; it will become noble and spotless; all intellectual, moral, and bodily inadequacies will fall away from mankind. What flourishes for the German hero in Valhalla, for the Christian in God's bosom, for the Moslem in Mohammed's paradise — socialism will realize all that on earth.

The Utopians, above all Fourier, were insatiable in wanting to paint the details of this life of ease. Marxism has most strictly tabooed every sketch of the state of the future. But this prohibition referred only to description of the economic, governmental, and legal order of the socialist state and was a masterful propaganda gambit. Since the arrangements of the future state were left in mysterious obscurity, the opponents of socialism were deprived of all possibility of criticizing them and perhaps showing that their realization could in no way create a paradise on earth. Depicting the favorable consequences of the socialization of property, on the contrary, was by no means proscribed by Marxism as was the demonstration of the ways and means by which it could be accomplished. By representing all earthly evils as necessary concomitants of the capitalist social order and further declaring that they would be absent from the state of the future, it has, in utopian depiction of the happiness that it promises to bring, again and again outdone the most imaginative authors of utopian novels. Mysterious intimation and mystical allusion have far stronger effect than open explanation.

That socialism appeared as a doctrine of salvation made its struggle against liberalism easy. Whoever seeks to refute socialism rationally encounters among most socialists not rational considerations, as he expects, but rather a belief, not derived from experience, in redemption by socialism. One undoubtedly can also defend socialism rationally. Yet for the great mass of its adherents it is a doctrine of salvation; they believe in it. For those for whom the religious gospels have lost force, it is, in place of faith, a consolation and hope in the difficulties of life. In the face of such conviction, all rationalist criticism fails. Whoever comes to the socialist of this sort with rational objections finds the same lack of understanding that rationalist criticism of the doctrines of faith encounters with the believing Christian.

In this sense, comparing socialism with Christianity was thoroughly justified. Yet the Kingdom of Christ is not of this world; socialism, on the contrary, wants to establish the kingdom of salvation on earth. Therein lies its strength, therein, however, its weakness too, from which it will collapse some day just as quickly as it has triumphed. Even if the socialist method of production really could raise productivity and provide greater welfare for all than the liberal method, it would be bound bitterly to disappoint its adherents, who also expect the highest exaltation of the inner feeling of happiness from it. It will not be able to remove the inadequacy of everything earthly, not quiet the Faustian drive, not fulfill inner yearning. When socialism will have become reality, it will have to recognize that a religion not referring to the life to come is an absurdity.

Marxism is an evolutionary theory. Even the word "revolution" has the meaning "evolution" in the sense of the materialistic interpretation of history. Yet regard for the Messianic character of the socialist gospel was bound to drive Marxian socialism again and again to endorsing violent overthrow, revolution in the strict sense of the word. It could not admit that evolution was coming nearer to socialism in any other way than that the contradictions of the capitalist mode of production were becoming ever more glaring and thereby bringing the revolutionary overthrow of capitalism into the near future. If it had been willing to admit that evolution was leading to the realization of socialism step-by-step, then it would have gotten into the embarrassment of having to explain just why its prophecies of salvation were not also being fulfilled step by step to some extent. For that reason Marxism necessarily had to remain revolutionary if it did not want to give up the strongest device of its propaganda, the doctrine of salvation; for that reason, despite all science, it had to hold firm to its theory of increasing misery and collapse. For that reason it had to reject the revisionism of Bernstein; for that reason it had to let not one iota of its orthodoxy be stolen from it.

Now, however, socialism is the victor. The day of fulfillment has dawned. Millions stand around impetuously demanding the salvation that is supposed to await them; they demand riches, they demand happiness. And now shall the leaders come and console the multitude by saying that diligent labor, perhaps after decades or centuries, will become their reward and that inner happiness can never be attained with outward means? Yet how have they reproached liberalism because it recommended diligence and thrift to the poor! Yet how have they derided the doctrines that would not ascribe all earthly hardship to the deficiency of social arrangements!

Socialism has only *one* way out of this position. Regardless of the fact that it holds power, it must still keep trying to appear as an oppressed and persecuted sect, impeded by hostile powers from pushing through the essential parts of its program, and so shift onto others the responsibility for the nonappearance of the prophesied state of happiness. Along with that, however, the struggle against these enemies of general salvation becomes an unavoidable necessity for the socialist commonwealth. It must bloodily persecute the bourgeoisie at home; it must take the offensive against foreign countries that are not yet socialist. It cannot wait until the foreigners must turn to socialism voluntarily. Since it can explain the failure of socialism only by the machinations of foreign capitalism, it necessarily arrives at a new concept of the offensive socialist international. Socialism can be realized only if the whole world becomes socialist; an isolated socialism of one single nation is said to be impossible. Therefore, every socialist government must immediately concern itself with the extension of socialism abroad.

That is quite a different kind of internationalism from that of the *Communist Manifesto*. It is not defensively but offensively conceived. To help the idea of socialism to victory, however, it should suffice — one should think — for the socialist nations to arrange their societies so well that their example leads others to imitate them. Yet for the socialist state, attack on all capitalist states is a vital necessity. To maintain itself internally it must become aggressive externally. It cannot rest before it has socialized the whole world.

Socialist imperialism is also quite without a basis for economic policy. It is hard to see why a socialist commonwealth could not also acquire in trade with foreign countries all those goods that it could not produce itself. The socialist who is convinced of the higher productivity of communist production could dispute that least of all.[25]

Socialist imperialism outdoes every earlier imperialism in scope and depth. The inner necessity that has caused it to arise, rooted in the essence of the socialist gospel of salvation, drives it to fundamental boundlessness in every direction. It cannot rest before it has subjugated the entire inhabited world and before it has annihilated everything reminiscent of other forms of human society. Every earlier imperialism could do without further expansion as soon as it came up against obstacles to its spread that it could not overcome. Socialist imperialism could not do this; it would have to see such obstacles as difficulties not only for outward expansion but also for its development at home. It must try to annihilate them or itself disappear.

25. Note how deficient is the argument in Marxist literature before 1918 for the thesis that socialism is possible only as world socialism.

Concluding Observations

Rationalist utilitarianism rules out neither socialism nor imperialism on principle. Accepting it provides only a standpoint from which one can compare and evaluate the advantages and disadvantages of the various possibilities of social order; one could conceivably become a socialist or even an imperialist from the utilitarian standpoint. But whoever has once adopted this standpoint is compelled to present his program rationally. All resentment, every policy prompted by sentiment, and all mysticism is thereby rejected, regardless of whether it appears in the garb of racial belief or of any other gospel of salvation. The fundamentals of policy can be disputed, pro and con, on rational grounds. If agreement cannot be reached both over the ultimate goals and also, although more seldom, over the choice of means by which they shall be pursued, since their evaluation depends on subjective feelings, one must still succeed in this manner in sharply narrowing the scope of the dispute. The hopes of many rationalists go still further, of course. They think that every dispute can be resolved by intellectual means, since all disagreements arise only from errors and from inadequacy of knowledge. Yet in assuming this they already presuppose the thesis of the harmony of the rightly understood interests of individuals, and this is indeed disputed precisely by imperialists and socialists.

The entire nineteenth century is characterized by the struggle against rationalism, whose dominion seemed undisputed at its beginning. Even its assumption of a fundamental similarity in the way of thinking of all people is attacked. The German must think otherwise than the Briton, the dolichocephalic person otherwise than the brachycephalic; "proletarian" logic is contrasted with "bourgeois" logic.[1] Reason is denied the

1. [Mises criticizes this thesis as "polylogism" — that different groups, races, and classes think and reason differently, that they use different logic. See above, pp. 8–9, and his major economic treatise, *Human Action*, 4th ed. (Irvington-on-Hudson, N.Y., 1996), pp. 75–89.]

property of being able to decide all political questions; feeling and instinct must show men the path that they have to tread.

Rational policy and rational economic management have outwardly enriched beyond measure the lives of the individual and of nations. That could be overlooked, since attention was always paid only to the poverty of those still living outside the boundaries of the territories already won by the free economy and because the lot of the modern worker was always compared with that of the rich man of today, instead of the lots of both being compared with those of their ancestors. It is true that modern man is never content with his economic position, that he would like to have things still better. Yet precisely this incessant striving for more wealth is the driving force of our development; one cannot eliminate it without destroying the basis of our economic civilization. The contentment of the serf, who was happy when he did not suffer actual hunger and when his lord did not thrash him too badly, is no ideal state of affairs whose passing one could lament.

It is also true, however, that the rise of outward welfare corresponds to no increase of inner riches. The modern city-dweller is richer than the citizen of Periclean Athens and than the knightly troubadour of Provence, but his inner life exhausts itself in mechanical functions at work and in superficial dissipations of his leisure hours. From the pine torch to the incandescent lamp is a great step forward, from the folk song to the popular song a sad step backward. Nothing is more comforting than that people are beginning to become conscious of this lack. In that alone lies hope for a culture of the future that will put everything earlier in the shade.

Yet the reaction against inner impoverishment should not impugn the rationalization of outward life. The romantic longing for wild adventures, for quarreling and freedom from external restraint, is itself only a sign of inner emptiness; it clings to the superficial and does not strive for depth. Relief is not to be hoped for from a variety of colorful external experiences. The individual must seek by himself the way to find within himself the satisfaction that he expects in vain from outside. If we chose to deliver up politics and the economy to imperialism, to resentment, and to mystical feelings, then we would indeed become outwardly poorer but not inwardly richer.

Warlike activity assures a man of that deep satisfaction aroused by the highest straining of all forces in resistance to external dangers. That is no mere atavistic reawakening of impulses and instincts that have become pointless in changed circumstances. The inner feeling of happiness aroused not by victory and revenge but rather by struggle and danger originates in the vivid perception that exigency compels the person to the highest deployment of forces of which he is capable and that it makes everything that lies within him become effective.[2] It is characteristic of very great persons to move forward to highest accomplishment out of an inner drive; others require an external impulse to overcome deep-rooted inertia and to develop their own selves. The common man will never share the happiness that the creative person feels in devotion to his work unless extraordinary circumstances confront him, too, with tasks that demand and reward the commitment of the whole person. Here lies the source of all heroism. Not because the individual feels death and wounds as sweet but rather because, in the enrapturing experience of the deed, he puts them out of his mind does he assail the enemy. Bravery is an emanation of health and strength and is the rearing up of human nature against external adversity. Attack is the most primary initiative. In his feelings man is always an imperialist.[3]

But reason forbids giving free rein to feelings. To want to beat the world to ruins to let a romantic longing exhaust itself contradicts the simplest deliberation so much that no word need be wasted on it.

The rational policy that is commonly called the ideas of 1789 has been reproached for being unpatriotic — in Germany, un-German. It takes no regard of the special interests of the fatherland; beyond mankind and the individual, it forgets the nation. This reproach is understandable only if one accepts the view that there is an unbridgeable cleavage between the interest of the people as a whole on the one side and that of individuals and of all mankind on the other side. If one starts with the

2. . . . *der Krieg lässt die Kraft erscheinen,*
Alles erhebt er zum Ungemeinen,
Selber dem Feigen erzeugt er den Mut. (Die Braut von Messina)
[. . . war makes strength appear,
It raises everything to the extraordinary,
Even in the coward it creates courage. (*The Bride of Messina*)]
3. This does not refer to the glorification of war by weak-willed esthetes who admire in warlike activity the strength that they lack. This writing-table and coffee-house imperialism has no significance. With its paper effusions, it is only a fellow traveler.
    Games and sport represent an attempt to react from natural, emotional imperialism. It is no accident that England, the home of modern utilitarianism, is also the fatherland of modern sport and that precisely the Germans — and among them, again, the strata most averse to the utilitarian philosophy, university youth — have shut themselves off the longest from the spread of sports activity.

harmony of rightly understood interests, then one cannot comprehend this objection at all. The individualist will never be able to grasp how a nation can become great and rich and powerful at the expense of its members and how the welfare of mankind can obstruct that of individual peoples. In the hour of Germany's deepest degradation, may one raise the question whether the German nation would not have fared better by holding firm to the peaceful policy of much-reviled liberalism rather than to the war policy of the Hohenzollerns?

The utilitarian policy has further been reproached for aiming only at the satisfaction of material interests and neglecting the higher goals of human striving. The utilitarian supposedly thinks of coffee and cotton and on that account forgets the true values of life. Under the reign of such a policy all would have to be caught up in precipitous striving for the lower earthly pleasures, and the world would sink into crass materialism. Nothing is more absurd than this criticism. It is true that utilitarianism and liberalism postulate the attainment of the greatest possible productivity of labor as the first and most important goal of policy. But they in no way do this out of misunderstanding of the fact that human existence does not exhaust itself in material pleasures. They strive for welfare and for wealth not because they see the highest value in them but because they know that all higher and inner culture presupposes outward welfare. If they deny to the state the mission of furthering the realization of the values of life, they do so not out of want of esteem for true values but rather in the recognition that these values, as the most characteristic expression of inner life, are inaccessible to every influence by external forces. Not out of irreligiosity do they demand religious freedom but out of deepest intimacy of religious feeling, which wants to make inner experience free from every raw influence of outward power. They demand freedom of thought because they rank thought much too high to hand it over to the domination of magistrates and councils. They demand freedom of speech and of the press because they expect the triumph of truth only from the struggle of opposing opinions. They reject every authority because they believe in man.

Utilitarian policy is indeed policy for this earth. But that is inherent in all policy. The person who has a low opinion of the mind is not the one who wants to make it free from all external regulation but rather the one who wants to control it by penal laws and machine guns. The reproach of a materialistic way of thinking applies not to individualistic utilitarianism but to collectivistic imperialism.

With the World War mankind got into a crisis with which nothing that happened before in history can be compared. There were great wars before; flourishing states were annihilated, whole peoples exterminated. All that can in no way be compared with what is now occurring before our eyes. In the world crisis whose beginning we are experiencing, all peoples of the world are involved. None can stand aside; none can say that its cause too will not be decided along with the others. If in ancient times the destructive will of the more powerful met its limits in the inadequacy of the means of destruction and in the possibility available to the conquered of escaping persecution by moving away, then progress in the techniques of war and transportation and communication makes it impossible today for the defeated to evade the execution of the victor's sentence of annihilation.

War has become more fearful and destructive than ever before because it is now waged with all the means of the highly developed technique that the free economy has created. Bourgeois civilization has built railroads and electric power plants, has invented explosives and airplanes, in order to create wealth. Imperialism has placed the tools of peace in the service of destruction. With modern means it would be easy to wipe out humanity at one blow. In horrible madness Caligula wished that the entire Roman people had one head so that he could strike it off. The civilization of the twentieth century has made it possible for the raving madness of the modern imperialists to realize similar bloody dreams. By pressing a button one can expose thousands to destruction. It was the fate of civilization that it was unable to keep the external means that it had created out of the hands of those who had remained estranged from its spirit. Modern tyrants have things much easier than their predecessors. He who rules the means of exchange of ideas and of goods in the economy based on the division of labor has his rule more firmly grounded than ever an imperator before. The rotary press is easy to put into fetters, and whoever controls it need not fear the competition of the merely spoken or written word. Things were much more difficult for the Inquisition. No Philip II could paralyze freedom of thought more severely than a modern censor. How much more efficient than the guillotine of Robespierre are the machine guns of Trotsky! Never was the individual more tyrannized than since the outbreak of the World War and especially of the world revolution. One cannot escape the police and administrative technique of the present day.

Only one external limit is posed to this rage for destruction. In destroying the free cooperation of men, imperialism undercuts the material basis of its power. Economic civilization has forged the weapons for it. In using the weapons to blow up the forge and kill the smith, it makes itself defenseless in the future. The apparatus of the economy based on division of labor cannot be reproduced, let alone extended, if freedom and property have disappeared. It will die out, and the economy will sink back into primitive forms. Only then will mankind be able to breathe more freely. If the spirit of reflectiveness does not return sooner, imperialism and Bolshevism will be overcome at the latest when the means of power that they have wrested from liberalism will have been used up.

The unfortunate outcome of the war brings hundreds of thousands, even millions, of Germans under foreign rule and imposes tribute payments of unheard-of size on the rest of Germany. A legal order is being established in the world that permanently excludes the German people from possession of those parts of the earth that have the more favorable conditions of production. In the future, no German will be allowed to acquire ownership of land resources and means of production abroad; and millions of Germans, narrowly pushed together, will have to feed themselves badly on the niggardly soil of Germany, while, overseas, millions of square kilometers of the best land lie idle. Need and misery for the German people will emerge from this peace. The population will decline; and the German people, which before the war counted among the most numerous peoples of the earth, will in the future have to be numerically less significant than they once were.

All thinking and effort of the German people must be directed to getting out of this position. This goal can be reached in two ways. One is that of imperialistic policy. To grow strong militarily and to resume the war as soon as the opportunity for attack presents itself—that is the only means thought of today. Whether this way will be practicable at all is questionable. The nations that today have robbed and enslaved Germany are very many. The amount of power that they have exercised is so great that they will watch anxiously to prevent any strengthening of Germany again. A new war that Germany might wage could easily become a Third Punic War and end with the complete annihilation of the German people. But even if it should lead to victory, it would bring so much economic misery upon Germany that the success would not be worth the stakes; moreover, the danger would exist that the German people, in the ecstasy of victory, would fall again into that limitless and boundless madness of victory that has already repeatedly turned to misfortune for it, since it can finally lead again only to a great debacle.

The second course that the German people can take is that of completely turning away from imperialism. To strive for reconstruction only through productive labor, to make possible the development of all powers of the individual and of the nation as a whole by full freedom at home — that is the way that leads back to life. To set nothing against the efforts of imperialistic neighbor states to oppress and de-Germanize us other than productive labor, which makes one wealthy and thereby free, is a way that leads more quickly and surely to the goal than the policy of struggle and war. The Germans who have been subjugated to the Czechoslovak, Polish, Danish, French, Belgian, Italian, Rumanian, and Yugoslav states will better preserve their national character if they strive for democracy and self-government, which finally do lead to full national independence, than if they pin their hopes on a victory of weapons.

The policy that strove for the greatness of the German nation through outward means of force has broken down. It has not only diminished the German people as a whole but also brought the individual German into misery and need. Never has the German people sunk so low as today. If it is now to rise again, then it can no longer strive to make the whole great at the expense of individuals but rather must strive for a durable foundation of the well-being of the whole on the basis of the well-being of individuals. It must switch from the collectivistic policy that it has followed so far to an individualistic one.

Whether such a policy will be at all possible in the future, in view of the imperialism that is now asserting itself everywhere in the world, is another question. But if this should not be the case, then precisely all modern civilization faces downfall.

"The most virtuous person cannot live in peace if that does not please his evil neighbor." Imperialism presses weapons into the hands of all who do not want to be subjugated. To fight imperialism, the peaceful must employ all its means. If they then triumph in the struggle, they may indeed have crushed their opponent, yet themselves have been conquered by his methods and his way of thinking. They then do not lay down their weapons again; they themselves remain imperialists.

Englishmen, Frenchmen, and Americans had already shed all cravings for conquest in the nineteenth century and had made liberalism their first principle. To be sure, even in their liberal period their policy was not entirely free of imperialist deviations, and one cannot immediately chalk up every success of the imperialistic idea among them to the account of defense. But no doubt their imperialism drew its greatest strength from the necessity of warding off German and Russian imperialism. Now they stand as victors and are not willing to content themselves with what they indicated before their victory as their war aim. They have long since forgotten the fine programs with which they went to war. Now they have power and are not willing to let it get away. Perhaps they think that they will exercise power for the general good, but that is what all those with power have believed. Power is evil in itself, regardless of who exercises it.[4]

But if they now do want to adopt that policy with which we have suffered shipwreck, so much the worse for them; for us that can still be no reason for abstaining from what benefits us. We demand the policy of calm, peaceful development—not indeed for their sake but for our own sake. It was the greatest error of German imperialists that they accused those who had advised a policy of moderation of having unpatriotic sympathy for foreigners; the course of history has shown how much they thereby deluded themselves. Today we know best where imperialism leads.

It would be the most terrible misfortune for Germany and for all humanity if the idea of revenge should dominate the German policy of the future. To become free of the fetters that have been forced upon German development by the peace of Versailles, to free our fellow nationals from servitude and need, that alone should be the goal of the new German policy. To retaliate for wrong suffered, to take revenge and to punish, does satisfy lower instincts, but in politics the avenger harms himself no less than the enemy. The world community of labor is based on the reciprocal advantage of all participants. Whoever wants to maintain and extend it must renounce all resentment in advance. What would he gain from quenching his thirst for revenge at the cost of his own welfare?

In the League of Nations of Versailles the ideas of 1914 are in truth triumphing over those of 1789; that it is not we who have helped them to victory, but rather our enemies, and that the oppression turns back against us is important for us but less decisive from the standpoint of

4. Cf. J. Burckhardt, *Weltgeschichtliche Betrachtungen* (Berlin, 1905), p. 96.

world history. The chief point remains that nations are being "punished" and that the forfeiture theory comes to life again. If one admits exceptions to the right of self-determination of nations to the disadvantage of "evil" nations, one has overturned the first principle of the free community of nations. That Englishmen, North Americans, French, and Belgians, those chief exporters of capital, thereby help gain recognition for the principle that owning capital abroad represents a form of rule and that its expropriation is the natural consequence of political changes shows how blind rage and the desire for momentary enrichment repress rational considerations among them today. Cool reflection would be bound to lead precisely these peoples to quite other behavior in questions of international capital movements.

The way that leads us and all humanity out of the danger that world imperialism signifies for the productive and cultural community of nations and so for the fate of civilization is rejection of the policy of feeling and instinct and return to political rationalism. If we wanted to throw ourselves into the arms of Bolshevism merely for the purpose of annoying our enemies, the robbers of our freedom and our property, or to set their house on fire too, that would not help us in the least. It should not be the goal of our policy to drag our enemies into our destruction with us. We should try not to be destroyed ourselves and try to rise again out of servitude and misery. That, however, we can attain neither by warlike actions nor by revenge and the policy of despair. For us and for humanity there is only one salvation: return to the rationalistic liberalism of the ideas of 1789.

It may be that socialism represents a better form of organization of human labor. Let whoever asserts this try to prove it rationally. If the proof should succeed, then the world, democratically united by liberalism, will not hesitate to implement the communist community. In a democratic state, who could oppose a reform that would be bound to bring the greatest gain to by far the overwhelming majority? Political rationalism does not reject socialism on principle. But it does reject in advance the socialism that hinges not on cool understanding but rather on unclear feelings, that works not with logic but rather with the mysticism of a gospel of salvation, the socialism that does not proceed from the free will of the majority of the people but rather from the terrorism of wild fanatics.

INDEX

accounting in war economy, xii, 132–33, 134n16

Adler, Max, 143n21

agricultural vs. industrial areas, 121, 136, 140, 167–68, 170

Alexander I, Czar of Russia, xvi

alphabets and national identity, 15

Alsace-Lorraine, changing ownership of, xxii

ancestry and nationality, 8–9

Anglo-Saxon nation, 15–16, 51–52. *See also* England; United States

arbitration in international disputes, 73–75

aristocracy, xi, xiii–xxiii. *See also* authoritarian states; Habsburg dynasty; Hohenzollern dynasty; princely state

armaments industry, advantages of war economy for, 127–28

Arndt, Ernst, 10n4, 65–66n49

assimilation, national, 19–20, 24, 64–65. *See also* migration; mixed populations

attack theory of war, 114n4

ausgleich, xxi

Auspitz, Rudolf, 130

Australia, 75

Austria (Austria-Hungary)*: fear of power loss to Germany, 88–100; and German Liberal Party, 93, 102–6; and German Nationalist Party, 104–6; historical overview, xiv–xv, xvii–xix,

xx–xxi, xxii–xxiv, 100–102; and Italy, xxi, 83; national autonomy within, 42–44, 45, 67–68, 107–9; and proportional representation, 42; Reussen movement, 20–21; and social democracy, 106–7, 108. *See also* war economy

Austro-Prussian War, xx–xxi, 101

autarky, 69–70, 111, 112, 121–25

authoritarian states: advantages in mixed population states, 37, 41; as cause of World War I, 1, 2–3; as focus for freedom movements, 27–28; inability to create national assimilation, 24; pre–World War I Germany, xxiii–xxiv; Prussian triumph of, xxiv, 80–88; Social Democracy's common ground with, 147–50; vs. syndicalist socialism, 166, 167. *See also* Austria

autonomy, national (Austria), 42–44, 45, 67–68, 107–9. *See also* self-determination

Badeni, Count Kazimierz Felix, xxiii, 104

Bauer, Otto, 43, 76

Benedek, Gen. Ludwig von, xxi

Bentham, Jeremy, 151

Berlin, Congress of, xxii–xxiii

Bernhardi, Friedrich A. J. von, 113n3, 114n4

bilingualism and nationality, 11–12

---

*The geographical designation "Austria" denotes territories belonging to the Austro-Hungarian Empire before World War I.

The typeface used in setting this book is Electra, designed in 1935 by the great American typographer William Addison Dwiggins. Dwiggins was a student and associate of Frederic Goudy and served for a time as acting director of Harvard University Press. In his illustrious career as typographer and book designer (he coined the term "graphic designer"), Dwiggins created a number of typefaces, including Metro and Caledonia, and designed as well many of the typographic ornaments or "dingbats" familiar to readers.

Electra is a crisp, elegant and readable typeface, strongly suggestive of calligraphy. The contrast between its strokes is relatively muted, and it produces an even but still "active" impression in text. Interestingly, the design of the *italic* form — called "cursive" in this typeface — is less calligraphic than the italic of many faces, and more closely resembles the roman.

This book is printed on paper that is acid-free and meets the requirements of the American National Standard for Permanence of Paper for Printed Library Materials, z39.48 –1992. ∞

Book design adapted by Erin Kirk New, Watkinsville, Georgia, after a design by Martin Lubin Graphic Design, Jackson Heights, New York

Typography by G & S Typesetters, Inc., Austin, Texas

Printed and bound by Edwards Brothers, Inc., Ann Arbor, Michigan